Erotic Revelations

Erotic Revelations: Clinical Applications and Perverse Scenarios delves into erotic desires and fantasies . . . above all, how our sexuality expresses our inner being and defines the ways in which we engage in the psychoanalytic situation. Andrea Celenza addresses the 'desexualization' of the psychoanalytic field by reclaiming sexuality as one of the many nexes that are of central concern to the patient. She illustrates a wide range of erotic manifestations (for both therapist and patient) and offers recommendations to practitioners for dealing with erotic material when it arises.

Andrea Celenza has divided this book into two parts, with clinical, theoretical, and technical discussions in each chapter:

Part I: Erotics embodied: transferences and countertransferences

- Presents the varieties and meanings of erotic transferences and countertransferences common in clinical situations
- Includes case studies of erotic material used as examples of phases in treatment as well as moments of defensive impasse
- Includes discussions of the management of aggression, underlying merger fantasies, uses of countertransferences (in multiple forms), and dilemmas surrounding self-disclosure

Part II: Perverse scenarios revisited

- Reconceptualizes and restores the term perversion into the clinical lexicon
- Views perversion as a quality of relating rather than a specific action or behavior
- Presents a wide range of clinical illustrations that demonstrates the usefulness of this reformulation

Erotic Revelations puts sexuality back into psychoanalytic theorizing and makes a place for erotic transferences, of whatever shape, in every analysis or therapy. With a strong clinical focus, this book will redefine how to work with many aspects of sex and gender in clinical psychoanalytic practice and will be an essential resource for psychoanalysts, psychotherapists, psychologists, educators, trainers, students, and those with an interest in the mental health field.

Andrea Celenza is a Training and Supervising Analyst at the Boston Psychoanalytic Society and Institute, and Assistant Clinical Professor at Harvard Medical School. She has authored numerous papers and two books on psychoanalysis and psychoanalytic psychotherapy. She is the recipient of several awards and is in private practice in Lexington, Massachusetts.

Erotic Revelations

Clinical applications and perverse scenarios

Andrea Celenza

LONDON AND NEW YORK

First published 2014
by Routledge
27 Church Road, Hove, East Sussex BN3 2FA

and by Routledge
711 Third Avenue, New York, NY 10017

Routledge is an imprint of the Taylor & Francis Group, an informa business

© 2014 Andrea Celenza

The right of Andrea Celenza to be identified as author of this work has been asserted by her in accordance with sections 77 and 78 of the Copyright, Designs and Patents Act 1988.

All rights reserved. No part of this book may be reprinted or reproduced or utilised in any form or by any electronic, mechanical, or other means, now known or hereafter invented, including photocopying and recording, or in any information storage or retrieval system, without permission in writing from the publishers.

Trademark notice: Product or corporate names may be trademarks or registered trademarks, and are used only for identification and explanation without intent to infringe.

British Library Cataloguing in Publication Data
A catalogue record for this book is available from the British Library

Library of Congress Cataloging-in-Publication Data
Celenza, Andrea, 1954–
 Erotic revelations : clinical applications and perverse scenarios / Andrea Celenza.—First Edition.
 pages cm
 1. Sex (Psychology) 2. Psychoanalysis. 3. Psychotherapist and patient. 4. Sexual excitement. I. Title.
 BF175.5.S48C4285 2014
 155.3'1—dc23
 2014011582

ISBN: 978-1-138-77673-9 (hbk)
ISBN: 978-1-138-77674-6 (pbk)
ISBN: 978-1-315-77305-6 (ebk)

Typeset in Times New Roman
by Swales & Willis Ltd, Exeter, Devon

To Bruce, Derek, and Ethan.

Contents

Acknowledgments		ix
Introduction: transcending binaries		1

PART I
Erotics embodied: transferences and countertransferences — 13

Introduction — 15

1. Maternal erotic transferences and merger wishes — 25
2. Maternal erotic transferences: engaging the mother within — 37
3. Erotic transferences and the role of aggression — 47
4. The guilty pleasure of erotic countertransference: searching for radial true — 59
5. Erotic countertransference revelations — 71

PART II
Perverse scenarios revisited — 85

Introduction — 87

6. Perverse female scenarios: the Objectified Self — 99
7. Sadomasochistic relating: what's sex got to do with it? — 113
8. Fetishes, the anal universe, and other fantasies of one-person relating — 125

Conclusion: positions of subjectivity—the ineluctable
construction of the self   137

References   147
Index   163

Acknowledgments

I owe a profound debt of gratitude to all my patients, necessarily anonymous, who have honored me by sharing their private desires and longings. It is a privilege to be welcomed into that level of intimacy and I hope I have done this honor justice.

In innumerable ways, psychoanalytic writing grows out from the scholarship of others: we stand on the shoulders of giants from whom our work is inevitably derived. I hope I have cited all of the colleagues whose thinking has inevitably, consciously and unconsciously, permeated my own. In particular, my writing has been in intimate conversation with the writings of Jessica Benjamin for decades and I thank her especially for her rigorous scholarship and theorizing. Reading Jessica's work has included gratifying moments of synchrony that have been hugely generative for me. My longstanding admiration of Jessica's boldness has facilitated my ability to speak my own mind. I am honored to receive her acknowledgment of this book as well as her friendship—I could not have hoped for more.

I could not have evolved in my theoretical understanding, now reflected in this book, without the immensely valuable assistance of two distinguished colleagues and friends, Adrienne Harris and Muriel Dimen, in whose debt I remain. Inherent in their careful reading (and sometimes re-reading) of this work are their considerable deliberations, judicious feedback, constructive critique, and a profoundly felt respect for our abiding differences. I view this aspect of their help as an utmost and crucial act of friendship—I thank them both especially for that. I look forward to continued enjoyment and debate on the ways in which our ideas overlap, intersect, and diverge.

As with many of my writings, I rely on the ongoing involvement and intellectual rigor of several lifelong friends and colleagues: Lew Aron, Baird Brightman, Steven Cooper, Jennifer Ellwood, Jack Foehl, Ellen Golding, and Martha Stark. This book is a tribute to their unflagging guidance and support. Thank you, all. I also thank Murray Cohen for sharing a case and for his continued friendship and mentoring.

To my peer group, in whose trust I have placed my clinical thinking, creative risks, and emotional investment in this work, I give you my gratitude and love. Thank you for your help and support over many years and I look forward to many more years to come: Jack Foehl, Ellen Golding, Chris Lovett, and Joan Wheelis.

Many thanks to my editor, Kate Hawes, and her responsive assistant, Kirsten Buchanan, for their guidance, editorial suggestions, and unceasing respect for my writing and judgment.

My husband, Bruce, remains my most ardent supporter and critical editor. To write without jargon or pretense is a shared goal; I hope I have met his standard. To all my boys, whose love I cannot live without, thank you for your constancy, unerring faith in me, and loving devotion.

I gratefully acknowledge the following publications in whose pages versions of many chapters first appeared:

Contemporary Psychoanalysis: Celenza, A. (2013). Perverse female relating: The objectified self. *Contemporary Psychoanalysis, 49* (4). By permission of the editors, Don Greif and Ruth Livingston. (Chapter 6.)

Journal of the American Psychoanalytic Association: Celenza, A. (2006). The threat of male-to-female erotic transference. *Journal of the American Psychoanalytic Association, 54* (4), 1207–1231. By permission of Sage Publications. (Chapters 2 and 3.)

Psychoanalytic Quarterly: Celenza, A. (2012). Sadomasochistic relating: What's sex got to do with it? *Psychoanalytic Quarterly, 69* (3), 527–543. By permission of John Wiley and Sons. (Chapter 7.)

Rivista di Psicoanalisi: Celenza, A. (2013) Maternal erotic transferences and merger wishes. *Rivista di Psicoanalisi, LIX* (4), 821–838. (Chapter 1.)

Studies in Gender and Sexuality: Celenza, A. (2010). The guilty pleasure of erotic countertransference: Searching for radial true. *Studies in Gender and Sexuality, 11* (4), 175–183. Reprinted by permission of the publisher (Taylor & Francis Ltd, http://www.tandf.co.uk/journals). (Chapter 4.)

I also acknowledge, with appreciation, the following publishing or film companies for permission to reprint excerpts from:

Fight Club: A Novel by Chuck Palahniuk. Copyright © 1996 by Chuck Palahniuk. Used by permission of W. W. Norton & Company.

Closer by Patrick Marber. Copyright © 1997 by Patrick Marber. Used by permission of Bloomsbury Methuen.

Gravity's Rainbow by Thomas Pynchon. Copyright © 1973 by Thomas Pynchon. Used by permission of Viking Penguin, a division of Penguin Group (USA) LLC and Copyright © 1973, 2001 by Thomas Pynchon. Reprinted with permission of Melanie Jackson Agency, LLC.

Assassination Tango by Robert Duvall, copyright © 2003 United Artists Film Inc., courtesy of MGM Media Licensing.

My gratitude also goes to Elizabeth Wallace for allowing me to reprint her poem "Girl, Edited," which first appeared in *The American Psychoanalyst*, Vol. 38, 2004.

Introduction
Transcending binaries

> *The sexual is not the genital . . .*
> *It is what causes [one] to have a history. . .*
> *provides a key to [one's] life,*
> *It is because in his sexuality*
> *is projected his manner of being towards the world.*
>
> M. Merleau-Ponty, 1962

To encounter another person is to experience their being, to perceive their way of relating to others and the world. It is to engage their humanity in their own particularized manner and style. When we 'see' another person, we immediately perceive their way of thinking and *feeling into* their aliveness, their relationship to their body, and their relationship with their intelligence and desires. When we touch another, we don't just touch their body, we touch their being (Celenza, 2012). A universal, primal presentation, the other is present to us from the beginning as the mother transmits her enigmatic, sexual unconscious to the infant (Laplanche, 1997).[1]

In these ways, several categories of being are immediately present and emerge, including one's gender[2] and one's sexuality. Even when someone's gender is ambiguous to the perceiver, this is registered as such. Encountering another is reciprocal as well, in that we also experience ourselves *being experienced*. All of these ways of experiencing ourselves in relation to others are captured in the essential fact of how we enter into the world, always embodied, always sentient. *Embodiment* is an existential fact of our being, our relationship to others and the outside world. "Precisely because my body can shut itself off from the world, it is also what opens me out upon the world and places me in a situation there" (Merleau-Ponty, 1962, p. 191).

Gender is a distinguishing characteristic of a person, a difference marker (Goldner, 1991) that is immediately present. Even trans persons use gender to (re)categorize, as they both undermine and ratify the gender binary (see Goldner, 2011). Harris (2005b) makes the point that many tomboy experiences are both conforming and resistive at the same time; gender refusals while swallowing convention wholesale. To register a person's gender goes beyond categorizing a nominal or anatomical fact. When we encounter another, we see *their relationship to* their gender; we see *how they feel about* the imposed cultural expectations of their gender.[3] In this way, being a woman or a man in Western societies is more than a nominal or anatomical fact; we have a relationship to this fact, including choices about how one's gender is cultivated and expressed in relation to the imposed cultural expectations upon one's gender and other categories of identity as well.[4] Does she display it stereotypically? Does he obscure it? Does it appear to be minimally relevant? Does she hide or disclaim it? Does he express his 'maleness' overtly, conventionally, or transgressively? Since we are embodied and born into a Western culture, the expression of one's gender and one's sexuality is inescapable, whether it is derived from convention, liberated, or contested.

Postmodern and, in particular, post-structural critiques of psychological theories of development, including and perhaps especially feminist influences on psychoanalytic theories, have contested the ways in which an individual is described by normative, universalist, and paternalistic or patriarchical gender categories that hide and constrain (through social regulation [Corbett, 2009] or surveillance [Foucault, 1978; Butler, 2006]) more than reveal or liberate. Naming itself reflects membership in a group that denotes *this* (some particular way of being) and not *that* (usually its polar opposite).[5] Hence a binary surfaces along with a relentless or seemingly inevitable tendency to privilege one pole over the other, thus refracting through and instantiating within a hierarchical relation. These power hierarchies then become accepted and embedded in discourse, cultural practices, and rituals that are so commonplace as to disappear from view. In these ways, many types of subjugation are nonreflectively perpetuated through the social and cultural order.

There are many outstanding critiques targeting and deconstructing these politics of gender (Birksted-Breen, 1993; Benjamin, 1998; Dimen, 1998; Dimen and Goldner, 2002; Layton, 2004; Harris, 2005a), especially the ways in which the individual is subjected to and created by power relations. Among the various contested themes, all discussions rest on some notion of the ways in which culture and relationality intertwine and inflect gendered experience, including the ways in which "solution[s] of gender problems sometimes involve the solution of general problems of personal subjectivity and capacities for intersubjectivity" (Chodorow, 1995, p. 297; see also Flax, 1996). We have tended to see the body as an anatomical fact rather than as a surface inscribed with factoids whose meanings, constructed rather than essential, have become reified over time (Fausto-Sterling, 2000; Saketopoulou, 2013).

As a psychoanalyst, I am interested in the ways in which a particular individual and her or his internalized self and object representations embody these culturally imposed power relations, since the instantiation of these will vary across individuals. These frame desire in highly individual ways (Chodorow, 1995; see Yanof, 2000, for a child case report), including how each individual embodies femininity and masculinity as both culturally defined and relationally particularized. These then become the structures of subjectivity.

The binary is not dead; it is not even binary

Contemporary psychoanalytic theorists have employed a variety of evocative images to depict human development in its complexity across time and space. Metaphors such as kaleidoscopes (Davies, 1998a), bridges connecting countries (Bromberg, 1998), fractals amid chaos (Harris, 2005a; Levine, 2009), a bicycle wheel with multiple spokes (see Chapter 4, this volume) and the general idea of multiplicity (Mitchell, 1993; Stern, 2010) have all been used to capture the big picture of psychological development.

If we take one step in and attempt to discern an organizing principle, it is possible (in broad strokes) to view a variety of developmental imperatives rotating around a binary, e.g., relationality and autonomy or intimacy and solitude. The mind naturally perceives contrasts, but in reality there is a multidimensionality and seemingly endless variety within. So we must hold these polarities lightly, always with the knowledge that the reality is much more complex. A postmodern epistemology reframes the entire project of understanding human development; still, a variety of dialectics can be situated within it, where moments in psychoanalytic theorizing have their place. The individual *embedded in culture, embodied and emergent in relation* is a cornerstone of contemporary epistemology, especially in relational perspectives. Through this lens, a retrospective view on psychoanalytic theorizing situates and signifies early classical theories as attempts to explain the individual's striving for autonomy, separateness, and psychic differentiation. In this way, it can be viewed that early phallocentric theorizing called out for the revolution that eventually toppled its dominance; some gynocentrist views of feminist theorizing engaged in the same polarization from the other end.[6]

My stance is inclusive, finding a place for each end of the polarity as the individual struggles to resolve conflicting needs or opposing wishes. No dialectics exemplify this inclusive approach better than those that revolve around gender (see Goldner, 1991; Benjamin, 1995; Dimen, 2003; Harris, 2005a; Thurer 2005). Further, it is in the sexual arena that core conflicts and personality schisms are played out in a variety of adaptive and maladaptive efforts at resolution. Gender and sexuality, together, form a nexus around which privately held fantasies display their inhibiting and destructive power. It is psychologically and emotionally healthy *to include*, yet we are often moved *to exclude*. Inclusiveness, embodiedness, intensity, flexibility, and range in one's affective life—these are the components of healthy psychological functioning and the aims around which treatment is focused.

In my clinical experience, I have come to believe that everyone must reckon with, must come to terms with, as a developmental imperative, their capacity for *receptivity and potency*, accessibility and force, openness and backbone. Put as a more traditional stereotype: the feminine and masculine within us all. These binaries, split in two for psychic clarity only, function in dialectic relation; that is, they define and imply each other by contrast and play against each other as they mutually deepen.

Various self-states can be described in terms of the degree to which the phenomenal experience is *receptive* (feelingful) and *potent* (agentic). A healthy state of mind is maximally both, and the embodied subject is defined by these two characteristics. *Embodiment* is sensate *receptivity* to feeling and affective aliveness. The capacity to harness one's *potency* (or authority) is what is meant by being a *subject*, the experience of articulated selfhood. Taken together in a feelingful agency is what I mean by *embodied subjectivity*. (In the concluding chapter of this book, I offer a schematic that depicts several subjective positions, elaborating on this central position and how the recognition of these various self-states can clarify an individual's relationship to various capacities and inhibitions.)

In an overall way, and from within the position of the experiencing self (the experiencer/agent or embodied subject), individual experience can be described as some amalgam of *receptivity and potency*—in the language of sexuality, *holding and penetration* or, in the language of the body, *openness and backbone*. Put as a more traditional stereotype: the feminine and masculine,[7] but here representing bi-gendered aspects of the self as opposed to one over the other. Indeed, to describe phenomenal experience from the position of the *embodied subject*, I am describing this dialectic, the experiencer/agent as a position where one has achieved some blend of access to feeling (*receptivity*) and articulated selfhood (*potency*).

And so we have a number of dialectics held as complementary developmental imperatives: autonomy and intimacy, relationality and solitude, fortitude and receptivity, to name a few. These too can be gendered, but again, this is a facility of our own making and not to be viewed as inherent.[8] Fortitude/receptivity can be viewed through the traditional gender stereotype of a phallic/receptive dialectic, summoning the now well-worn and politically tainted masculine/feminine iconography.

Gender is one of many difference markers (Goldner, 1991) that poses a binary facilitating the organization of an early self, as the preoedipal child awakens to gender differences. In Goldner's (2002) words, "Gender [is] a transcendent social category whose truth, though false, remains central to thought" (p. 70). Other binaries may serve the same purpose (see, for example, Stoller, 1968, Chodorow, 1978, and Holzman and Kulish, 2000, for a discussion of the way gender may be used as an organizer of separation, Chodorow, 2004, 2011, for a discussion of the little girl/mother polarity, Chassegeut-Smirgel,1984, for a discussion of generational difference, and Laplanche, 1997, for a discussion of the child's negotiation of the primal scene). These gendered splits often form the basis of segregated or dissociated aspects of the self that need to be recuperated and reconnected, as in the post-oedipal recuperation of earlier bi-sexual self-other identifications (Bassin, 1996; Benjamin, 1998; Elise, 2002b; see Celenza, 2012 for a discussion of how gendered splits can collude in the organization of cross-gendered identifications). These gendered dualities can sequester nonconscious, body-based aspects of self that may be unconsciously communicated in the "intermediacy" (Civitarese, in press) of the clinical setting.

The TV series *Mad Men* makes use of such stereotypy, and another artful illustration is the movie *Flawless*. This Tribeca sleeper centers around two characters

Introduction: transcending binaries   5

each of whom embodies a gendered extreme: the hyper-masculine war hero, Walt Koontz (played by Robert De Niro), who has little patience for human frailty and a 'pre-op' transsexual, Rusty (played by Phillip Seymour Hoffman) who is saving money for her sex-change operation. Both of these characters depict real life efforts at stereotyping: Walt is the prototypical male chauvinist and Rusty wants to be 'all she.' By some strange coincidence of fate, they live in the same apartment building in the meat-packing district of Greenwich Village. They hate each other, of course, each embodying the essence of what the other is attempting to disavow. A cerebral aneurism bursts their respective bubbles (so to speak) as Walt finds himself unable to speak from a stroke. His doctor suggests he take singing lessons to regain his ability to articulate. Rusty happens to teach singing. Through their mutual need, each gives the other a priceless gift—Rusty becomes more courageous, more able to forcefully stand up for what she wants (a touch of maleness, despite herself) and Walt finds his humanity in all its vulnerability. Through mutual identifications, each one gives something vital to the other that crosses the boundaries of the forced polarity, at least in this film, of classical gender stereotyping.

It can be argued that the use of classical gender stereotyping harkens back to outmoded conceptualizations, and phallocentric theorizing in particular. I believe we can avoid the past adverse effects of patriarchy and male hegemony (see Reis and Grossmark, 2009) especially pejorative connotations toward either gender and the ways in which these imply power hierarchies, while restoring useful but presently taboo concepts by placing them in a contemporary and depoliticized context. I am attempting to correct what I see as a tendency to discard concepts wholesale when certain meanings have become outmoded while leaving our patients to struggle alone with their imbalanced reckonings. It is not merely an intellectual problem, since language structures, and is structured by, unconscious processes. The gendered referents of masculinity and femininity need such reformulation, as does the word 'phallic' itself. Rather than omitting these words from our lexicon, I have chosen to use terms such as 'phallic' *precisely because* it conjures the associations of masculinity, but I have a different purpose and context in mind.

I am aiming at a similarity with a crucial difference (Celenza, 2010b)—recontextualized and patient-driven. Michael (described extensively in Chapters 2 and 3) conceived of himself in traditionally gendered ways; that is, he defined his masculinity (or lack thereof) in terms of his potency and phallic prowess—these words conveyed his subjective experience from his point of view. Likewise, his way of being receptive was wholesale. He didn't associate these impulses with femininity, but had he, the problem would not have been in the naming; it was the *lack of balance* between his desire for the other and his own subjectivity. These issues were reflected in both sexual and nonsexual realms. Once named, they could be accessed and explored in multiple realms more easily.

Beyond the specific case, I aim to expand the vision of the self in an inclusive and gendered multiplicity (Benjamin, 1995; Harris, 2005a; Reis and Grossmark, 2009). We women have men (and boys, little, old, adolescent, and so on) within us, as well as the anatomically concordant gendered beings.[9] Similar to Diamond's (2004, 2009) plea to "make room for the mother in the man" and Fogel's (1998) conception of male 'inner genitality,' I hold that phallic striving and active receptivity, mother and father, man and woman, girl and boy, are part of a gendered multiplicity within us all. Just as heterosexual males have been reduced, homogenized, unmarked, and foreclosed (Reis, 2009), I seek to describe both genders with heterogeneity, contradiction, and ambiguity while striving for holism in an ongoing lifelong process. At the same time, I understand that this effort, especially in gendered form, will not resonate with everyone. I recognize that gender as a difference marker (Goldner, 1991) is only one way of organizing experience. I continue to believe, however, that depoliticizing a variety of terms makes them once again available for use in everyday imaginings.

My stance is to engage this polarity (receptivity and potency), stereotypically definitional of femininity and masculinity, in order to expose this polarity as a false dichotomy, the poles of which are not actually opposite (thereby are not mutually exclusive) in any register of meaning. These reckonings and the particular individual's negotiation of each may define the ways in which gender is instantiated, experienced and expressed from within the embodied subject.[10] They may also vary *intra*-individually as relational patterns shift and self-experience multiplies and expands. *Most importantly, I view these poles as liberated from any hierarchic power relation, in that neither pole is privileged*, though in any particular individual one may be.[11] Even in its disavowal, each pole of this duality will be relevant, along with multiple gendered and nongendered dualities revolving around this "force field" (Dimen, 1991). This is what I mean to convey with the play on Faulkner's (1951) phrase, *the binary is not dead; it is not even binary.*

One aim of clinical practice is to liberate our patients from constraint and degradation in the construction of self-referents, of which gender is a foundational organizer. An aspect of the initial engagement in the clinical setting involves the adoption (temporarily) of our patients' language (gender stereotypes being "available as consensual linguistic categories" [Stein, 1995b, p. 308]) in order to join each individual in her or his way of organizing subjective experience and their relation to the world. As treatment progresses, it becomes possible to transcend cultural stereotypes (of gender, race, ethnicity, age, etc.) and expand self-experience and gender repertoire (Elise, 1998; see Stein, 1995a, for an elaboration of clinical process with a transsexual patient; see Long, 2005, for a panel report on the function of binary systems in promoting cross-classification). This expansion involves the acceptance and inclusion of binarial, oppositional categories in a 'both/and' multiplicity, in effect to achieve a *unique gender blend*.[12] This blend reveals the binary as a false dichotomy and guards against polarization in favor of a playful oscillation between the two and the many (see Goldner, 1991, and Harris, 2005a, for extensive development of this idea).

As an example of the clinical use of a patient's problematic binarial construction, Paul, who has diagnosed himself with erectile dysfunction and who relies on Viagra, spoke about his envy of his wife's business accomplishments. He had just read *Mating in Captivity* by Esther Perel (2007) and disagreed with her findings about what makes one's partner sexually appealing to the other. He said, "I'm not attracted to Jeannie [his wife] because she's successful. I think it makes her masculine, not feminine or attractive to me." I saw my patient's dilemma: trapped in the captivity of traditional masculine/feminine gendered splits, he felt that his wife's gain was his loss. In yesterday's session, he remembered disliking coed camps growing up. He said he preferred all-boys camps where, "it was all about sports. That's what boys did in the boys' camps; and the girls, I don't know what they did." We used the language of the body in the ensuing discussion, a language he is comfortable with, in which I posed his dilemma as a forced choice between openness and backbone: he should have the backbone; his wife should be all openness and lace. He saw his unconscious gendered split and his disclaimed struggle for vulnerability and affective intensity.

Further, as difference feminism (Miller, 1976; Gilligan, 1982; Kestenberg, 1982; Jordan, 1992) and many other gender critiques (Goldner, 1991; Kaplan, 1991; Benjamin, 1998; Dimen, 2003; Harris, 2005a; Aron, 2011) confront and attempt to liberate the repudiation of femininity in cultural practices, I am also attempting to return the 'phallus' to our clinical vocabulary, not as a privileged signifier, but as a developmentally meaningful signifier for both genders.[13] (Corbett [2009] speaks of the expansive relational potential of phallic, aggressive, assertive, extending, and thrusting play and wonders about a kind of *phallophobia* that has crept into our theorizing.) Embedded in the idea of potency, thrust, penetration, and assertion, the signification of the phallus and traditionally feminine signifiers can be traced to early self-other identifications, all of which derive from primary bisexuality (see, for example, Kubie, 1974; Samuels, 2000a; Schaverien, 2006b), a kind of equipotentiality and polymorphous erotic potential in us all.

Case illustration

Becky is a 53-year-old married woman with three children. She is a highly placed executive in a Fortune 500 company. She is having an affair with a bouncer/bodybuilder whom she met at a bar and revels in the way he "makes her feel feminine." From the start, Becky has struggled to break up with him, readily admitting to me, "He has no place in my life and could be dangerous to my marriage and family." Each session she tells me and herself that she will stop seeing him yet ends up having sex with him, sometimes directly after our session, despite her conviction never to see him again. He is unreliable, self-centered, and controlling; he causes her much emotional distress in his unavailability except when he spontaneously calls her for a quickie.

Becky also has a fetishistic attachment to her lover's body, and in this sense he is objectified. She describes his very large penis and his musculature, the way in which she does not have to display any aspect of her desire—he takes her, he dominates the interaction and it is always on his terms. Otherwise, their liaisons are disappointing, frustrating, or infuriating. She describes him as "not good enough but *just enough* . . . actually *barely* enough" where his ways of contacting her are so infrequent that Becky's relationship with him never threatens to upset her marriage and life, yet *just enough* to keep her titillated and wanting more.

We have come to realize that these are the very qualities that described her father from whom she was traumatically separated in her pre-adolescent years. He had a series of affairs during her childhood that placed her mother in a chronically helpless and distraught frame of mind. In this way, we surmise that Becky makes contact with her little girl self—waiting for her philandering father, experiencing his disappointing unreliability—and obtains a sexual satiation by feeling his macho domination (especially contrasted with her disclaimed desire and agency in relation to him), which is intense but fleeting. In all of this, she experiences herself as feminine in the repudiated, passive, and degraded sense. *We could say that this aspect of herself in relation to him is trapped in the feminine side of a traditional masculine/feminine binary*; her lack of agency is a reflection of the inadequate development of her *potency* or strength.

Becky's inability to "cut the relationship off" refers to another aspect of the traditional passive feminine ideal as well. Derived from her inability to be forceful, potent, or assertive on her own behalf, she cannot bear to conceive of hurting or separating from him *for fear of damaging him*. She disclaims her own desire to end the relationship by maintaining an empathic connection with *his* desire. She harms herself in order to avoid harming him.[14]

In all of the foregoing, we see how Becky disclaims her authorized subjectivity, projecting her desires and agency into her lover, as she constructs his body as a ready container for her own 'too big' and too potent desires. She reveals her anxiety about being 'too big' through her mode of relating to him. When she receives accolades at work, she becomes anxious, feeling as if the image of herself as highly successful is "not really her." At these times, she often has the urge to view a picture of her lover's naked body. She finds relief when she gazes at its intactness and beauty. We have speculated that unconsciously, as a result of her professional successes, she may be checking his picture to be reassured he is not castrated. If she succeeds, does he fail? If she is potent (phallic), is he castrated? And more pointedly, did she *do that to* him, i.e., does her potency make her too powerful?

In subsequent years, Becky has experienced increasing success at work (including awards and public prominence). When these occur, she has the urge to have sex with her lover in a celebratory way—to see him ejaculate like an uncorked bottle of champagne. The polarization of their roles (he the dominator, taker, über-male) reassures her that she remains a (degraded, i.e., small, impotent) woman, incapable of harming him. In this way, her actions have the structure of harming (i.e., diminishing) *her*, not him. He is used to externalize her dangerous desire which is then disclaimed. At least for Becky, this seems to reflect a wish to control a self-experience of wanting too much, desiring too much or becoming or being too potent. We can see an unconscious fear of authorizing her 'phallic' power, a struggle with assertion, potency, and the dread of being too big or too strong.

Becky recently remarked,

> The more I recognize my power, the less I feel I need him. At the same time, I can see how he brings me down. No, I debase myself by being with him. It's almost as if I am acting like a man . . . I get a bonus and I start having an affair. Maybe it's a fantasy of *being* a man too. He's like my penis.

We see the challenge ahead as Becky's need to contain and tolerate, actively authorize her own power as a strong, successful woman without fear of damaging either herself or anyone else.

In relation to me, it appears I hold the maternal transference in both positive and negative aspects. Though she frustrates me with her 'philandering' like her mother was frustrated with her father's affairs, I am also a mother who admires and enjoys her accomplishments. She tearfully states,

> It's lonely being successful. I can't tell my mother, she can't handle it and be happy for me. You don't withdraw or retreat in envy, like she does. My challenge is to embrace power without feeling narcissistic, like my father, or castrating because I am so angry, or like a thief, taking success away from somebody else. Who is that anyway? It's mine, it's all mine.

Recently, Becky was asked to give a speech extemporaneously in front of a very large audience. She described the experience to me.

> It wasn't scripted and I was proud. It was spur of the moment and I felt it was really me. Like me there and me here are the same. You know that side of me; it's separate yet connected. Afterwards, I thought of sending you a picture of Frank (her lover), then I realized I wanted you to see *me*. So you would be proud of me and for yourself too. I couldn't have done this 5 years ago, speaking my mind with such confidence. Just being myself.

Discussion

I am proposing the clinical engagement of a binary, receptivity and potency, because of the way in which it conjures bodily language, not in an essentialist manner but expressive of where the individual positions herself or himself within this dialectic and how each pole is experienced and actualized through embodied experience; i.e., the extent to which one's phenomenal subjectivity is characterized by receptivity to (feelingful) experience and agency (potency). Given the socially constructed nature of desire, excessive and enigmatic (Stein, 1998), it often becomes organized along this binarial axis at different points in different mental states, each with its own unique gender blend. In Kaplan's (1991) words,

A female's forbidden masculine wishes have the same disastrous impact on her life as the analogous forbidden feminine wishes have on the life of a male. What adult women and men want is to regain access to the parts of themselves that they have learned to distrust and fear in the course of growing up from childhood to adulthood... powers, ambitions, longings that they had regarded as intrinsic to the little person they were—and that these precious treasures were stolen away. In a society where there are real and considerable disparities between the powers granted to men and the powers granted to women, the distinctions between male genitals and female genitals are a convenient way to symbolize all sorts of dissatisfactions, injustices, and disappointments.

(p. 182)

By stating *the binary is not dead, it is not even binary*, I aim to call attention to the fact that there is no inherent opposition between (phallic) potency and (feminine) receptivity, but an imperative to reckon with each that is beyond gendered complementarity. Striving for 'integration' might be translated into a striving to expand one's gender multiplicity (Aron, 1995), gender repertoire (Elise, 1998), gender portrait (Balsam, 2001), the capacity for gender mobility or gender variance (Corbett, 2009) and the achievement of postoedipal overinclusiveness, including "gender ambiguity and uncertainty" (Benjamin, 1998, p. 73); i.e., each person's unique gender blend. Along these lines, there is a way in which gendered dichotomies collapse unrelated aspects of selfhood (Dimen, 1991; Harris, 1991; Stein, 1995a; Chodorow, 1995, 2011), such as intimacy (receptivity) or assertion (potency), that are thereby disguised through stereotyped, gender roles (see Sherfey, 1966; Lerner, 1976; Fogel, 1998; and Hartman, 2010b, for discussions in terms of inner-directed and outer-directed genital sensations).

In the ongoing striving for a unified or core self, this differentiated but connected self system reflects a multi-faceted network with permeability and access to a variety of self-states that are variously gendered and sexed. The recuperation of bisexual potential (Aron, 1995; Bassin, 1996; Benjamin, 1998; Elise, 1998; Fogel, 1998; Suchet, 2011) might be further expanded as well, to a multi-gendered and multi-sexual self-system. At some point, the gendered or sexed language, mired in binary opposition and culturally encoded power gradients, loses its efficacy in conveying the ultimately individualistic ways in which each person inhabits her/his multiple potentials (Chodorow, 2004, 2011; Goldner, 2011).[15] There is no resolution that points toward becoming an essence of one thing (gender or otherwise) but a greater tolerance for ambiguity and contradiction across the broad spectrum.

Notes

1 Similarly, Samuels (2000b) suggests that a function of the good enough parent is to communicate to children (of both sexes) that they are admirable, physically desirable, and erotically viable creatures.

2 I realize in posing gender as an immediate, defining characteristic of an individual, I am asserting a universalist claim that disregards alternative cultures where gender divisions are not relevant or primary categories. If, however, it can be asserted that Western cultural regulatory practices are drenched in gender, then my arguments may at least be applied to those cultures where binarial divisions of gender lay claims on the unconscious of the individual. Interestingly, Young-Breuhl (1996) emphatically states, "No society is without its 'sex/gender system'; there are no ungendered destinies" (p. 9). In contrast, Dimen (2011, personal communication) speaks of cultures where gender divisions (or further, 'self and other') are not opposed.

3 Eve Sedgwick's (1990) felicitous phrase, "Some people are more gender-y than others" comes to mind here. What I aim to describe are the variety of ways in which persons may present themselves that aim (consciously and unconsciously) to convey the gendered aspects of their being in a more or less distinctive (singular or multiple) manner. For example, in styles of dress, displaying one's gender in America would be those styles of dress that traditionally represent the male/female distinction—high heels, a short skirt, and a bustier exaggerate the female body in traditionally Western ways that contrast to the American male. While these choices vary intra-individually and across contexts, I aim here to capture a moment in time, i.e., upon meeting another person in a particular time and place.

4 Indeed, there is a "porosity" among all identity categories (e.g., race, class, gender, ethnicity) that mutually influence the construction of identity (see Munoz, 1999; Halberstam, 2005; and Saketopoulou, 2011).

5 I confine my arguments to those (primarily Western) cultures that foreground individuation in some dialectical relational process, where the establishment of boundaries around early experiences of selfhood necessarily requires the negotiation of difference (hence, a binarial construction of self vs. other). Because my concern is in clinical matters, the clinical setting will always be embedded within a particular cultural context that requires, at least initially, shared linguistic categories (see Stein, 1995b), and these may include a division in gender categories.

6 Dimen (1998) cogently argues that relational theory itself is the site of excess, a theory which can only be practiced in the tension between one and two person psychologies. In relational theorizing, the binary is 'overcome.' "If you look deeply enough into one, you come upon the other" (p. 70).

7 I realize articulating this binary can be misunderstood as promoting one pole over the other, in line with the ways in which Western culture traditionally organizes sexual and gendered splits. I am not supporting the traditional delegation of a host of (gendered and nongendered) relations associated with each pole to either female or male (e.g., femininity with passivity, to name the most prevalent). Risking this misunderstanding, I am proposing the articulation of this binary because it is helpful in describing clinical problems, ways in which individuals are trapped in gender polarities and splits, with the clinical aim of transcending these (see Dimen [1991] and Benjamin [1998] for further discussion of splitting and its interface with gender polarity).

8 Compare, for example, Schiller's (2012) labial framework of sexuality as a specifically female form of desire.

9 The case of intersexed persons presents an interesting challenge as well. At the very least, they demonstrate that there are no lines in nature, reflecting the need for more than two categories, a move from the binary to multiplicity in the conception of gendered selves (Fausto-Sterling, 2008). Intersexed persons, however, are the rare case (.1%–1.7% depending on the criteria used); my arguments are derived from the great majority of persons where gender is split, however artificially, in two.

10 See the concluding chapter for an elaboration of this subjective position.

11 Compare Schiller's (2012) framework of female sexuality that she conceives as 'existing alongside' the traditional phallicentric framework.

12 Along similar lines, Lingiardi (2007) discusses the ways in which refusing forced binaries does not mean defending the gray area equidistant from the two extremes.
13 Likewise, Schaverien (2006b) refers to the phallus as embodying the paternal function and other qualities associated with the law, which are not necessarily the province of men.
14 For interesting distinctions, see Kaplan's (1991) depiction of Emma Bovary, Janet and others, all of whom unconsciously use their lover's phallus to confirm their femininity and defend against abandonment. Similarly, compare Riviere (1929) who formulated a woman's response to her exhibitionistic urges as a fear of male reprisal for having castrated him.
15 See Diamond (2004) for a compatible discussion in relation to male identity and multiple gender identifications that are reworked in mid-life.

Part I

Erotics embodied

Transferences and countertransferences

Introduction to Part I

*Thus the significance of psychoanalysis
is less to make psychology biological
than to discover a dialectical process
in functions thought of as 'purely bodily',
and to reintegrate sexuality into the human being.*

M. Merleau-Ponty, 1962

There is an amusing story of two friends in a nudist colony. They are walking together, naked, around the grounds. One has a band-aid on his upper arm. The other asks, "Can I see what's under that band-aid?" We are drawn to the hidden and mysterious; we are tempted to push boundaries, even in the most permissive contexts. Erotic experience exemplifies this urge (Stein, 1998). What is the nature of this push, this urge to get beyond the immediate and concrete? What are we looking for, what does it feel like? These are some of the questions that pertain to the present exploration into erotic life in the psychoanalytic and psychotherapeutic situation.

Given sexuality's ubiquity in our culture and private fantasy life, it is remarkable to note the pervasive desexualization of psychoanalysis, a once sex-infused theory of human development. Indeed, Mann (1997) claims the erotic is the heart of one's unconscious fantasy life. We, as psychoanalysts, seemed to have known this at one time, but have forgotten it now. There was a time when psychoanalysis was viewed as 'all about sex.' In recent decades, however, it seems not to be about sex at all.[1] This ironic desexualization of psychoanalytic theory is thought to be an unintended consequence of the emergence of the interpersonal and object relations theories,[2] along with the two-person paradigm shift in psychoanalytic theorizing. Fonagy (2008) quantified the apparent decline in interest in sexuality by examining word usage in electronically searchable journals of psychoanalysis. He found that the decline in sexual word usage is inversely related to the rise in relational word usage. So it appears that the decline in interest in sexuality has come about through, at least in part, the emphasis on object relational and especially preoedipal strains in human development and the therapeutic setting.

Similarly, sexuality has virtually disappeared from much of the writings on sadomasochistic relating, with an emphasis instead on pregenital, non-erotic needs. As Green (1995) stated, it is as if the etiologic determinants of psychopathology are thought to be located 'before' or 'beyond' sexuality. Dimen (1999) attributed much of the desexualization of psychoanalysis to the paradigm shift in contemporary theory from drive to object relations, noting that "where libido was, there shall objects be" (p. 417).

Despite the de-emphasis, underestimation, or outright neglect, I doubt that sex has ever budged from the forefront of anyone's mind. In only the last few decades, sexualization, both in its defensive function and as an intrinsic aspect of human relating, has begun to be refound. In particular, the maternal erotic transference has been reconceptualized as another version of erotic desire, leading to explorations of the erotic nature of preoedipal sexuality (e.g., Chassaguet-Smirgel, 1970, 1993; McDougall, 1992; Benjamin, 1994a; Wrye and Welles, 1994; Dimen, 2003; Harris, 2005a). Space has also been cleared for the possibility of genuine, non-neurotic loving aspects of attachment. Bolognini (1994) describes erotic transferences along a developmental continuum (from erotized, to erotic, to loving, and finally affectionate), comprising a broader range of meanings for erotic transferences (see also Bonasia, 2001; De Masi, 2012). Subsequently, Bolognini (2011) has delineated the multiple roles of the analyst in relation to the patient as well. All of these, from both the analyst's and the patient's perspectives, should make their appearance in the evolving phases of a *thorough-going* therapeutic treatment.[3]

Intimacy embodied

With the assumption of the individual as embedded in culture, embodied and emergent in relation, I conceive of healthy sexuality as a capacity for *intimacy embodied*, rendering any discussion of sexuality as referencing a body/being in relation to another body/being. I do not mean to imply that every healthy sexual *act* should involve an intimate union with another person, but that healthy sexual functioning must include *the capacity* for intimate sexual union. Simon (2013) traces the defining characteristics of healthy sexuality throughout the history of psychoanalytic theorizing and notes a tension between two registers of sexual functioning: mutual, reciprocal and whole object *relationality* along with the capacity for intense bodily *pleasure*. Note that these registers do not prescribe particular attitudes or behaviors per se, with the exception of privileging freedom, excitement, and pleasure within bodily and relational domains (Kernberg, 1991a). Sexuality, then, is not about anatomy or the genitals; the body is not separate or distant from one's experience of it. Healthy sexuality is a capacity for body-based erotic union with another. Psychoanalytic theorizing, however, has gradually lost its emphasis on sexuality in recent decades. My intent is to re-engage theorizing of sexuality within this holistic paradigm.

It's been said that in psychoanalysis, everything is about sex . . . except for sex; that's about aggression. It is true to the point of cliché that psychoanalysis, as a hermeneutic discipline, has revolved around the discovery or construction of meaning behind or underneath, an infinite project which changes and evolves with new perspectives, different lenses, and personal transformations. There is an ever-present temptation to use visuo-spatial metaphors, analogizing to the concrete world, where different locations shift one's perspective, where the construction of meaning can be categorized as surface to depth. There has been a sense in which psychoanalysis has had the *feel* of depth as elusive meanings were constructed from the previously unthought. The idea of a hidden, as in 'there but not visible,' proved heuristic and became bedrock, easier to imagine as concretized levels. Thus Freud's unconscious was almost a place . . . if not found, at least imagined as under, buried inside the depths of one's being, waiting to be discovered.

Layers became part of the leveled, hierarchical structure, with the more primitive envisioned as further away, earlier in time, and deeper in inward space. Psychoanalytic explorations searched for meaning beyond the surface; an ulterior and interiorized motive, as it were. Everything became about something else and sex, already complex, forbidden, and fascinating, was a particular source of mystery. But is there a place for erotic longing in our minds and bodies that does not point elsewhere?[4] And what about that surface? The surface reveals the depth itself, more as a quality of beyond in a transcendent, meaning-making effort whose limit is infinite. It is through the exploration of erotics in clinical process that I address my first purpose: sex can be viewed holistically as *intimacy embodied*. It is at once a two-person embedded and embodied relational experience. It is concrete in the sense that it is a body-based experience, and in that sense, it is surface yet at the same time expresses the full intensity and depth of feeling for the individual.

Eros embodied

Second, my focus on the erotic nature of the therapeutic situation is an effort to *reclaim sexuality* as one of the many nexes that are of central concern to our patients. As mentioned, I am asserting that erotic transferences, of whatever shape, should make their way into every *thorough-going* analysis or therapy at some point. For over a century now, the prospect of placing erotic life front and center has been akin to holding down a scared rabbit in the woods. It has eluded even the psychoanalysts for which the tendency to search for meaning behind or beyond the manifest[5] is almost routine. Deconstructing sexuality by searching beyond it has virtually, and I believe unintentionally (at least on a conscious level), made it disappear from our writings and thinking. Psychoanalysis developed through Freud's shocking discoveries of the erotic nature of his patients' symptomatology, all within the context of a repressive cultural time. Freud's main intent throughout his writings has been to legitimize psychoanalysis as a 'hard' science despite its scandalous content. In the past few decades, emphasis on object relational theories, the maternal/preoedipal, and otherwise unintentionally desexualized relational theories have once again relegated sexuality to the background as the maternal figure and her containing function became the primary focus (Green, 1995; Celenza, 2000; Dimen, 2003; Fonagy, 2008). So, what's sex got to do with it?

Desire structures perception and, given this, it is easy to understand how the therapeutic structure can provide an igniting spark to erotic excitement. Our patients come to the therapeutic setting with unfulfilled longing on conscious and unconscious levels. Analysts and therapists also have wishes and levels of comfort that influence what is seen, heard, and said. Many behaviors and statements made by the therapist are accompanied by rationalizations that serve to justify (in the moment) their expression. It is only after the fact that the analyst may become aware of a self-serving or defensive aspect to his/her expression that prevented the therapist from seeing its inadvisability. Many self-disclosures fall into this category (see Chapter 5 for an elaboration of this issue). The context that is likely to provide the fodder for a defensive, erotic reaction on the therapist's part may be the patient's emerging disappointment, sometimes stated directly but often just subliminally sensed by the therapist.[6] If the therapist is unable to explore and tolerate the patient's frustration, he/she may react with a conscious rationale to become more revealing, perhaps by disclosing some personal information with the idea that the patient will benefit from learning of some similarity between them.

Consider the following: An analyst had a dream in which the last patient from his workday (who happens to look like his daughter) appears. The dream involves a pertinent theme for the patient that, coincidentally, is also a timely conflict for the analyst. He decides to disclose the dream in the next session with the conscious rationale that the patient may see her conflict from a new perspective. What does she hear? Only, "You are in my dreams," when, in fact, it is not at all clear that the patient was the relevant person for this analyst, on this particular night and in this particular circumstance.

Yet, our theories have become desexualized to an extent that fails to prepare clinicians with the necessary armamentarium to cope with the level of desire and erotic material likely to emerge. This is even more ironic when we consider how easily the treatment situation (perhaps any intimate relationship) lends itself to sexual metaphor. The dialectic between holding and penetration fosters a mutual deepening and this dialectic is itself a sexual metaphor. For both therapist and patient, the psychotherapeutic work is penetrating and enveloping, incisive and holding, a firm receptivity that retains, envelops, and holds the other in mind.[7]

From the patient's point of view, resistance to the erotic transference can take many forms: the inability to process or hold the analyst's insights; warding off the invasive, penetrating mother; or being unable to feel the analyst's receptivity to the patient's prowess or insight. Criticisms of the analyst as uncaring, unsupportive, not listening, not recognizing, or wielding her authority to dominate, or remain superior are all phenomenal experiences that may reflect such dynamics. Alternatively, being unable to perceive the analyst's ability to *hold him*, retain what has been said, or contain the patient's aggression (without retaliation) can become allusions to an underlying aggressivized erotic transference.

Erotic transferences and countertransferences

Throughout this book, I will be referring to erotic transferences and countertransferences and their therapeutic usage in contrast to sexual or sexualized transferences. The latter are more simple and straightforward, emerging as the expressed desire to have sexual intercourse with the analyst or therapist. These do not necessarily reflect an erotic relation, but an urgent need and demand to have sex with the analyst that is unelaborated and unrepresented. Erotic transferences are more complex and involve the patient's incorporation of the therapist or analyst into their private erotic fantasies (Bollas, 1994; Mann, 1997), i.e., the imaginative use of the analyst as an object of desire. These reflect erotic transferences and can then become grist for the analytic mill. Therefore, *the first step in the treatment setting is to elaborate the sexual transference into an erotic transference*, i.e., to explore the patient's fantasies as they are associated with the wish to have sexual relations with the therapist or analyst.

No matter what variety or form, erotic transferences are intensely challenging. There quickly arises a pressing need to manage the blossoming transference, as clinicians urgently want to prevent the patient from engaging in some threatening behavior—either to the analyst/therapist or to him/herself—losing the capacity to think or, in the extreme, having a psychotic breakdown. But before any of these questions can be addressed, there must be an adequate understanding of what a particular erotic transference means, i.e., what is your patient desiring, and what is being expressed when the patient makes a plea for (sexualized) love?

Along these lines, it is incumbent upon the analyst or therapist to remember that in many (if not most) instances, *erotic longing is a demand for love in the absence of a capacity for loving* (Frayn and Silberfeld, 1986). As in all transferences that are particularly intense, the strength of the demand signifies a host of unresolved, conflicted feelings or developmental deficits that drive and motivate manifest longings. Though the patient demands (and thinks he or she needs) a sexual relationship, sexualization may be a masquerade, a way of expressing as yet intolerable or otherwise unexpressable longings or vulnerabilities.

Sexuality has many guises and is commonly used in a wide range of defensive efforts. It is remarkably easy to transform a variety of tensions (abhorrences or excitements) to sexual longing. Yet the question to be posed is not simple. If sexualization is apparent and functioning as a defense, it must be asked, "Defense against what?" Here, there is virtually no limit to the variety of needs that may underlie sexualization. Self-object needs, hatred, separation, loss, a desire to destroy, envy, and so on, may all be eroticized as the patient (unconsciously) looks to divert her/his own and the analyst's attention.

To this list must also be added a pure and healthy desire (Bolognini, 2011) for erotic union with the analyst, experienced as an ideal potential lover. As I have written elsewhere (Celenza, 2007), these moments raise a fundamental question, asked most often in unconscious ways: "Why can't we be lovers?" This fundamental question can be posed even between the most unlikely pairs.[8] A useful exercise for the analyst is to wonder why there might be an absence of sexual desire with a particular patient. Why does this patient fail to erotically arouse, and might this be related to the issues of the treatment?

Every thoroughgoing analysis explores the full range of affects, and each in their full intensity. Indeed, this constitutes the definition of health, and its counterpart, the absence of neurotic (unnecessary, irrational, or vitality-constraining) inhibitions. As analysts, we welcome whatever our patients bring through an essentially affirmative attitude toward their symptomatology and problems in living. This is the basis of a nonjudgmental stance. In this spirit, we have to be able to bear intense hatred, contempt, devaluing, and rage, to name a few of the more problematic relational engagements. These affects are brought to the fore so that our patients can deepen their self-understanding and self-acceptance. In this way, we help our patients reckon with dissociated self-states so they can gain access to these parts of themselves and take responsibility for them. In essence, this is what is meant by the striving toward integration.

When sexualization functions as a defense, it is a signification of unresolved affects or modes of relating seeking to hide or evade (Coen, 1992; Kernberg, 1994) and this can be evident in the countertransference as well (Mann, 1997). These often include a repetitive, defensive attempt to magically transform destructive feelings into excitement. Depending on the developmental press, sexualization can function to transform vital urges, preoedipal issues, grief, loss, competitiveness, envy, hatred, and so on. In self-psychological language, Stolorow (1975) and Kohut (1977) speak of *sexually expressed neediness*. In short, "sexual feelings seem so effectively to transform one's perceptions and feelings from bad to good" (Coen, 1992).

I have found it helpful to conceptualize sexualization as either being subtracted from, or added to, a mode of experiencing. For example, erotic longing can be displaced onto alternative mental processes (and, thereby, subtracted from intimate contexts) in order to find expression without being noticed. So-called mental masturbation or the libidinization of thought is a way of using thinking to displace a more threatening erotic engagement in intimate contexts. Money and food are often sexualized, as are many hobbies and sports.[9] As in all defenses, this displacement serves to express erotic longing in a safe arena, thereby evading the vulnerability and threat of intimacy. In these examples, gratification is thereby diverted from a two-person arena and added to a one-person arena (see Part II: Perverse scenarios revisited for elaboration of these ideas).

In contrast, sexualization may be added to a psychological process, transforming an otherwise noxious experience into a pleasurable one. The eroticization of reminiscence can be a defense against mourning and grief; the libidinization of perception (as in sexualized looking or voyeurism) adding or intensifying an already erotic activity. In all of these examples, sexualization may be viewed as being added to a psychological function or experience to effect a transformation by masking an otherwise noxious or forbidden expression.

As in most defenses, sexualization as a defense precludes integration. It is prominently involved in perverse modes of relating, sadomasochistic relations, and pathological dependency (Coen, 1992), but can be used in any developmental constellation where there is an attempt to transform a noxious, intolerable or otherwise distasteful experience into something pleasurable and exciting. Incest, for example, can function as sexualizing in order to defend against separation (especially in the parent's inability to allow the child's resolution of oedipal conflict).

In a more adaptive use, erotic excitement can function to recenter us by locating our experience in our bodies. As I have written elsewhere (Celenza, 2007), many treatments will revolve, at some level, around the question, "Why can't we be lovers?" This question must then be reckoned with, and will involve the use of erotic arousal in the dyad. This experience may dovetail with the analyst's need to recenter him or herself (Sinsheimner, 2008), situate, or ground himself in his body.

Gender embodied

The treatment setting is characterized by asymmetry between analyst and patient, and there is a mystique associated with this asymmetry, especially the way in which the exploration (discovered or co-constructed) is purposefully focused on the patient. This asymmetry leaves the analyst in the shadows, a dark, enigmatic figure that unconsciously reverberates with the vastly superior knowledge and maturity of the parent in the eyes of the child. To stereotype these along the typical Western bifurcation (in terms of gender roles), it is the penetrating, omnipotent gaze of the father as he admires his daughter or the enveloping receptivity of the mother to the son, either of which may coincide with sexual/oedipal and erotic/preoedipal dynamics. It is a sign of a healthy outcome in analysis that the analysand can experience these gendered roles with more fluidity and play, detached from the anatomically based and culturally encoded gender stereotyping.

Over time, the analyst's authority, based on having greater psychological knowledge of the patient, gradually becomes an undeniable reality in the sense that the analyst increasingly broadens and deepens his knowledge of the patient. This parallels another idealization associated with a sexual ideal—the mysterious nature of sexuality itself and the illusion of romantic perfection coinciding with the universal wish to be recognized and known. This is an inherent feature of romantic idealization that is not only structured with the analytic dyad, but in the parent/child dyad, as well (see Stein, 1998, and Davies, 2001, for similar observations). All of these factors, namely the power asymmetry, the mystique of the relatively unknown analyst, and the universal wish to be known, contribute to the seductive aspects of the analytic situation.

If desire structures perception, the body contains, feels, and expresses it. And the body is gendered, at least on an anatomical level. Sex, then, as intimacy embodied, has gender implications. This brings me to my third purpose for this book: to *resurrect, transform, and restore certain terms* and ways of conceptualizing from classical literature by viewing them through a contemporary lens. Terms such as 'perversion' and 'phallic striving' warrant reformulation into more useful ways of conceptualizing, and should not be discarded entirely (see Diamond, 2009, for a similar approach toward masculinity). I hope to salvage the clinical utility of such terms.

Lisa Folkmarson Kall (2009), a contemporary philosopher in Merleau-Ponty's existential phenomenological tradition, writes of the ways in which the self-in-relation experiences and shapes emergent aspects of being:

> The *force* by which the other draws me toward meaning and toward herself is equally a force which *draws me out* of myself and back again. It is paralleled by and in dialogue with an active force by which I draw the other out of herself and toward me. We are each *exposed* to one another, each vulnerable to the other, each *soliciting the awareness and attention* of the other as that off of which we feed for our sense of self and identity. As the other draws me out of myself toward her, I am already *reaching out*, extended into the world through my embodiment. Instead of being passively frozen by the other's activity, I am actively *meeting* her, taking up and responding to her expressions, attempting to understand her and *letting myself be* understood by her, drawing her toward me as she draws me toward her.
>
> (pp. 22–23, italics added)

I especially appreciate, in this deeply evocative language, the immediacy of Folkmarson Kall's description and the 'given' that gender is not a defining characteristic as the two play out an actively receptive and forceful dance. She goes on,

> We resist being determined by others and are driven to expression by the urge 'to explain things we have said that have not been properly understood [and] to reveal what is hidden within us' [Merleau-Ponty, p. 87f/50]. By taking perspective on us, others bring to light our limits and by contesting what we say about them, point to the limits of our own perspectives. I see myself limited by the other and, yet, I nevertheless need the other to give birth to me through dialogue and interaction. I need the other to strengthen and validate as well as doubt and context my experience of the world and of myself.
>
> (Folkmarson Kall, p. 23)

A conversation, then, is made up of ongoing dialectics, one of which can be characterized by the tension between receptivity and potent force. To acquire skill in this interaction, each speaker must also be a listener; the task is not to choose between but to find the balance, the ratio of which will change depending on the particular dyad.

In any examination of sexuality, gender issues arise, since gender identity and gender role development are intrinsic to self-experience and self-expression. This does not imply a singular notion of self, however. The postmodern awareness of multiple potentiality and the multiplicity in self development has expanded our notions of what it means to foster growth in clinical practice along with widening social norms and normative behaviors. Even ideas of true and false selves fall into a restricted binary and unnecessarily truncate "gender's wide arc" (Corbett, 2008).

If the question, "Why can't we be lovers?" is applied to a relational matrix, there arises the specter of the universal longing (and perhaps the universal potential) to infinitely love in multiply configured relational contexts. One way in which these ideas can be usefully translated to the clinical situation is by transcribing the idea of a true or core self to ideas of first or old selves; new or emerging capacities often feel alien simply because they are, as yet, unfamiliar but may hold greater promise for creative potentials than identities or selves that feel more familiar. In this way, the familiar is not necessarily more true, earlier, or core.

Still, the search for realness (or authenticity) is a persistent effort. Some selves feel more real than others; some are rooted (i.e., integrated) within a larger self-system framework, while others are unmistakeably disavowed. The idea of vertical splits, spaces between selves that are bridged (or not), selves hiding behind other, more superficial and less rooted selves, and the distinctive, phenomenal experience of falseness, all continue to have clinical utility.

Opposite gendered selves

As will be repeated throughout this book, we all need to come to terms with our ability to stand erect, while remaining open and receptive to all manner of feeling. These are developmental imperatives for us all—this dialectic, in particular, is easily gendered, but may not be for any one particular individual and is not inherently so. Associating the phallus with a concrete anatomical part (the penis) is an infantile fantasy and reflects the gender and social order of many cultures (Kaplan, 2006). To subscribe to this ideal reflects a nontranscendence of these forced polarities.

More often than not, I have found that an individual's need for treatment presents itself in an imbalanced gendered form and in the literally sexual realm. Along with this, there is a tendency to de-eroticize material. Symptoms are enacted in a dissociated state or are described symbolically, without bodily pleasure. Gendered experience is imbalanced and erotic life is disembodied. Treatment revolves around re-eroticization and re-embodiment. The fundamental imperatives of autonomy and intimacy can easily be translated into a sexual metaphor: the need to stand up, to display one's prowess along with the capacity to hold, sustain, and be accessible to others. In clinical work, the challenge is to be open to sexual metaphor and thereby, to organize an individual's experience revolving around these crucial dialectics: receptivity and thrust, holding and penetration, vulnerability and (phallic) force. Especially for those patients coming to treatment with sexual problems, the sexual symptomatology may be elaborated in other aspects of their functioning. For example, a patient with erectile dysfunction and a lifelong urge toward exhibitionism talks about being quoted for his professional work in a magazine. He was intensely excited in anticipation of the publication, but found himself disappointed, even "deflated" after receiving the issue in the mail. He said, "I knew it was coming, but it didn't last." This statement could just as easily be applied to his sexual functioning, where he anticipates his exposure with great excitement and then loses intensity of feeling when he is actually having sexual relations. All of this is related to the way this patient experiences himself as a 'man' and his difficulty remaining receptive to feelings that he associates with 'femininity.' Harkening back to the dialectical consideration of the stereotypic gender binary, it is impossible to privilege masculinity over femininity (or the other way around). It is a both/and constellation: could anyone choose between assertion and receptivity?

For some patients, this challenge will be translated in a traditional way—hardness and penetration will stand for masculinity, as they did for Michael (see Chapters 2 and 3), traditional stereotyping install and reflect these nongendered strivings. Though Michael would use the traditional masculine/feminine iconography, the analytic work revolved around moving beyond this bifurcation and comprehending the dialectical intertwining of the two.

In the chapters that follow, I present a variety of erotic transference and countertransference experiences as they emerged with several patients in psychoanalysis or psychoanalytic psychotherapy. Different gender mixes are considered and discussed at length with an eye toward reformulation of clinical theory.

Notes

1 See Lichtenberg's (2008) account of sensuality and sexuality "across the divide of shame" and Pajaczkowska and Ward (2008), all of whom posit a central role for shame in the experience of sexual and sensual attachments.
2 Bonasia (2001) wonders if relational models perform a defensive function in eliminating the sexual altogether.
3 Not everyone enters treatment with sexual concerns, however a *thorough-going analysis*, where one's subjective experience and personality organization as a whole is at issue, should, for some period of time, revolve around one's sexuality and erotic life.
4 It can be argued that the search for the underlying meaning of erotic transferences, especially in its defensive usages, is derived from the classical view of the erotic transference as resistance, rather than as an opportunity for transformation (see Mann, 1997).
5 Kernberg (2011) has recently discussed the interpenetration of aggression in sexuality, as in the desire to invade or penetrate.
6 Many sexual boundary transgressions are motivated to manage this clinical situation (Celenza, 2007).
7 See Holtzman and Kulish (1997) for clinical process as a metaphor for defloration.
8 Similarly, Searles (1959) wrote of his experience treating severely disturbed patients and his belief that there needs to come a time in all of these treatments where the analyst can imagine marrying the patient. I contend that the more general question, "Why can't we be lovers?" is potentially present in the analytic couple and, universally, between two people at different times throughout life.
9 The argument could be made that all activities have an erotic component because our bodies perform the activity and our bodies are inherently erotic. Sexualization as used here, however, is observed as a defense by the intensity of investment or interest along with the absence of gratification in otherwise erotic contexts.

Chapter 1

Maternal erotic transferences and merger wishes

> *When we say that the life of the body or the flesh,*
> *and the life of the psyche are involved*
> *in a relationship of reciprocal expression,*
> *or that the bodily event always has a psychic meaning...*
> *[It is] the body's role ... to ensure this metamorphosis.*
> *It transforms ideas into things...*
> *The body can symbolize existence*
> *because it realizes it and is its actuality.*
>
> M. Merleau-Ponty, 1962

Classical models of erotic transferences have historically revolved around oedipal themes in the sense that these transferences are comprised of a reawakening of oedipal desire and its attendant defensive organization. With the burgeoning interest in object relations, interpersonal, and relational theories of development, these models have sensitized us to the emergence of preoedipal desires expressed through the oedipal structure, often as an attempt to use sexuality to disguise earlier wishes and needs.[1] Such preoedipal themes harken back to the maternal/infant dyad and, generally, the literature has not taken into account the sensual and erotic nature of mother/infant interaction in and of itself. One little known exception, however, is Hilferding (1911) who emphasized the erogenous breast.[2]

Contemporary writers aim to elaborate the maternal as erotic. Benjamin (1994a, b) artfully observes the sexuality inherent in the erotic dance of healthy mother-infant interaction (e.g., mutual gazing, gesturing, and vocalizing). She regards the desexualization of preoedipal maternal representation as consistent with the more generalized desexualization and de-erotization of the mother in Western culture. Similarly, Taniguchi (2012) discusses the mother as the object of erotic fantasy and the subject who is doing the fantasizing.

In the last decade, Wrye and Welles (1994) emphasize erotic tonalities in their focus on the sensual bonding between a mother and her baby. They and others (see, for example, Chassaguet-Smirgel, 1970; McDougall, 1992; Benjamin, 1994a, b; Elise, 2002b; Dimen, 2003; Harris, 2005a; Atlas, 2012, 2013; and a series of papers on women working with women in Schaverien, 1995, 2006b) affirm the erotic nature of the early bond with the mother or primary caregiver, wresting eros from the oedipal structure and widening its presence throughout development. These authors suggest early determinants of erotic transferences as present from the beginning and erotic in their own right. Consistent with this assertion is Laplanche's (1997) general theory of seduction, in which he claims that the mother, the universal driving force of all scenes of seduction, presents the infant with her enigmatic, sexual unconscious. These affects and longings are then rekindled in later genital sexuality yet retain the maternal-infant dyad to serve as their template.

Wrye and Welles (1994) use the term "body loveprinting" (p. 34) to refer to interactions derived from maternal ministrations with the infant's body fluids and skin. Referents include experiences as juicy, gooey, and messy as well as fantasies with powerful, sensory imagery of nursing, putting together, getting inside, pouring, patting, poking, smearing, and messing (p. 36). These types of interactions are focused on body sensualities and are decidedly nonverbal, perhaps only 'remembered' or re-experienced through bodily reenactments.

On the maternal side, whether in the therapeutic setting (as in countertransference) or as a conscious or unconscious natural response to the infant, the mother participates in the child's gooey, messy world in an essentially tactile, embodied way. A patient who was severely deprived of tactile affection, literal holding, hugging, and affectionate embraces from his withholding, sterile mother, stirred in me a powerful sense of wanting to touch him, to soothe or stroke his hair in reassuring gestures that might convey a sense of my acceptance of him. Similarly, when my children were young, a poem came to me that I repeated to them often: "Nothing is *ewe* that comes out of *you*." McDougall (1992) states that the baby's earliest reality is his mother's unconscious and, in these ways, the mother provides a nonverbal, receptivity to the primitive communication of "neo-needs" (p 274).

Writers in this area delineate different experiences of the mother at different phases of development, all of which encompass a multi-layered maternal icon. At the most primitive or early developmental level, there is the mother of body ministrations. This mother gives the infant the experience and containment of early sensory impulses. Wrye and Welles (1994) posit these experiences as the seat for the birth of desire at its most primitive level. As is well known, patients with a history of intrusion, neglect, or over-conscientiousness (e.g., in cleaning or hygiene) in relation to their early bodily experiences carry a host of anxieties and discomfort in later life. These anxieties are often located in specific places on their bodies and may become a locus of obsessional activity or sites of impairment in the capacity for sexual excitement (either inhibitions or over-excitations).

Wrye and Welles (1994) elaborate four interrelated narratives manifest in maternal erotic transference, the first of which describes the early, body-based, experience of the mother.[3] These are body-based aspects of self, including active seeking of sensual reciprocity through feeding, bathing, cooing, and holding.

The adult counterpart is recognized in the analysand's expressions of longing for an erotic sensual relationship with the analyst in concrete, nonverbal forms. "These bodily sensations are not symbolic of sexual contact; they *are* the contact . . . bodily feelings are the stuff of these archaic transferences" (p. 58). This quest attempts to re-create the earliest experience of the transformational environmental mother, who is less an object than a process, who is able, through her bodily ministrations to the infant, to "alter self experience" (Bollas, 1987, p. 14).

The underlying erotic elements constituting (preoedipal) maternal longings often go unanalyzed since the erotic in the maternal tends not to be viewed as erotic per se and are distinguished from oedipal strivings by virtue of non-erotic referents. When eros is recognized, however, the nature of bodily experience in relation to another body becomes highly relevant for, and the background to, early identity formation.

In addition, we cannot experience our sexuality without thinking about gender identity, i.e., the body in the sense of who one is in relation to another body, another sex (same or different), and the use of multiple narratives or lexicons in placing oneself in one's own private fantasy world within one's skin. Identifications based on parental relations and the interweaving of gender-based associations can be usefully explored as richly imbued with meaning. Since the body is anatomically gendered and one's body is the foundation upon which identity is based, what mother and father come to represent (boy/girl, masculine/feminine) is shaped through one's experience of the body in these relationships as well.[4]

Jordan (1992) distinguishes two modes of knowing: an empathic/love mode and an objectifying/power/control mode. Similarly, sameness and difference, inside versus outside or other binary categorizations are easily (mis)associated with femaleness versus maleness. For example, the maternal figure can come to represent empathic attunement, resonance, sameness, and the enveloping aspect of understanding. For a little girl, identifications based on sameness may also be viewed as either inherently erotic or defensively eroticized. In the latter case, if parental relations are polarized, there can be an underlying denial of difference and a defensively split transference wherein the positive maternal object is experienced as the empathic, attuned, and desired object, where as the negative paternal object is experienced as intrusively penetrating, disruptive, and unempathically different (see e.g., Britton, 2004).

Still, a question might be asked, Do we need to label these experiences erotic? Does 'sensual' suffice to describe the interactions between mother and infant, then by extension, later forms of non-erotic affection in certain dyads? I suggest that the desire for skin contact, touching, sucking, licking, and ultimately merger (the desire to be inside the other) are so much a part of lovemaking that it is incumbent upon us to acknowledge the essentially erotic nature of these experiences. This chapter aims to bring to the foreground the maternal erotic transference as another version of erotic desire, adding to the literature exploring the erotic nature of early, maternal-infant sexualities.

Longing for sameness and merger wishes

"I'm happy for her, she's always wanted to be married. But I don't want that for myself." Julia, a single woman painter, will now be living alone as her roommate is moving out of their apartment to live with her fiancé. Suddenly, I'm aware of my wedding band on this, our first session, and I feel Julia's gaze weighing heavily on my finger. "I want a steady boyfriend but haven't been able to find one. It upsets me but, mostly, I'm worried about my career. I hate the spotlight and don't like to show my work. I just give my paintings away."

Despite these initial complaints, Julia's appeal to me was a feeling of her basic sense of optimism, which I saw as poignant and charming, yet also naïve. She talked of her childhood as uneventful and happy, recounting, in a blasé way, stories that to me held potentially traumatic aspects. She told me of her birth, "I was planned. My parents were hoping for a boy." Perhaps in a deft move of exacting revenge in the present, she then described her mother's experience in labor (long and painful).

At the start of analysis, Julia did not identify her sexuality as a problem area despite coming to analysis for problems with intimacy. She saw her difficulty with intimacy as separate from her sexuality, preferring to view herself as sexually unconventional and uninhibited. She told me that, in the past, she had enjoyed sexual experiences that involved multiple partners and, at times, recreational drugs (specifically, marijuana and ecstasy). She did not view either as problematic yet worried that I might see it that way. She grew up with many siblings in a fairly chaotic home atmosphere; I wondered what she was recreating through her sexuality and drug use, thinking which was perhaps in line with her worries.

Julia's first sexual experience as a teenager was (in her mind at the time) consciously designed to experiment with her body and break down inhibitions. This experience involved seducing three men sequentially on the same day (privately, in different locations, and none knew of the others). In her young adulthood, she continued to experiment sexually, but often in a distanced, sometimes drug-induced state. Jealousies and competitive feelings conflicted with her desires to be uninhibited and sexually carefree, so she gradually became monogamous; however, she then experienced difficulty sustaining a relationship, as either she or the man would lose interest.

Given that Julia had identified a problem with intimacy, I wondered what psychic purposes her previous sexual behavior may have served, what feelings she was trying to enhance or diminish by using substances, and how her intimacy fears, or perhaps fears about sexual intensity, may have been warded off by having relations with men she didn't care for or by engaging with multiple partners. I wondered if she was attempting to diffuse the intensity of her feelings and expected this would come up between us. She acknowledged that she was trying to avoid feelings of vulnerability or potential rejection. She also acknowledged doubts about whether she was capable of caring deeply or intensely about any man.

"I usually want things men don't. I want a *merger*," Julia told me one day. She described this longing—her word was merger—as a quasi-hypnotic experience of being totally understood, known, and cared for without having to do anything herself. Months later, she would tell me how frustrated she was that I could not automatically know her mind. She felt frustrated at the effort it took to speak her thoughts and feelings. She expressed a desire for me to know her through some kind of body therapy or touch therapy; some way to magically bypass having to speak. She expressed wishes that I could read her mind, get inside her skin, and know her without her having to say anything.

Julia's expressed frustrations and wishes might be conceptualized psychogenically as deriving from the negative preoedipal maternal transference; however, I did not think this fully captured the picture. She continued to complain that talking was too intellectual and 'left-brain.' During this time, she frequently sought out therapies that were more body-oriented, involving massage and the reading of 'auras' around her body. I said, "It's wonderful to be touched without words, to be understood effortlessly, totally." She said words divided us and that they did not describe how she wanted to be transformed. She wanted to *feel* different and she wanted me to *make her feel* different without her having to say anything, by touching her body, or in some spiritual, ineffable way. She said she didn't care about knowing *why, how*, or even *what* she wanted; she just wanted me to *do it*. I felt the intensity of her frustrations and wishes; there was urgency. I acknowledged her wish that I change her and how powerful that would make me. (I felt her wish for my power yet, at the same time, I felt powerless and constrained. Just what was it she wanted me to *do*?) She said she felt exhausted with being the powerful one and wanted me to take over. She wanted to say nothing and do nothing herself.

At the same time, Julia expressed the feeling that I was hurting her with insights, 'doing to her' by making *observations of* her that may have held some truth on an intellectual level but did not change how she felt in her real life. I suggested that words made her feel I was outside of her, *not in it with her*, so that she felt alone in my presence. She said this was similar to her experience of her father, an intellectual man who would regularly conduct experiments in the kitchen (i.e., in the family eating and living space). She felt this was a way he ignored her basic needs and displayed his self-centeredness. Maleness came to be defined to Julia as intrusive, self-absorbed, intellectually aggressive, and disconnected. I felt as if I could hurt her with my 'male' tools of analysis and insights that were different from her (i.e., outside of her perspective). In contrast, she wanted a 'female' kind of loving from me, one where I shared her perspective completely, non-intellectually, and nonverbally. To Julia, sameness was maternal and healing.

Viewing Julia's desires refracted through an oedipal structure, it is possible to posit that her frustrations (with the non-tactile, verbal nature of analysis) functioned as a screen for disguised competitive and envious feelings of me. If she spoke, would her words stand up to mine? Could she know as much or more than, she wanted me to know? However, I felt there was an unmistakable quality of unfulfilled longing in Julia's pleas, specifically for me to touch her . . . she wanted something she had not gotten in childhood and the analysis was stirring up these longings.

Soon it became clear that among the reasons for Julia's objections to analysis was a deep sadness that she could not *be inside my womb*.[5] Together, we recognized the sensual aspects of her desires, her wish that she were my baby, that I might give her my breast, she feeding on my body, that she could *be inside my body* and I inside her, to touch her, and feel her being from the inside. I became increasingly sensitized to her need for me to express my recognition of her internal states, especially painful experiences, such as the birth of her siblings, and other experiences that reflected early deprivations. I became more expressive to her of these needs and linked them to her mother's passivity and seeming lack of interest in her. I appreciated the erotic nature of these longings in her as well, i.e., longings to be touched, stimulated, or sensually aroused by my body, to be lost in the feelings of it and her desires to have me long for her in the same ways.

As the analysis proceeded, Julia began to wonder if she wanted to be with a man at all. She expressed the desire to be loved by a man who was more like a woman. She understood her desire (for a 'womanly' man) as expressing a frustration in the way men are socialized in our culture and not as a homosexual longing because she was not aware of being stimulated by or erotically fantasizing about me or other women. She had many close women friends and had experimented sexually with one, but stated that she did not fantasize about women erotically, the way she fantasized about men. She realized that what she longed for was "not a man; I want a mouth."

I wondered about possible oral needs being expressed behind the bodily meaning. I also recognized the allusion to our talking—oral—therapy. I told her I recognized her hunger and that she wanted me to touch her deeply, in a way that was beyond words. She stated again that she was frustrated by analysis and that she didn't want 'talking'; she wanted 'doing.' I asked her what she wanted me to 'do,' which led to wishes to be comforted by me, that I would make her feel better and soothe her in ways that did not involve insight. She reiterated that she wanted to be transformed in a feelingful and spiritual way, without knowledge or insight.

One way to understand Julia's longings coincides with an hysterical formulation. She desired *not to know*, perhaps comprising a regressive defense against becoming separate and autonomous, at least insofar as growing up meant knowing the full extent of her trauma and disillusionments. I wondered too if her demand was a regressive defense against competitive and envious feelings toward me (for instance, that I was married and had a family), tinged with a defensive sexualization. I made statements about the pain of separation, including the responsibility and loneliness of taking care of oneself. These elaborated aspects of her depression, leading back to memories of the loneliness of her childhood and the premature pressure she had felt to be self-sufficient.

Yet, another lens through which it is possible to view Julia's dynamic organization takes into account the more erotic nature of her desires. Despite her protests to the contrary, there were clear homoerotic intonations in her experience of me as strong and attuned to her. At the same time, she also experienced me as persistently frustrating as I continued to press her to put her feelings into words. I felt she was expressing both 'male' and 'female' modes of relating (as she had come to define these). First, (and by now a familiar pattern) was the desire to be merged with me as a denial of our separateness; Julia associated these desires with a maternal or female mode of relating, us being inside each other, *a taking in*. She told childhood stories of being left alone, a constant feeling of not being loved or cared for by her mother, whom she increasingly appreciated was chronically depressed. In contrast (and with much complaint and discomfort for Julia) was the persistently frustrating, insight-oriented mode of relating in which she felt pressured *to speak* and *to know* the meaning of her desires. Julia associated this form of relating with maleness, a kind of intellectual and disconnected, intrusive, and penetrating form of engagement, a *doing to.*

Paradoxically, I reminded Julia that 'being done to' was something she had persistently demanded of me—she wanted me to *do something to* her without her having to do anything in return. Receptivity took on more complexity: she realized being receptive to my attunement meant allowing penetration of *both my sameness and difference.* She began to notice that indeed she wanted both: attunement and penetration, sameness and difference, me inside her and she inside me. (This eventually led to an expansion of her self-experience and a manner of her phenomenal experiencing beyond a simple male/female or masculine/feminine binary.)

In the last year of analysis, Julia began to express increasing curiosity about my sexuality. She wondered if my husband understood my sexual needs and how we communicate in bed. She assumed having children had interfered with our sex life and associated to memories of her parents never kissing or finding time to be alone with so much chaos at home. She also wondered how I relate to my husband as a strong woman and, in particular, *wondered if my strength overpowered him.* We explored the extent to which this fantasy might be related to her anxiety about showing and selling her paintings. If she displayed her strength, might she overpower? She replied, "I'm always trying to hold myself back. I'm so tired of these small men who can't seem to match me. How do you handle that? I don't seem to have the same problem with you or my women friends. I either feel men are not big enough or that I am too big."[6]

Julia wondered if I shared similar conflicts and how I might manage them with my husband. She said, "Well, I know you're a professional and you stand for things. But we're in such different worlds. I don't want what you want. I don't want kids, living in the suburbs, a house, and conventional-type things. Your husband is probably Caucasian. I am turned on by ethnic types. Diversity is very important to me."

I noted her tendency to become involved with exotic-looking men, whom she experienced as masculine but narcissistic, "in their own world." Alternatively, she experienced "WASP-y" men as passive and effeminate; she became frustrated and then experienced them as too weak. She felt confused about desiring too much, of being too hungry; either she was attracted to men who couldn't return her interest or who didn't seem to want enough and couldn't match the intensity of her passion. She began to question how to resolve being a strong woman without fearing overpowering a man.

At this time, Julia became more curious about my 'insides,' asking questions about what I feel toward men, how I express my needs sexually, and whether I am satisfied. I heard these questions on two levels: both as a question about her 'feminine' sexuality (i.e., what was inside her and whether any man could satisfy her needs) and as an expression of how she fantasized we were negotiating our needs together. While in the past, the question was, Were we one person or two?, now the question was gendered: Were we two women or a man and a woman? Who would be on top? She previously had longed to merge with me in a nongendered way, as person to person. Now, not only was her experience with me gendered, Julia seemed interested in me *as a man.* What was inside me? Was I big and powerful? How does a man satisfy me? On an unconscious level, was there a man inside me that she could access?

In reflecting these ideas back to her, she began to wonder whether she was "filling me up enough." Did she satisfy me given her low fee? In effect, was she big enough for me, i.e., enough of a 'man' for me? She expressed a conviction that, since I had children, I had less to give her. At the same time, she began to wonder about my family without negation, considering whether she could have what I have. These were the syncopations in her experience of me as either gender—could she be a woman/mother yet be a strong person/man at the same time? What did it mean to be a strong woman and what about that little boy inside?

While in the past, ideas of having her own family would lead to emphatic denials and statements about her friends' unhappy marriages and overburdened families, at this point in the analysis Julia was able to admit that it was painful to think about what she might be missing. This led to more open admissions that she wanted a husband and children as well as more fantasies about my body. Being inside my skin took on a different meaning at this time; whereas in the early phases of the analysis she wanted a feeling of merger with me, now she expressed curiosity about what she might find inside me. She painted a picture of a well with treasures in the deepest part. We talked of this as evidence of her increasing curiosity about and acceptance of her own sexuality, both 'maleness' and 'femaleness' (accordingly in her own lexicon), what's inside her body and mine, along with the pleasures each gives.

Julia began to show her work publically. She sold many paintings and won awards. She began to feel 'big' inside herself.[7] As these changes took place in her outside life, she also began to experience herself as a strong woman, a 'manly' woman, yet 'feminine' at the same time. It's possible to play with these emerging self-states in a gendered way: The man inside the woman, the womanly man, the mother and the little boy inside, the little girl—all of them reflecting a partial truth and none comprising, by itself, the whole. As the analysis drew to a close, it was evident that Julia had increasing access to the full range.

* * *

The presentation of Julia's fantasies and desires, emerging in her predominantly maternal transference to me, illustrate the essentially erotic nature of such longings. Below is another presentation of a female patient's longings, similar in some ways to Julia's fantasies (especially with regard to her desire for merger); however, this presentation involves the patient's fantasies in relation to a male therapist, necessitating a more predominant reckoning with the analyst's difference.

Romance with difference as erotic merger

Malika is a dark, exotic-looking Indian woman in treatment with a male analyst, Dr. Vogel. He is German, blonde, and muscular with pale skin. They are both married, and each has two children but, beyond that, their ethnic and cultural heritages, as well as their lives and families, could not be more different. Given this great divergence, you might suspect that they (together and mutually) could represent safe targets for each other; that is, safe repositories for disavowed wishes. To use a different framework, you might suspect an impending danger that each might come to represent important but dissociated parts of themselves emerging as unresolved longings from childhood. These patterns are likely to be unconsciously categorized as 'not me' and represent potentials over which they have little control. This indeed came to be true, at least in an overtly discussed manner for Malika, as the attachment took the form of an intense romance.

The treatment began to take shape with a particular form of interaction in which Malika would often express her great satisfaction about the way the process was going. In response to almost anything Dr. Vogel might say, she would say, "Oh, you're so right," "This work is so stimulating," or "Yes, that's exactly what I meant." These expressions began with a mutual appreciation for ways in which they were indeed similar, usually referring to outward style and aesthetic preferences. Malika loved Dr. Vogel's selections of paintings, for example, eventually linking these up with similar visions of "how to make a life in this world." Dr. Vogel was pleased with Malika's strong engagement in the treatment and felt greatly appreciated. He knew there were important corrective aspects to the relationship as Malika's mother had been chronically depressed and unavailable, rarely seeming to understand her. (Malika would often wonder why others talked of homesickness since to her, home was an empty, lonely place.) Dr. Vogel thought he was engaging her maternal transference as the empathic mother for whom Malika had long been searching.

About a year into the treatment, Dr. Vogel took a two-week holiday and, when he returned, he found Malika in a very different state. Where she had been animated and talkative before, now there were long pauses and many silences during the sessions. She was not unhappy, but seemed in a kind of dissociated state. She would say there was "a lot going on" yet she would not express what this was, either in detail or in general. Instead, she would mysteriously state, "I see a lot of connections . . . everything is clear . . . I almost don't have to speak, you already know everything." These phrases were punctuated with long silences where Malika would stare at Dr. Vogel in a kind of ecstatic reverie. She did hint at "powerful sexual fantasies"; however, she refused to say anything further.

This went on for several months and Dr. Vogel wondered if the treatment was foundering, given that Malika was having such trouble verbalizing her thoughts and feelings. Gradually, this mode of interacting shifted to one in which Malika could once again bring up issues from her outside life. Dr. Vogel was relieved that the focus was no longer so confusing and paralyzing for him; at the same time, however, he felt an ironic loss at this change, the loss of her flattering attention, but assumed her current transformation was for the best. With this measure of greater distance, they each seemed more comfortable talking about what had happened (in retrospect and from her perspective) in those months just after his apparently significant vacation.

Malika referred to these months as being overcome with "that feeling." She said she was having erotic fantasies about Dr. Vogel but also stressed that she did not want to have sex with him. She revealed her fantasy that Dr. Vogel was gay and childless (both untrue). He surmised that she had constructed this image of him to reduce the threat of him as an erotic object; indeed, we could say she had desexualized him to create a safe repository for her longings. These seemed to revolve around a desire for merger, as reflected in her frequent utterances about Dr. Vogel's knowing her feelings without her having to state them. Dr. Vogel's physical appearance was handy in this effort as well—*his dissimilarity created a barrier to engulfment*, i.e., she need not risk a total loss of separateness.

In the months following, Malika continued to describe her phenomenal experience of that time with even more precision. She stated, "It was a kind of love, erotic, but I didn't want to have sex with you. I didn't need that. It was a room filled with love. A kind of floaty feeling that involved my whole body. It now energizes me for my life too."

During this time, Malika demonstrated important gains in her life and marriage that could be linked to the phenomenal experience in her analysis. She reported feeling increasingly recognized and intimate in her relationship with her husband, as if she felt a more substantive presence in her own identity.

* * *

To be seen and to be heard is to be touched, held, and loved. There is a way in which these longings can be experienced and gratified nonverbally as they emerge in the treatment in a subsymbolic register. Perhaps every treatment 'touches' our patients in similar unspoken ways. For patients like Malika, this profound level of therapeutic action can be absorbed in a state of dissociation. Rachel who feels an insistent urge to disrobe in sessions, (see Chapter 4) says that my eyes on her body feel like a touch; it is erotically pressing, yet not about 'genital sexuality' per se. It is an erotic aspect of intimacy. These urges, because they reside at a fundamental level of intimacy, often arise in nonverbal and/or subsymbolic form. These urges can be experienced as erotic, ultimately beyond words, but no less a significant part of treatment.

Notes

1 Compare, for example, Kavaler-Adler (1992) who claims that mourning of the preoedipal object facilitates the emergence of erotic transferences.
2 Margaret Hilferding was the first woman to be admitted to the Vienna Psychoanalytic Society. In a paper on maternal love (1911), she observed that maternal love is not innate but is intimately connected to the bodily pain or pleasure of the delivery and nursing experience (cited in Balsam, 2012, and Laplanche, 1997).
3 The others include: anal erotism, the sensual matrix in the formation of object relations, and the solidification of gender identity through erotic experience (pp. 36–44).
4 The experience of children with a single parent or same-sexed parents need not be excluded from these theoretical propositions. The 'male' and 'female' aspects of the analyst, as perceived, experienced, and bisected by the analysand, parallel the ways in which children can bifurcate and gender their experiences with primary caregiver(s). The clinical illustration below demonstrates this capacity as well. The proposed binary, receptivity and potency, especially if considered as a nongendered developmental imperative, remains enduringly relevant regardless of the sex of primary caregivers.
5 Likewise, Balsam (2012) argues that castration anxiety has no relevance for women, that it is a fantasy based on another fantasy, and that the pregnant body would be a natural place for the body ego.
6 See Chapter 6 for further discussion of women's fears of being 'too big.'
7 Balsam's (2012) references to the female's relationship to her (potentially) pregnant body and a mature identity portrait come to mind here.

Chapter 2

Maternal erotic transferences

Engaging the mother within

Labour is blossoming or dancing where
The body is not bruised to pleasure soul.
Nor beauty born out of its own despair,
Nor blear-eyed wisdom out of midnight oil.
O chestnut-tree, great-rooted blossomer,
Are you the leaf, the blossom or the bole?
O body swayed to music, O brightening glance,
How can we know the dancer from the dance?

W. B. Yeats, *Among School Children*, 1928

Within sexual symptoms and, in particular, those revolving around inhibited sexual desire (such as the variety of forms of impotence in men or inhibited sexual desire in women), there can be discerned some difficulty with the dialectical experience of receptivity and/or potency, both in affective experience and bodily behavior. The fear of the power of sexuality, for example, affects the active attainment of orgasm and, dialectically, the receptivity to the intensity of the (embodied) attendant feelings. With the structure of this formulation in mind, the following case[1] is discussed, as Michael found his way toward greater receptivity to feeling and was eventually able to harness his power as he increasingly viewed himself as a potent person (see Chapter 3 for the resolution of this treatment). Given the use of rather stereotypical gendered metaphors (his way of conceptualizing masculinity and femininity), Michael's ability to embrace, surrender, and express feeling was easily metaphorized by him as embracing the 'woman' inside him. In counterpoint, his increased capacity to use his body in a forceful, thrusting manner was viewed by him as accessing his 'manliness' (primarily elaborated in Chapter 3). The analyst's openness to embracing the power of these attitudes and *finding them equally within herself* were as much a part of the process, given that the engagement of these feelings emerged in multiple self-object identifications and patterns of relating between the two of us.

Though these ideas are presented sequentially, i.e., the accessing of maternal erotic (in the present chapter) and the harnessing of the paternal erotic (in Chapter 3), the development of these capacities did not follow an orderly linear pattern or fall into such neat categories. In broad strokes, two phases of the treatment could be discerned; however, the attainment of these capacities is best *viewed dialectically*, the capacity to experience, sustain, and express affective experience in one realm leading to the deepening awareness and emerging capacity in the other.

* * *

Up to the mid-eighties, the psychoanalytic literature generally reflected the belief that the development of an erotic transference rarely occurs between female therapists and male patients (Lester, 1985; Person, 1985). This notion arose out of a comparison with the dynamics of the opposite gender pairing (male therapists with female patients), for whom an erotic transference is not only a frequent occurrence, but is viewed (in classical theory) as replicating oedipal power dynamics as well. Because psychological development has been thought to require 'passing through' an oedipal phase, the development of an erotic transference with a male therapist falls into developmental line and has been viewed not only as part of, but essential to, a healthy progression. In contrast, female therapists were thought to promote a *regressive* preoedipal maternal transference, seemingly counter to therapeutic progress, with the implication that, for this gender pair, sexualized or erotic aspects of a healthy progression may be more difficult to access.

Writers in the last few decades have reflected a more frequent occurrence of erotic transference in male analysands toward their female analysts (Goldberger and Evans, 1985; Gornick, 1986; Myers, 1987; Kavaler-Adler, 1992; Diamond, 1993; Davies, 1994, 1998b; Wrye and Welles, 1994; Atkinson and Gabbard, 1995; Stein, 2000; Elise, 2002a; de Peyer, 2002; Schaverien, 2002, 2006a; Knafo, 2008). Many of these authors acknowledge, however, apparent resistances to the emergence of the full intensity of erotic transference in this particular gender pairing. Goldberger and Evans (1985) cite five examples of erotic (and paternal) transferences in female analyst-male analysand dyads. They conclude that, while these dyads may generally represent the full spectrum of transference manifestations, they tend to express transferences in the more constricted range of the spectrum for both erotic and aggressive manifestations. Along these lines, Person (1985) observed that male analysands tend to displace erotic feelings to extra-analytic figures. Noting a more general absence of erotic transferences, Schaverien (2006b) suggests female analysts may collude with their male patients' fears of their sexuality and aggression by acquiescing when they make a move to leave treatment.

It has been suggested that the more frequent occurrence of the erotic dimension of various transferences (muted though it may be) has emerged in recent years as a result of the enhanced relational engagement of therapists with their patients in general. Coen (1994) suggests that the classical analytic ego-ideal has tended to encourage constriction and discomfort on the part of the analyst, especially in regard to loving feelings toward patients. The barriers that prevent loving feelings in the analytic setting, Coen adds, are mutually constructed. In contrast,

Goldberger and Holmes (1993) observe that it is the countertransference of a particular analyst, rather than the biases of analysis and of culture, that tends to be the major determining factor in eliciting or constricting the emergence of particular transferences.

Several authors have speculated on the dynamic factors that mute or inhibit erotic transference in female analysts with male analysands. These include the difficulty a male patient has in identifying with his female analyst, difficulties resolving the 'negative oedipal position' (Karme, 1979), and fear of the patient's aggression (by either analyst or patient) that influences the unfolding of the erotic transference (Goldberger and Evans, 1985; Stein, 2000; de Peyer, 2002). Lester (1985) argues that primitive anxieties, stirred by the fantasy of the overwhelming preoedipal mother, tend to inhibit the full expression of sexualized impulses. Atkinson and Gabbard (1995) suggest fear of regressive symbiosis may be particularly prominent in adolescent male analysands.

Case illustration

Michael is a 45-year-old Mathematics Professor who has been in analysis for four years. His concerns initially revolved around longstanding problems with impotence and difficulty accessing his desires in general. He has always been successful at work but had difficulty sustaining romantic relationships. Historically, he has become involved with women he desired but quickly felt dominated by, prompting the ending of the relationship, usually by her. He inevitably felt demeaned and humiliated. He noticed that his relationships lasted longer if he did not fall in love. In his mid-30s, he married a female friend, sustaining a constricted, passionless relationship for about 5 years. They divorced having never consummated their marriage. Michael then retreated into relative isolation.

About the middle of the year 1999, Michael became increasingly preoccupied with the Y2K crisis and became convinced that civilization was about to end. He stockpiled food and water. It was around this time that he began treatment with me as his anxiety over Y2K mounted. Several months later, and still a few months shy of the turn of the century, he bought a gun in the belief that he would need to defend his stockpiles from desperately starving people. He also began taking shooting lessons.

Michael became obsessed with the idea that the world was going to be caught unaware and that, though there was talk of fixing the computer problem, in reality no one was helping. He was convinced there was going to be a panic. Desperately needy people were going to break into his house, kill him, and steal his supplies. He dug a trench in the backyard, in which he buried his canned food. He worried for my safety. I wondered if he were psychotic.

Throughout this early and intensely anxious period, we worked on establishing links from his current ruminations to his childhood experience. His mother was a "desperately needy" woman who demanded high achievements but displayed no interest in his emotional well-being. She would burst into his room "catching him unaware" and rant about some chore he hadn't finished. His father was of "no help," uninvolved, and living apart since his parents divorced. I noted too that it was Michael, himself, who was furious, wanting to kill people, but he denied this.

As Michael grew older, he felt exploited and enslaved. As an example, his mother would have dinner parties at which he would be required to greet the guests, hang up their coats, and serve dinner. He felt particularly demeaned when his mother insisted he wear a napkin over his arm, which he thought made the guests laugh at him. He took refuge in his schoolwork. He was a math prodigy, so he set off for college at 16, relieved but tremendously emotionally and psychologically unprepared.

Michael's anxiety began to settle down as we made the links from childhood to his Y2K construction. He said these links "made sense" and he began to feel less crazy. Several weeks before New Year's Eve, he turned his gun over to the police. When Y2K fantasies never materialized, he was embarrassed but also curious about how he could have gone to such extremes. This prompted his desire for psychoanalysis and, though I wondered about his stability, I agreed.

Unrequited (analytic) love

Early on, it became clear that issues of power and Michael's various reactions to feeling disempowered were going to be prominent themes. His erotic desires encompassed multiple ways of expressing power, at different levels, depending on the phase of treatment. Merger fantasies, sadomasochistic dynamics, and aggressive strains each played a prominent role as the treatment unfolded. I wanted Michael to feel free to express the full intensity of his desires and I wanted to be open to them. The literature on erotic transferences, especially in the female analyst-male patient configuration, alerted me to the possible inhibitory influence of my anxieties as they came up.

Many of the speculations about the facilitation or inhibition of an erotic transference (in either opposite-gender pairing) revolve around experiences and reactions vis-à-vis empowerment, the patient's experience with an empowered other, and the therapist's experience of the self as empowered. Idealization, an aspect of loving, endows the beloved with empowering attributes, especially the power to hurt or reject. Since the treatment setting has its own power structure, empowerment is an ineluctable part of the context within which transferences and countertransferences develop. At the same time, gender configurations unconsciously confer power in unique and culturally determined ways.

The power inherent in (and essential to) the therapeutic matrix is derived from the asymmetric distribution of attention between analyst and analysand (Aron, 1996; Hoffer, 1996). The power conferred on the analyst through this matrix thereby establishes a hierarchy. This power differential coincides with the familiar power differential between parent and child (e.g., the generational difference [see Chassageut-Smirgel, 1984] inherently set up and based on the parent's 'coming before' the child, a temporal advantage so to speak). When the analyst is male and the analysand female, this power differential coincides with traditional gender stereotypes. The psychoanalytic setting, for this gender pairing, is a powerful instigator of traditional developmental and societal expectations, especially as these expectations were conceived by classical theorists (see Benjamin, 1998, and Harris 2005a, for a critique of traditional developmental paradigms in psychoanalytic theorizing).

Thus, the structure of the therapeutic setting provides the template for activation of the full spectrum of unresolved conflicts associated with early parent/child relations and the ways in which these experiences are organized by gender. For some analysands, both aggressive and erotized strivings will be activated and experienced specifically in relation to this power differential. The power that the analyst embodies can become an erotic icon that symbolizes both the old templates and the hoped for potential of a new form of erotic desire. Needless to say, the analyst's comfort with this power will have profound implications for the nature of the countertransference, as well as for the extent to which certain transferences are facilitated or foreclosed (see Hirsch, 2008).

During the first year of analysis, Michael revealed, "I have a conflict. On the one hand, I feel you're a good analyst. You strive to help me. But it feels like love. And you will not reveal anything about your personal life. Like a blind man develops a heightened sense of hearing or touch, I read you. I want to praise you and tell you about all of your qualities. But you won't give anything back. How am I supposed to do this one-sided thing?"

Here, Michael explicitly referred to the structured imbalance in the analytic dyad and the way he experienced the asymmetric distribution of attention. I thought he was telling me that this felt simultaneously stimulating, gratifying, and frustrating. Michael specifically articulated these factors over time and, as his frustration grew, he developed a shorthand for his experience of 'the analytic set-up.' He became fond of rephrasing the Hippocratic Oath as my "Hypocritical Oath," referring to my refusal to engage in a sexual relationship with him as hypocritical, given the seductive and tempting aspects of the psychoanalytic situation.

At this point in the treatment, I was aware of some discomfort when Michael referred to the power imbalance between us. Was I more anonymous than necessary for him? Did my relatively greater knowledge of him and continual focus on him unduly empower me? I was reminded of the demands made by many patients who become sexually involved with their analysts at early stages of the slippery slope: "I must know X or I can't work with you!" Or, "I can't tell you X about me unless you tell me Y about you!" In these contexts, disclosures on the analyst's part inevitably lead to more demands and more disclosures. I sensed this would happen with Michael were I to turn down this path.

Interestingly, I noticed that I was actually *less* revealing and more constrained with Michael than is typical of my style, despite the fact that he demanded more and seemed particularly pained by my reserve. What was the nature of this aspect of my countertransference? I did not know yet, but the awareness of my relatively greater constraint with Michael increased my guilt.

I recognized the cautionary themes in the literature, especially the potential inhibitory effects of the female analyst's discomfort with power, so I stood my ground. I also recognized an unmistakable feeling that I was *doing something to* Michael, as if, by virtue of being his analyst, I was hurting him. He seemed to blame me for paying exclusive attention to him, for doing the very job he had hired me to do. In order to tolerate my guilt, I frequently reminded myself that his humiliation and difficulty accepting the treatment frame derived from his childhood experiences. He was not wrong in what he was saying, he was just stuck on it. I openly acknowledged the accuracy of his observations about the power imbalance between us, but I maintained my analytic stance and steeled myself for a fight.

The temptation of the maternal/containing transference

Many authors suggest that the female analyst's psychological and culturally determined countertransference may inhibit the full development of erotized transference (Tyson, 1986; Russ, 1993). They suggest that dependency longings and pre-oedipal transferences may be fostered to avoid more ambivalent images of the empowered female (Szmarag, 1982). Still others (e.g., Chasseguet-Smirgel, 1970; Wrye and Welles, 1994) have identified underlying erotic elements as constituting preoedipal maternal longings that often go unanalyzed, bringing to the foreground the maternal erotic transference as another version of erotic desire. These reports have paralleled and, in some cases, stimulated the exploration of the erotic nature of preoedipal sexuality (e.g., Chassaguet-Smirgel, 1970; McDougall, 1992; Wrye and Welles, 1994; Benjamin, 1995; Dimen, 2003; Harris, 2005a).

These feminist writers have also elaborated an erotic aspect of the preoedipal transferences. As noted in Chapter 1, the maternal figure can come to represent empathic attunement, resonance, sameness, and the enveloping aspect of understanding. Identification on the basis of sameness, then, is viewed as either inherently erotic or defensively eroticized. In the latter case, there can be an underlying denial of difference and a defensively split transference in which the positive maternal object is experienced as the empathic, attuned and desired object, whereas the negative paternal object is experienced as intrusively penetrating, disruptive, nonempathic, and intolerably different (see e.g., Britton, 2004). In opposite-gendered pairings, the female analyst may symbolize an all-encompassing maternal refuge, a safe haven from more conflict-laden urges to explore difference.

Michael tells me he is thinking about me entirely too much. He describes aching, longing fantasies of making love with me, of talking to me about his desires, and states, "I'm imagining you watching me. I have a fantasy about you. We have sex. It's mutual, ecstatic, loving. We each leave our partners and live together forever. I want that. But I worry I may not be able to keep up with you. You have so many interests. And sexually too." Noting the allusion to his performance anxiety, I say, "You worry you won't be able to keep up?" He responds, "I do tend to feed off the other person's life. I'd get involved in what you like. I'd be interested—I'd be your surrogate."

In this interchange, Michael revealed a merger fantasy underlying his erotic experience. The merger fantasy had a sadomasochistic structure and represented a defensive move whereby he subjugated himself to sidestep the exploration and expression of his own subjective desire. The awareness of my countertransference helped me understand this formulation, especially from the way in which I experienced his attempts to penetrate me.[2] Specifically, I was not excited by Michael's aggressive or more phallic presentations. Rather, it was as if his penetrations were too soft or weak. He seemed to lack substance or hardness; it was not possible for me to feel *him*.

I recognized the more primitive, narcissistic level of his manifestly sexual demand. I said, "You'd leave your desires out of it," to which he responded, "I tend not to explore my own wishes. I'd use your life to give juice to mine."

At this phase of the treatment, I understood Michael's interest in me as a substitute for his interest in himself. Along the same lines, I was aware that I did not feel a trace of erotic arousal at Michael's attempts to 'get inside me.' Rather than being excited by his interest, I felt closed in, even suffocated. There was a way in which his examination of me felt *too* in me, appropriating, as if he wanted to take me over or *become* me. To say I felt an over-dependency is not exactly right—it was as if he was trying (psychically) to *take something from me*, like the desperately starving people he had imagined clamoring at his door during the Y2K crisis.

For the first two years of the treatment, we explored the way in which Michael's erotic transference seemed to cover over an insufficiently elaborated sense of his identity, his desires in general, and his difficulty sustaining or holding onto his sexual longing. I saw his desire to merge with me as a defensive effort to find refuge in the maternal/containing transference, an effort to substantiate himself through a kind of 'borrowed subjectivity,' giving him the illusion of strength and agency at the expense of his own autonomy. In the past, this had led to intolerable feelings of submission or submersion of himself in the woman, a both desired and feared annihilation. He was afraid to be receptive to this manner of feeling because of the ways in which he either felt annihilated as a man or too identified as a woman. Michael's tendency to focus his attention on the woman's desire empowered her to an intolerable degree, causing him to feel dominated, emasculated, or annihilated in her presence.

We understood this as, largely, a repetition of his relationship with his mother. Michael remembered the time spent with her as always revolving around her interests and needs. Even his studies and school achievements were experienced as for, or about, her. It was her wishes he strove to fulfill and he was unable to recognize his own.

At this juncture, it was unclear whether Michael was struggling with a deficient sense of agency in himself or a disavowed aggressive self that he wished to defensively disown. Perhaps one was due to the other, as in a denial of his capacity for thrust due to his fear that his thrust might murder. Most importantly, I wondered if the maternal/containing transference represented a way in which I too might be tempted to collude with his longings for merger and thereby sidestep his aggression, especially his potential to be aggressive toward me. The literature on the muted transference with female analysts alerted me not to back away from his aggression due to my own anxiety. I wondered if my focus on his wish to be recognized, 'watched,' understood, or held was doing just this, by viewing his sexual longings as a defensive sexualization against these more early narcissistic wishes. Still, this was my predominant formulation in the early years of the analysis. I kept in mind, however, the question of whether I was minimizing his more anxiety-ridden urges to be distinct, to stick out, and, in Michael's case, to dominate or thrust in a 'manly' and overpowering way. I was aware that these more aggressive urges might involve a desire to control or hurt me, but these were discomforts I had to tolerate if and when we were both ready (see Chapter 3 for an elaboration of this aspect of Michael's treatment).

In summary, intense, erotic feelings associated with early, maternal fantasies that emerge in the clinical setting can be formulated as representing the struggle to be receptive to a new range of feeling, perhaps those traditionally associated with femininity. Patients and therapists alike struggle to avoid the elaboration of these wishes, especially in their full intensity. The fantasies associated with this early transference are different from more neurotic, oedipal level desires, i.e., those involving the shame and humiliation of being the small, inadequate loser in the oedipal contest for the same-gendered parent (Kumin, 1985). Maternal erotic transferences are often due to unmet desire and the need for sensual body-based contact. The primal panic in the face of early erotic (preoedipal) transferences may involve the threat of disappearing into the mother's body, leading to psychic annihilation (as opposed to castration), or the fear of losing one's (nominal) gender identity, especially if these feelings rest on polarized stereotypic gender categorizations. According to Wrye and Welles, "For male and female patients alike, the maternal erotic transference threatens to suck them back into the intense body feelings toward the early mother and is thus a threat to separateness. Because girls' core gender identity, however, is not threatened by merger with the maternal body, they seldom exhibit the degree of erotic terror seen in males" (1994, p. 162).

Wrye and Welles (1994) emphasize maternal erotic fantasies as involving feeding, bathing, and diapering (as opposed to genital activity). These fantasies are then associated with vulnerability, shame, humiliation, and abandonment. There is usually a mix of memories and a resurgence of unmet need. Wrye and Welles (1994) emphasize the importance of correctly interpreting this phenomenon, especially as it makes re-experiencing more tolerable. It is important not to over-emphasize the usefulness of the correct interpretation, however. Much is accomplished in the acceptance, tolerance, and bearing of these longings alone, as these feelings are elaborated and sustained in the context of an accepting, holding relationship with the analyst. The emergence of this transference and its transformational properties can and often do resolve at a subsymbolic register (see Chapter 1). In the case discussed, Michael's transference unfolded as a defensive effort to sexualize his maternal longings, thereby using eroticization to mask wishes for merger or union. To effect the important transformational work associated with this transference, it is essential that the analyst have the capacity to tolerate and sustain these feelings in conjunction with the analysand.

Notes

1 An earlier version of this chapter, together with Chapter 3, won the Karl A. Menninger Memorial Award (conferred by the American Psychoanalytic Association) and the Felix and Helena Deutsch Prize (awarded by the Boston Psychoanalytic Society and Institute).
2 See also Bonasia (2001) for another illustration of erotic countertransference and its usefulness in formulating the patient's dynamics.

Chapter 3

Erotic transferences and the role of aggression

> *Tango is love, it's hate*
> *[You forgot to mention love]*
> *It's love, I did say it*
> *Don't interrupt me!*
> *They dance, hot like their mother*
> *It's in their blood*
> *And the blood runs...*
>
> R. Duvall, *Assassination Tango*, 2002

In this chapter,[1] I will begin by discussing the second half of my analysis with Michael, introduced in Chapter 2 with the emergence of a maternal erotic transference. In the second half of his analysis as explicated here, there emerged a quite different form of desire that had a transformative effect on his ability to experience and develop his capacity for intimacy. Though it might be said that Michael consistently expressed the same desire throughout his analysis with me (to have sexual intercourse with me), his erotic transferences took different forms as they unfolded over time.[2] Finally, I will briefly describe the most common form of sexual boundary transgression in which the seduction of the patient is used to manage a therapeutic impasse and to transform a hostile-aggressive transference into an erotic transference.[3]

As noted in Chapter 2, there has been a dearth of literature on erotic transferences in female analyst-male patient dyads. Kernberg (1994) attributes the absence or muted manifestation of erotic transferences in these dyads to narcissistic resistances against dependency and envy in which sexualized longings for the analyst are experienced as humiliating or degrading (see, for example, Schaverien's (2006a) paper, *Men who leave too soon*). In some cases, sexual longing may arouse intense anxieties over sexual inferiority or insufficiency as part of the reactivation of 'normal' oedipal dynamics (see Chasseguet-Smirgel, 1970, 1984). Kernberg notes, in particular, the incidence of an intense form of transference love in narcissistic male patients with female analysts whereby the transference masks and defends against an "aggressive sexualized seductiveness reflecting transference resistance against feeling dependent on an idealized analyst and an effort to reproduce a conventional cultural situation in which the powerful, seductive male relates to the passive and idealizing female" (Kernberg, 1994, p. 1140). Chassegeut-Smirgel (1970) noted the problem of male fantasies about terrifying females, as well as women's guilty fantasies about their instinctual impulses (which she called feminine guilt), both of which she felt played a part in the muted nature of male to female erotic transferences. For some men to allow their erotic desires to emerge, aggressive thoughts and feelings must be conjured up to counter the undue vulnerability and the emasculating effect of erotic desires for a woman.

In more contemporary writings on this subject, erotic transferences (and countertransferences) are viewed as reviving dissociated modes of relating based on disavowed or repudiated self-other identifications that may or may not be gendered in some problematic way. I am proposing that the dual developmental imperative, the cultivation of the capacities for receptivity and potency, are easily associated with body-based and gendered stereotypy, namely the 'feminine' and 'masculine' within us all. When these emerge as conflicted or repudiated identifications, often associated with problematic parental and gendered identifications, a variety of symptomatology may result, which can be expected to emerge in the form of erotic transferences. This chapter focuses on the transformation of Michael's erotic transference that served to manage Michael's fears of his own power, aggression, and potency (in relation to a woman), his 'thrust,' as it emerged in relation to me.

The sexualization of aggression

Michael said, "I think I'm sexually competent. But what do women want? I think women want to be raped. A void to be filled. Women like men to be strong. An 'I'm taking you,' Tony Soprano kind of thing. But technique is a question—how long, what to touch, how to touch." I said, "You have a lot of curiosity about who wants what, sexually, aggressively . . ." to which he responded, "I don't want to be a man that doesn't regulate, modulate, control." I said, "How to feel your thrust, fill your own void, and at the same time give a woman what she wants?" He went on, "You make it sound as if it's okay to use force. I don't know if I feel that. Maybe I do. It's a man thing. You want me to be a man." I said, "In whatever way you define that."[4]

In the third year of analysis, Michael began to express his longings in a more explicitly hostile way. This was first expressed masochistically: he wanted me to hurt and reject him in ways that both punished him and, in a fantasied way, would transform his loving feelings toward me into hateful ones. Suicidality became a constant feature. On one occasion, Michael said, "I'm worried I'm getting into a kind of frenzy. A crazy, negative state. I want you to tell me that you won't kiss me, you won't touch me, you won't have sexual intercourse with me. I want you to hurt me. I want you to help me turn off this primitive part of me. I want to fall into a zone of anger and destruction. I want to get angry with you. I want to harden my heart to you."

At this juncture, I understood Michael's increasing suicidality as an aggressivization of the erotic transference, initially directed inward in a defensive effort to give him the illusion of strength (hardening himself) in relation to me. The more he could take, the stronger he might feel. The more I hurt him, the more monstrous I became. He asked, "Do you take pleasure in your success at not telling me things about you? It is skillful." To which I responded, "You think I take pleasure in the very thing that causes you pain." He said, "Yes, it is a thrill for you that you can use your skill to help me with the pain you cause . . . You should say rejecting things to me. I would feel bad at first, but I need to get closure. I want to be indifferent to you. I want to fall out of love with you . . . Love is a humiliation."

Over time, there was an accentuated shift from masochistic to more outwardly directed aggression. This shift brought with it a set of feelings that were, to Michael, less emasculating, less subjugated, and internally strengthening, yet more threatening to me. On one occasion, he said, "I want to show you my best self. If I wanted, I could do that, but I would be holding back. I can be mean, vicious, sarcastic. It's enticing, because a part of me doesn't want to make myself attractive to you. I can let it fly. Attack you."

I welcomed (at least consciously) the emerging negative transference and expected that, as Michael's aggression surfaced and was expressed more directly toward me, my challenge would be to receive it without retaliating. I hoped too that we would see a diminishment of his suicidality and self-destructive wishes, along with a strengthened sense of inner presence as he became increasingly comfortable with his aggression.

As this work progressed, many treatment goals were accomplished. Michael expanded his social world, broadening friendships and beginning to date women. He took greater pleasure in his academic achievements and displayed more confidence at work, e.g., incorporating more humor in his papers and presentations.

Michael also began seeing prostitutes (high priced escorts), with whom he revealed his problems with sexual potency. Most of these women were happy to try to help him with it. Though this was unsuccessful, he was able to keep his sense of humor about it all. One day, he began a session by stating, "Your fees are low because your services are limited." The association to me as a prostitute was not lost on either of us.

There were some developments in my countertransference as well. For one, I was aware of experiencing Michael as more appealing. I felt less closed in or suffocated, as if his more differentiated presence allowed me greater room to breathe and to experience him at a distance, ironically making a new kind of closeness possible. At the same time, his hostility seemed to intensify and I was aware of an increasing discomfort in me.

Murderous wishes

For certain male analysands, an erotic transference experienced within the asymmetric power distribution of the treatment setting will engender feelings of dependency, humiliation, powerlessness, and degradation. In such cases, erotic longings can become defensively aggressivized, serving to substantiate the self in relation to the more powerful (female) analyst. Murderous, envious, and vengeful feelings can become activated, serving to foster the illusion of becoming 'harder' or firmer in the analyst's presence. These feelings in turn can promote powerful feelings of self-hatred associated with destructiveness.

By the end of the third year of treatment, Michael's analysis revolved around his feelings of love, humiliation, anger, and his attempts to harden himself in relation to me. He continued to be depressed, although there were also times when he seemed to feel a sense of himself as a desiring, romantic, and desirable man. These were easily counteracted by a relentless hopelessness that he could ever be sufficiently fulfilled.

Michael then revealed a murderous, vengeful fantasy about me that he said had been in his mind a year earlier. He said, "I want you to hurt the way I do. I want things to go wrong in your life. I want you to feel similar pain." Momentarily retreating from his attack, I restated his wish and said, "You want me to understand." He corrected me, "No, I want your marriage to go bad." I felt a bit rattled at the intensity of his hostility. Lamely, I responded, "You want me to feel your pain." He nodded. I continued, "You want what you think I have, but you feel hopeless to get it for yourself. So you want to destroy it in me. This is envy." He then said, "Yes, surely. I feel violent toward you. It's a temporary pleasure too. If I say I want to kill you, it's not a friendly thing to say. If I kill you, then I'll have to kill myself. It's a logistical necessity. I've thought of this several times. Pills are not a definitive way to kill myself. Most men kill themselves with a gun. I don't have a gun now." Bracing myself against how frightened I was becoming, I pursued these thoughts further. I said, "And killing me?"

Michael responded, "I thought of stabbing you. That is metaphoric. A gun is fast, decisive. But it's just killing. A knife is more expressive. It links to feelings. More cathartic. Releases what you feel. It's prolonged. More interactive. You'd say something. I'd have to deal with that. You'd scream." I imagine now that Michael could sense the increased adrenaline in the atmosphere. He became interested in my reaction. He asked, "What are you thinking? I need to know."

I was aware of being frightened and began wondering whether the treatment was proving to be harmful for Michael (and possibly me). I wondered if Michael was able to withstand the feelings (especially envious and vengeful feelings) aroused in the process of uncovering his desires. Perhaps I had overestimated his capacities to tolerate the frustrating effects of the treatment. It also seemed to me, in this moment at least, that the treatment structure itself had evaporated in Michael's mind, devolving into a basic and personal rejection of him by me. It was becoming clear to me that the tension between the professional and the personal relationship had collapsed (perhaps for both him and me), and I did not know if it could be reestablished. Most importantly, I couldn't ignore the memory of his buying a gun just a few years ago. It occurred to me that perhaps this was the threat some female analysts might want to foreclose when hints of an erotic transference begin to appear.

In the moment, I thought Michael needed to see his effect on me to counter the utter helplessness that cut across his humiliation, envy, and feelings of rejection. I also needed to find a way to reestablish a safe structure around our work. So I responded from a personal level, disclosing my concerns. I told Michael I was frightened and that I felt threatened. Then I said, "I am worried maybe you can't handle the feelings that are being stirred up. Still, I believe putting all this into words is important. You want to communicate . . . you want me to understand the pain you're in and that's what killing with a knife would do. And you want to have a reaction from me."

He responded at first in a dismissive manner, but then demonstrated an ability to reflect on what I had said. He said, "Oh, here we go with my mother," but then added, "It did come to my mind too, though, the way I felt trapped and unable to get anything from her. She never understood how I felt. I was some kind of surrogate to her. But there's also something about envy. I'll never have what you have." I said, "So you'd rather no one has it, than I have it and not you." He said, "Yes, that's the feeling." I continued, "So, for a moment, you can believe there's nothing you're missing." He said, "You think knowing your desires, feeling your desires is a great big help. A great big step for mankind." I responded, "Yes, I do. But I know it's painful to realize what you want, especially if you feel hopeless about getting these things for yourself." He said, "In my real life, I am hopeless, but with you, if I stabbed you, there would at least be one minute when *you* needed *me*."

I then turned to the moment in his fantasy where, 'I would say something.' Exploration of this did not reveal a specific statement, but rather an experience, for Michael, where I would plead with him. He said he wanted to see my need of him and to see me be as utterly helpless as he was as a child. I do not remember how the session ended.

Not surprisingly, after this session I felt the need for a consultation. I checked my appointment book and noticed a fortuitous coincidence of timing—the next meeting of my peer supervision group was to occur in just a few days. As it happened, I had been presenting Michael and was scheduled to continue. I braced myself for the next several days.

In the next session and for the remainder of the week, Michael expressed enormous regret at the, "insane, awful things" he had said, referring specifically to the fantasy of killing me. He insisted these were not in his mind presently. He said that he was simply remembering these fantasies from a year ago. This did not reassure me at all. Even if I took his words at face value, I was not comforted by the thought that these fantasies were no longer operative on some level. I was afraid that he might not be telling me the truth or that he might not know the extent to which he could be overcome with murderous impulses at any time. I felt somewhat reassured that Michael was remorseful, but I did not know to what extent he or I were in safe territory. Though I believed it was best for him to verbalize his thoughts and wishes, it was undeniable that we had lost the feeling of playfulness between us. Images of him stalking me or accosting me on the street kept intruding into my mind. I wanted to involve others and decided that I would, but I also worried that it might be too late. There was a dreadful feeling that this was now between him and me; on a personal level, that the treatment frame had been irrevocably lost and that it would not matter what steps I might take.[5]

I looked over my process notes of our work from the prior year. I came across Michael's words as he described lovesick images of himself as "a man lurching around" with "sensual stabs in my heart." I realized the fantasy of stabbing me represented these feelings and noted the phrase "sensual stabs" as expressing an aggressive penetration.

Michael continued to express regret at frightening me and a grave concern that I would decide I could no longer work with him. He worried that, even if we continued, I would now see him as crazy or as a "pathological threat" and no longer hold him in a respectful light. He was afraid he had destroyed something between us and that I disliked him intensely. Though I did not state anything of the sort, I did notice I had become very constricted in my manner. I assumed my anxiety was apparent to him.

In the immediate aftermath, I felt a need to ground our discussion in a framework of concrete safety. I asked Michael if he could gauge the relative weight of fantasy versus action in what he had said. He responded that it was, "way into the fantasy camp. The reality is I don't have the courage even to commit suicide, even though I talk about it a lot." He then offered several examples of his pacifist nature, citing a lifetime of inhibition in many realms. Still, images of old ladies feeding arsenic to unsuspecting strangers plagued me. On a more realistic level, I could not forget that he had previously bought a gun.

I presented Michael to my peer group, which proved essential in reestablishing my own sense of balance. The reactions and thoughts of individual members spanned the full range of formulations. One member thought this was no different from treating his suicidality, another thought Michael was more primitive and action-prone than I was appreciating, and the third felt cautiously optimistic. Rather than being confused or frustrated by the contradictions, I found myself welcoming the differences. I wanted to hold a variety of dialogues along different pathways and I also knew any single formulation of the case would have been unconvincing.

Then I did one more thing—a final step in the enactment. I disclosed to Michael that I had presented the material to my peer supervision group and that I would continue to do so for some time. I knew my disclosure was a direct result of my residual feeling of threat and an attempt to reestablish safety for myself. Through our subsequent discussions, Michael and I have also recognized a repetition of bringing in superego figures, much like his turning his gun over to the police. The need for a third presence, an overseeing body, a limit, a vortex establishing a triangle, or at least a father figure are all meanings we have explored (Britton, 2004; Aron, 2006).

At the time, Michael was visibly relieved by my disclosure and stated that he was interested in what the group had to say, feeling this was a way to get more help. I had the fantasy that the group served a paternal function, like the third vortex, a symbol of the protective and corrective influence of the analytic community for both Michael and me (Spezzano, 1998). This had a relieving effect on our ability to be together without undue tension and fear. Not only was it essential to have the support for myself, but the ability to bring the peer group's presence and super-ego into the treatment served to counterbalance the dyadically organized closed system we seemed to be viciously re-creating.

Continuing resolution

With the safety of the frame reestablished, we could resume the work of analysis. Michael's destructive envy remained the primary focus. And, because his desire was paired with an irrational and destructive hopelessness which I saw as a major contributor to his depression, we continued to examine his hopelessness in both its present defensive function and historical roots.

Similarly, we examined Michael's idealization of me, his tendency to imagine that I had everything in my life and that I was totally fulfilled, especially sexually. He seemed fixated on these images of me, which seemed to have the character of a fetish. He seemed to torture himself with exaggerated sexual images of me—not the images themselves but his use of them as a way to compare himself with me and find himself wanting. He imagined that I was, "fucking [my] brains out all the time" and that he was the only man in the world who did not have satisfactory sex. I observed that he was torturing himself with these ideas, perhaps as a way to punish himself for past failings, but also to avoid the responsibility of addressing these concerns in the present. Unconscious punitive self-criticism, passive longings, and envious fantasies were paired with an inability to accept what I could offer him, leaving him feeling chronically unsatisfied (Kris, 1976).

The examination of Michael's fantasies, desires, and hopelessness coincided with continuing improvement in his external life, including the establishment of long-term male and female friendships, a sustained romance with a woman, and greater vitality in his career.

Michael also demonstrated evidence of moving beyond the fantasy of killing me and other consequences of his destructive envy by imagining scenarios where he would "overcome my will" in more benign ways. These apparently functioned to redress the power imbalance between us. For example, he talked about giving me expensive gifts, despite the fact that he knew I would not accept them. He chose to sit up and commented that he felt too submissive on the couch. In all of these scenarios, it was an important feature of his behavior that he thought he was defying my wishes—a display of his own power that would redress the disempowerment and utter helplessness he felt. I pointed out to him that, though he seemed to be tortured with love for me and wanting love from me, what he really wanted and seemed to need was not love at all, but power. He insightfully added, "Well, I suppose you can't have one without the other."

In the fourth year, Michael and I engaged in a series of interactions that had a similar structure to the murder fantasy and my subsequent consultation. One involved the suggestion, by Michael, that we have a consultation on whether the analysis should be terminated. On several occasions throughout the analysis, Michael had brought up the wish for a consultation. It is undeniable, however, that raising it again now, after I had disclosed my consultation with my peer group, added a new meaning of 'payback.' He wanted the consultant to be a male analyst with whom he would also consider entering treatment. I responded (as I had always done in the past) by affirming the idea of a consultation; however, I also informed him that if the consultant agreed that we should terminate, the consultant himself could not become Michael's analyst due to a conflict of interest. Though less enthralled with the idea, he persisted with the wish for a consultation. I contacted a few colleagues. I informed Michael of their availability. He then said he had observed in me some distress over the fact that he seemed to be seriously considering termination (he was correct about this) and he changed his mind about having a consultation. He said that the distress he observed in me became the confirmation he needed to continue the treatment. I asked what he had observed and, in response, he stated, "I saw evidence of pain in you. I thought you might miss me. I saw that you didn't want me to terminate—even that feels loving. When you told me in the past that you had consulted with people about me, I felt visible and important to you. I feel that now too. All of this makes me feel your involvement with me."

Approximately a year after he shared the murder fantasy with me, Michael demonstrated a shift in his ability to accept the power imbalance between us. He said, "This is an uneven situation, but that is characteristic of everything. My goal is to accept my own experience and separate it from yours. It's limited, but it's all I have to work with."

In the ensuing months, Michael met a woman with whom he enjoys a vibrant and full sexual life. His impotence has resolved and they are now married.[6]

Discussion

The insularity of the treatment dyad is implicated in many discussions of the role of the third, as in dyadic versus triangular relations (Britton, 2004; Aron, 2006; Celenza, 2006). Most psychoanalyses and psychotherapies are conducted with at least a tacit understanding that the treatment will be periodically and anonymously reviewed in such contexts as consultation, peer groups, and/or supervision. It could be argued that the presence of others creates a safety net and represents the outside world to the treatment dyad. The illusion of a treatment dyad outside of temporal and spatial constraints can foster unrealistic treatment goals and may be a cause of extensively protracted treatments (Cooper, 2001; Renik, 2004; Celenza, 2006, 2007). Further, the absence of any type of consultation has been noted as a risk factor, part of the slippery slope, in cases of sexual boundary violations between therapists and patients (Gabbard and Lester, 1995; Celenza and Gabbard, 2003; Celenza, 2007).

Any moment in treatment can be explored for meaning; likewise, there is no moment that is not enactive. The question is which enactment would most facilitate a deepening of the analytic process. If an analyst seeks consultation but does not disclose this to the patient (as is usual practice), the nondisclosure may be maintaining a certain fantasy in the patient's mind. Is the dyad a secret to the outside world, the 'collegial other,' and/or the father? What is the meaning of that enactment?

Whether my disclosure to Michael opened things up or closed things down, the fact remains that this is what happened and, in that sense, my disclosure was part of a meaningful enactment. The 'third' in its paternal function is one meaning that seems particularly relevant. Why did I need to turn to others, to 'tell on' Michael, so to speak? Despite that I don't scare easily, I was very frightened. I felt physically threatened, I felt trapped, and I wanted to stop the action. I had the sense that we had lost our ability to relate on multiple levels. I could no longer access myself as analyst. I felt disempowered.

It can be said that, not only did the dyad need a third, not only did Michael need a father, but I needed a 'man.' What was this move and how does it connect with the erotic dimension of the treatment? I have discussed the nature of the female analyst's countertransference and its potential inhibitory influence on erotic transferences in male patients. As I have outlined, fear of the male patient's aggression may cause the female analyst to emphasize the maternal containing aspects of her functioning, the so-called 'mother/woman' in the analyst, in order to sidestep and assuage the full force of the male/patient's aggression, to have the 'woman' in the woman engage with the 'woman' in the man, so to speak, and to keep that dimension of their relating in the foreground.

But I wanted to engage the 'man' in Michael and facilitate his emergence. In so doing, Michael's aggression came through in full force; perhaps the 'man' in the man then needed to make contact with the 'man' in me. In retrospect, at the moment when he described his wish to stab me, I would now have me say, "Yes, we want to kill the person who humiliates us, rejects us. More than that, you wanted to make me spill my guts the way you feel you have done with me." Would it take a man to be able to say that? Now, in retrospect, I think not, but apparently it did at that time for me.[7]

In the past few decades much progress has been made in developing the 'woman' in all of us, a feminization of the profession, i.e., the maternal and relational side of the analytic process (in traditional gender stereotyped language). What is involved in counterbalancing the 'woman' with the so-called 'male' aspects of our role? As much as Michael did not want to experience me as a paternal (empowered) woman, I too was resisting accessing the 'male' in me. Though this discussion attempts to open up traditional, stereotypic gender connotations, Michael and I were dancing to a fairly traditional tango. That was the song he wanted to hear and, apparently, I heard it too.

Aggressive erotic moves

As I have written elsewhere (Celenza, 2007), there is a special quality of aggressiveness that, when combined with erotic desire, makes for a particularly combustible blend. This is not to imply that an explosion is inevitable or that patients with this character feature are untreatable . . . it takes two to tango. Yet, there are therapists and analysts[8] who will interlock with these patients in a kind of death-grip, with both parties seeming to hold on until 'total destruction do they part.' Essentially, I am describing the sadomasochistic tie that is associated with a very common (the most common) form of sexual boundary transgression.

These treatments usually begin benignly enough, and it is understandable that many therapists do not realize how or when the basic dynamic seems to have changed. The treatments involve an early idealization of the therapist, one that is often enjoyed with an underlying, subliminal sense or conscious observation of relief by the therapist. Often only realized and exposed in retrospect, this relief is resultant from the sense by the therapist that the patient has a strong tendency to rely on splitting in her interpersonal relationships. The therapist usually hears a lot about a spouse or significant other who is chronically disappointing and who is repeatedly denigrated by the patient as she chronicles her frustrations. The underlying relief derives from the fact that the therapist is not, at the moment, the focus of her anger and hatred. Sometimes the therapist is not aware that the patient has this organization in her defensive tendencies though, when this is the case, one has to wonder about the selectivity in the analyst's attention and focus. It may also be true that otherwise highly competent caregivers reach a time in their life when they no longer have the stamina or steel reserve for this kind of splitting. In general, then, the therapist is enjoying the patient's admiration too much and may be exploiting her tendency to keep her anger outside the treatment context. I have described this transference/countertransference dance (from the therapist's point of view) as a tendency to transform countertransference hate to countertransference love, which basically represents the counterpart to the patient's splitting (Celenza, 2007). In the main, the therapist is making every effort to ensure that the patient does not turn her edgy, biting criticism on him.

These efforts, on the part of the therapist, are doomed to fail, and it is only a matter of time until the full weight of the patient's anger and hatred becomes rerouted to find its expression within the treatment dyad. Though a difficult time for the therapist, this is a turn of events that should be welcomed. This is the problem for which the patient came to treatment and signals the emergence of acute negative transference. If an otherwise competent therapist is at a fragile point in his life or under some kind of unusual stress, he may not be able to withstand the full brunt of what the patient has in store. Seduction of the patient at this moment of the treatment is a real risk and has been shown to be a common response to this phase of the work, culminating in the most common type of sexual boundary transgression (see Celenza, 2007 for a fuller description of many aspects of this outcome).

A safe context for therapeutic engagement cannot be maintained under threat. But, as the erotic desires heighten, so do frustration and humiliated rage when these desires are not fulfilled. Out of desperation and in order to stave off further humiliation, some patients will resort to threatening their therapist in order to get what they think they want and need. If they reflected upon their actions further, they would realize this is not the way they want their desires gratified but, in desperation, there is usually no room for such nuance. Some patients will threaten to abort the treatment, some will have particular requirements for a change in context (e.g., "I'll only continue to meet with you at a coffee shop," "I cannot talk here, only in my car," or "I'll only tell you X if you tell me Y"). These are all desperate attempts at leveling the inherent hierarchy in the treatment context, aimed as they are at the power imbalance resultant from the asymmetric distribution of attention between therapist and patient.

But threats can take a more dangerous shape. Threats to commit suicide are all too common and have been documented. In cases of sexual boundary transgressions where the analyst is male and the analysand female, it has been reported that over 50% of the patients were actively suicidal at the time of the seduction (Celenza and Gabbard, 2003).[9] Resorting to the woefully mistaken notion that "sex might cure suicide" (see Eyman and Gabbard, 1991) or that a "magically curative copulation" (Searles, 1959) might save the day, too many male therapists turn to seduction in these moments of crisis. As I have written (Celenza, 2007), one therapist cogently stated to me, "I was at the end of my rope. I didn't know how to help her. I knew how to seduce her, so that's what I did." As has long been suspected, the core dynamic in sexual boundary transgressions is not at all about sex, love, or erotics, but about power and control.

Sexual boundary transgressions are not inevitable in these situations and, in the best of circumstances, the road will be rocky and tumultuous, there will be an unmistakable feeling that the treatment is at times foundering, but both patient and therapist will ultimately survive it. I have written this chapter in hope of illustrating how to handle such combustible passions in the transference and countertransference.

Notes

1 An earlier version of this chapter, together with Chapter 2, won the Karl A. Menninger Memorial Award (conferred by the American Psychoanalytic Association) and the Felix and Helena Deutsch Prize (awarded by the Boston Psychoanalytic Society and Institute).
2 As noted in the Introduction to this Part, the expressed desire to have sexual intercourse with the analyst is best termed a 'sexual transference' in contrast to an erotic transference, which denotes the private imaginative use of the analyst in one's erotic life. It is the various erotic transferences that reveal unconscious meaning and that are the focus of psychoanalytic treatment.
3 Sexual boundary transgressions of all types are thoroughly described in my previous book (Celenza, 2007).
4 Though the defining reach of gender is currently undergoing radical transformation (see Dimen, 2003, and Harris, 2005a, for vibrant discussions), Michael's personal struggle to 'feel more male' coincided with traditional stereotypes of masculinity and femininity.
5 Recently, I discussed this vignette with a colleague, who shared an anecdote involving a similar clinical challenge experienced by a colleague of hers. When this colleague discussed her case with a supervisor, he purportedly said, "Don't worry—these things don't usually happen." (Evelyn Schwaber, personal communication, 2004). I doubt this would have reassured me at the time!

6 In 2007, I was awarded the Karl Menninger Memorial Award from the American Psychoanalytic Association for a paper on my treatment of Michael (Chapters 2 and 3 are derived from this paper). In a poetic moment of irony, I received the award from APsaA on the day Michael married his new wife.
7 Still, I am not convinced that, had I said this at the time, Michael would not have had to 'up the ante' in an effort to frighten me further.
8 For ease of writing, I will refer to 'therapist and/or analyst' as simply 'therapist.'
9 In contrast, I have observed that when the analyst is female and the analysand male, there is an equally common tendency for the analysand to aggressivize the essentially erotic tie, potentially culminating in threats to harm the analyst. This may account for the muted manifestation of erotic transferences, the ways in which female analysts may unconsciously register and subtly discourage the impending threat of an intense erotic transference because of the fear of the male patient's outwardly directed aggression. The maternal-containing transference can be used to manage, avoid, and transform the hostile-erotic transference into a more structurally benign transference. It is possible that Michael (this chapter) expressed these dynamics.

Chapter 4

The guilty pleasure of erotic countertransference
Searching for radial true[1]

> *A former self is a fool*
> *An insufferable ass, but he's still human.*
> *You'd no more turn him out than you'd turn out*
> *Any other kind of cripple.*
>
> T. Pynchon, *Gravity's Rainbow*, 1973

We think we want to talk about sex. We think we're comfortable with it. When my son Ethan was 8, he said, "Mom, I could never do what you do when I grow up. I'd have to read all those books with bad words in them." But *we* have no problem with that! And we know the famous caricature about psychoanalysis—'It's all about sex.' So who, if not us, should be comfortable talking about sex?

This reminds me of an episode that occurred during my own analysis. I'd had an erotic dream about my analyst and, when I awoke, I thought to myself, "Cool!" As far as I knew, I wanted this to happen, and I looked forward to telling my analyst all about it. So, I got in my car and began the drive to his office, as had become automatic, having driven there 4 times a week. This was the third year of that ritual; so, it's fair to say, I knew the way. On this particular morning, the 563rd time (I did the math, including Bunker Hill Day and Flag Day, which my analyst considered scam holidays, but I digress), I inexplicably, and for the first time in 3 years, missed the exit to Brookline off Storrow Drive. Further, I did not notice that I was on my way to downtown Boston until I arrived at none other than 'Government Center' . . . Super-ego City.

By the time I retraced my steps, chuckling all the while, yet also realizing I was more uncomfortable than I could admit, I finally arrived at my analyst's office with just enough time remaining to explain what had happened. No time to tell the dream on that day. Apparently, in its efforts to derail, my unconscious kept track of time too. When I left his office, my analyst said, "See you tomorrow . . . maybe."

So, we think we are comfortable talking about sex. Our bodily desires. Embodiment. Libido. Erotic countertransference. Big words about an everyday thing. And this was me, *as a patient*, when we're supposed to talk about sex. What about when we're the analyst? Not only are we not supposed to talk about it, we're not supposed to have those feelings at all. This is an impossible standard, and I doubt anyone really believes it. But there was a time when all countertransference feelings were thought to be a sign of something unanalyzed, forbidden, or taboo.

As we all know, countertransference has become a legitimate lens through which analysts monitor, explore, and analyze their patients' dynamics. Whether viewed as the container of disavowed wishes or as part of a co-created unconscious dance, analysts of all ilk now consider countertransference a crucial part of the clinical process. While the use of the analyst's countertransference remains a point of controversy, it is a rare analyst who would not consider such feelings useful fodder, at least for the analyst's private reverie. *But when the affective valence leans erotic, countertransference once again becomes taboo.* (For notable exceptions, see Davies, 1994; Gabbard, 1994; Tansey, 1994; Wrye and Welles, 1994; Dimen, 1999; Maroda, 2002, 2012; Phillips, 2002, 2003; Celenza, 2006; Hirsch, 2008, 2010; Wolfe, 2010; Atlas, 2012; Kuchuck, 2012; Gentile, 2013; Sherby, 2013.)

It is very difficult for analysts to admit having erotic feelings for a patient, even in the protected environment of a supervisory dyad. In my work with sexual boundary transgressors (Celenza, 2007), many have reported, "I tried to tell my supervisor, but he or she just said, "You should bring this to your analysis . . . oh, so sorry, times up." And it usually was, because the supervisee (now transgressor) brought it up at the end of the hour.

We want our patients to talk about their sexuality in a meaningful way that will evoke meaningful, analytic responses in us. What makes an experience meaningful? What is meant by the phrase, 'I know what you mean?' Psychoanalysis, an essentially hermeneutic discipline, specializes in the art of association—a 'this is like that' kind of endeavor based on analogic thinking. Characteristic of the nondominant (for most people), right hemisphere, the mode of cognition relied upon for our work is synthetic, gestalt oriented, associative, and integrative (see Watt, 1990, Celenza, 1993, and Schore, 2011, for a more elaborated discussion of the neurophysiology of cognition along these lines). This contrasts with the linear, cause-and-effect sequential logic of the left or dominant hemisphere. Our main tool, empathic listening, is based on the evocation of such associational links through affectively resonant self-other identifications contextualized within our own histories. Always relationally based, we call upon one or many self-other identifications in constructing an analytic response. Further, these self-other identifications are part of an overarching self-organization that contributes to a core feeling of self.[2]

To make analytic use of such associational links, we must have the capacity to examine the full range of countertransference responses, including erotic, within ourselves. For the purposes of this chapter, I make use of the metaphor of a bicycle wheel with multiple spokes, requiring periodic re-balancing or 'truing' to reset the delicate, counterbalanced tension among these spokes. But we have a moving core at the center capable of transformative evolution, along with some spokes that are only tenuously connected. It is these loosely connected spokes that, when evoked through associational links with our patients, may potentiate an intense, perhaps eroticized countertransference response in us.

Contacting me: the little girl inside

In 2007, I wrote that the question, 'Why can't we be lovers?' is calibrated and danced around in many relationships, sometimes regardless of age, gender, role, or context. After all, *our unconscious is never married*, and there are no boundaries or limits in our imagination. This question sometimes comes up heatedly, sometimes subtly, but, most often, it is not admitted, either verbally or consciously. In my writing, I went further still and suggested that this question should be a moment in most treatments—that the analyst should wonder where she stands in relation to each patient on this question, meaning what she erotically feels toward her patient. It is a meaningful question, especially for those patients in whom the capacity to erotically arouse seems dormant or dead.

Like the bicycle wheel with multiple spokes, the erotic dimension of our connection is one that adds to the balance, each spoke representing a crucial dimension in a pattern of relating that may repeat itself over and over. When these spokes are in balanced tension, we can call it *radial true*. Calling upon the multiplicity of roles we have for our patients, each spoke has its tension counterbalanced with the others.

Having put this question—Why can't we be lovers?—out there, I forgot to anticipate what might happen if one of my patients read it. Rachel enjoys showing her body; this is mostly to herself, but she also notices that she walks around the locker room in her gym a little too long. She can feel the gaze of other women on her skin. "It's like they're touching me," she says. Similarly, the heat of the sauna on her genitals arouses her, and she masturbates in the stall. She talks about this to me, knowing (and fearing) that she is on the verge of taking her clothes off during a session. Is this erotic? Yes, definitely. Is it an erotic move toward me? On one level, yes. I tell her she wants to be seen and touched; that her 17-year-old body is like a throbbing fire engine—both enflamed and calling out to be doused. The fact that she has not had sexual relations with her lover for several years is implicated, but is not the whole story. On another level, her disrobing is a flowering—she wants her erotic body to be seen in its pubescent glory; she wants her mother's admiration. She is also stoking her sexuality in order to distract herself from mourning her father's death. Coming, as it did, a few weeks before she began menstruating, he never got to see his little girl flowering into a woman, and she never felt his gaze on her nubile body.

Who am I to Rachel? At least a mother, father, lover, and her own pubescent self. Embedded within this formulation is the theoretical assumption of multiplicity (Mitchell, 1993; Bromberg, 1998; Davies, 1998a; Dimen, 2003; Harris, 2005a), based on the development of identity as deriving from multiple same-gendered and opposite-gendered identifications. These identifications arise through different processes, may be global or partial, metabolized, undigested, or alien (Harris,

2005a). Conscious or unconscious, these identifications comprise a mosaic that continually evolves and kaleidoscopically transforms as we explore "gender's wide arc and the corresponding wide arc of relationship structures and object ties," as Corbett (2008, p. 852) and others (Goldner, 1991, 2003; Elise, 1998; Dimen and Goldner, 2002; Roughton, 2002; Phillips, 2003) have described.

Being multiple selves is the human condition, and being multiple others to our patients is the analytic condition (see Bolognini, 2011). When multiple (emergent) selves are presumed in relation to the question, 'Why can't we be lovers?' we see that this is ultimately an unanswerable question. After all, to whom is the analyst speaking? And from where within herself? A response through one lens contradicts another. Thus, a helpful response to this question conveys the message, "I am many things to you, and I don't want to invalidate any one of them."

Judicious clinical technique respects the complexity of clinical process. So, when I feel an erotic counter-response to Rachel, I must also ask myself, in which dyad am I responding erotically, and what might it mean? As a parent, my erotic countertransference response might signal the repetition of an oedipal conquest or traumatic memory; as a lover, my countertransference may signal her emerging health, but also a way-station. Given the imbalanced, asymmetric structure in analysis (Aron, 1996; Hoffer, 1996), her erotic move toward me may signal a budding readiness for gratification in her real life;[3] as a child, my erotic countertransference may be her projected and unmourned longing for her father. And finally, there is a level at which my erotic countertransference is mine—arising from within me and reflecting my own needs and desires. Then, I must ask, Who is Rachel to me? The answer will have many spokes.

We more easily recognize lost, dissociated, or disclaimed selves in others. For most persons, the opposite-gendered self is more easily seen as 'not me' and can become a previously unformulated or disavowed self with whom we long to reconnect. Think of how poignantly, painfully even, we love our opposite-gendered children—he who looks like me, yet is not me—in his sweet innocence and vulnerability, that good little boy so devoted to pleasing. The same-gendered child resides in the self as well, though we are likely to have done more analysis with her. She's not as likely to be so dramatically disavowed or neglected. But this is not true for everyone; gender is a difference marker (Goldner, 1991) some more readily embrace (see Celenza, 2000, for a discussion of a case of same-gendered disavowal). As Blechner (2009) cautions, "The gender that the analyst is, male or female, is not necessarily the only gender the analyst can be in the erotic transference" (p. 175).

Our readiness to embrace the same-gendered child, however, does not mean the connection is uncomplicated. In my work with female sexual boundary transgressors, it is striking how often the erotic countertransference involves an over-identification with a female patient. One transgressor reported to me, "She was the child I was. I couldn't stand the pain she was in." Two thirds of female transgressors engage in sexual relations with a female patient; many of these transgressors are not previously self-identified as gay. As Sinsheimer (2010) notes, "unconscious homophobia is a risk factor for sexual boundary transgressions." Homoerotic identifications that drive us suddenly to act in unfamiliar or uncharacteristic ways (compared to the more patterned modes) can be conceived as disconnected spokes that have been recaptured and connected anew. We feel gleeful at the return of a prodigal child, a lost shoe that finds its mate in the closet (pun intended).

The development of erotic countertransference

Whether or not a patient arouses sexual desire in the analyst is an important indicator of the patient's vitality and strength, their sense of wholeness or coherence. What if there is *no* sexual desire in relation to the patient? This should not be confused with the analyst's subjective experience of neutrality or an easy route to abstinence. The absence of erotic energy (mutual and bi-directional) should prompt the analyst to explore inhibitions or other conflicts.

In Chapters 2 and 3, I discussed my analysis of Michael, whose erotic imaginings toward me became the central focus early on in his treatment. An inhibited, obsessional academic, who had grown up with divorced parents, largely in the care of his domineering, narcissistic mother, Michael became preoccupied with the wish to have sex with me after about a year into the treatment. Within this, I discerned a merger fantasy underlying his erotic longings. The merger fantasy had a sadomasochistic structure and represented a defensive move whereby he subjugated himself to me in order to sidestep the exploration and expression of his own subjective desire. It was largely through my countertransference that I understood this formulation, especially from the way in which I experienced Michael's attempts to penetrate me. Michael would demand that I have sexual relations with him and insist that my refusal was sadistic, following upon what he experienced as the hypocritical, seductive analytic set-up that had trapped him in a helpless and impotent position. But beyond the sex, what did he want? He was essentially pained and furious that I would not fill up the hours with stories about my life, my experiences outside, and my desires. He felt I deprived him. He said he wanted to take my lead, to be my surrogate.

In counterpoint, I was not excited by his aggressive or hapless pleas. Rather, it was as if his attempts to penetrate me were too soft or weak. He seemed to lack substance or hardness; it was not possible for me *to feel him*. He attempted to *'get inside me'* with an obsessive interest in my life but, rather than being excited, I felt closed in and suffocated. His examination of me felt *too in* me, appropriating, as if he wanted to take me over and *become* me. Though he explicitly only talked about sex—his wish to take me, all the time—it felt more like a desire to take my subjectivity, my being, from me.

In the middle phase of his analysis, I noticed a welcome shift in my countertransference. Michael had become more appealing. His more differentiated presence allowed me greater room to breathe and to see him from a crucial distance which, paradoxically, made intimacy possible. At the same time, his hostility seemed to intensify and I was aware of an increasing discomfort in me. These developments finally culminated in his sharing a fantasy to murder me, the crux of which revolved around stabbing me repeatedly until I cried out, in a lurching, bloody, and passionate plea. Orgasmic in nature, this also did not turn me on, but it did grip me so that I could not think of anyone or anything else except Michael for what seemed to me like a very long period of time.

Michael stirred me up so much, I needed others to calm me down. I got consultation from various 'thirds,' all phallic figures, to fortify my intimidated self. It can be said that not only did the dyad need a third, not only did Michael need a father, but I needed a 'man.' What was this movement in the analytic field, and how did it connect with the erotic dimension of the treatment?

I had wanted to engage the 'man' in Michael and facilitate his emergence. In so doing, Michael's aggression came through in full force; perhaps the 'man' in Michael then needed to make contact with the 'man' in me. Counterbalancing the 'feminine' with the so-called 'masculine' aspects of our role, we both needed more phallus—Michael had not wanted to experience me as an empowered, phallic woman earlier in the treatment because of its subjugating effects on him, and I too resisted access to the 'male' in me. It took a third to say, "Yes, we want to kill the person who humiliates and rejects us. More than that, you want to make me spill my guts the way you feel you have done with me." A third 'man,' and the 'man' in me.

As his analysis continued, Michael transformed in his ability to erotically excite me. Not that this was at the forefront all the time, but I did find myself imagining living with him, being his lover, and identifying with the women in his life. Non-pressured erotic musings emerged along with the full range of everyday concordant and complimentary affective experience. Michael had become whole—a bicycle wheel with all the spokes.

Multiplicity, lost selves, and opposite-gendered selves

Through the urge for integration, we can see a desire to recapture early, former, or lost parts of ourselves. As I have often said to my patients, we can't leave anyone behind. The striving to reconnect with earlier, lost, or disavowed selves, to recuperate our primary bisexuality (McDougall, 1992; Bassin, 1996; Benjamin, 1998; Elise, 1998), or the "phantasy of bisexual completeness" (Aron, 1995, p. 201), broadens the arena for creativity, play, thought, and symbolization. In keeping with the metaphor of a bicycle wheel with multiple spokes as representative of multiply constructed and coded self-states that cohere more or less in an ongoing search for *radial true*, we have a visuo-spatial representation of how we continuously find attachments that connect with old selves in an effort to achieve a better balance among the collection of all our parts. The parts, or, to stay in metaphor, the spokes, represent modes of relating that are differentiated by roles, ages, or dynamic (perhaps disavowed) self-object identifications that are more or less connected to a core feeling of self—the more continuous and present mode of embodied experience. It is the tenuously connected selves that press for expression in an unbidden, alien-feeling way and that are consciously considered 'not me.'[4]

Such is the fate of opposite-gendered selves that often find expression in a mother's opposite-gendered child or in relationships with another person of a markedly different age—perhaps a person who represents "the child I was." This latter statement comes from a female therapist who had become sexually involved with a female patient despite not being previously identified as gay. Along the same lines, it is a well known phenomenon that many heterosexual women become sexually involved with a woman in later years, often representing a reconnection with a self previously psychologically disavowed. This former, early self may alternatively be the opposite gender, a different age (Donnell, 2013), a different (often lower) socio-economic status, or different race or ethnicity. Such outward signs of 'otherness' make apt repositories for disavowed wishes and forbidden desires—attributing the urge or wish to the other and connecting with it at the same time. Or, in accord with the development of expanded self-experience discussed in this chapter, including those that may derive meaning from gendered attributes, same (nominal) gender relations may indicate an expansive gendered multiplicity in which anatomical sameness is no longer meaningful.

To the extent that these self-states are dissociated, repudiated (or, as in the metaphor of the bicycle wheel, tenuously connected), they, when enlivened, are characterized by a feeling of drivenness, compulsion, or feeling out of control as they push for expression, often culminating in an outwardly inexplicable crush or infatuation with a lover who seems to represent all that one has tried to repudiate or disavow. Lost or forgotten selves, ungrieved self-other identifications, connecting with others from whom one was traumatically separated, all find ways to re-emerge, often in the form of a mid-life affair.

Consider Christienne, a young mother of two, who secretly longs for her childhood home in France. She is happily married and has an apparently full life here in America. She comes to treatment after inexplicably becoming involved with a French colleague whom she met at a professional conference. All of her descriptions of this handsome adult man are oddly reminiscent of her own childhood dreams as a little girl. She is puzzled because her relocation to the United States at age 10 happened easily enough—she insists that she wanted to come to school here and was excited for the adventure. Of course, more exploration reveals traumatic separations from loved ones back home that she could not afford to process or feel at the time (see Harlem, 2010, for a more explicit discussion of the recapture of lost selves in relation to immigration).

The opposite gendered self: contacting 'not me'

It is in the psychoanalytic context (with the attendant assumptions of multiplicity, condensation of affects, multi-determinism, and ever-deepening layers of unconscious meaning) that the question of gender and homophobia becomes strained. As Michael made contact with the man in me, Thomas made contact with the boy. But not just the boy . . . the *little* boy. Opposite-gendered selves are often different ages—selves further away in time and gender make apt repositories for disavowed vulnerabiltities and wishes. The rescue of a lost self in whom we have located denied, unformulated, or disavowed experience can be a strange and potent attractor.

The psyche continually strives toward integration, and we are in love with our little boy and little girl selves. Sometimes love is primarily an identification with these lost selves and manifests as a mutual rescue fantasy, begging the question, Exactly whom are we saving? Leonard and Michelle (from *Two Lovers*, [Gray, 2009], played by Joaquin Phoenix and Gwyneth Paltrow) are such lost lovers—inexplicably drawn to each other because, in Leonard's words, "I'm fucked up too—I want to help you." Love is, in part, salvation.

Thomas is a successful attorney in his 40s. He has struggled all his life with premature ejaculation and, though he had some previous treatment for this problem, it had never resolved. He was in analysis with me for four and a half years. We explored his childhood, which was rife with trauma, his mother being a rageful alcoholic, and Thomas, an only child. He remembered curling up in a fetal position in his bed, shaking with anxiety when his parents would fight. They divorced when he was 6 years old, leaving Thomas alone with his mother. There were sadistic scenes, one including a breakfast incident when his mother forced him to eat. When he threw it up, she made him eat that too.

Dramatic maternal images developed in Thomas' dreams and reveries, alternating between a sucking, bottomless pit, needy woman/vagina to a sadistic, biting, castrating vagina. We understood these as reflective of his need to '*pull out of a woman*' or ways in which he '*didn't want to be inside.*' Not surprisingly, safety concerns were paramount in the early stages of the analysis. Thomas expressed his need to feel securely held in my office and, as he was able to feel safe '*in my hands*' (his idiom), I developed an intense, but pleasing, feeling of enveloping him, cradling him as he lay on the couch and securely holding him in the cavity of my office/vagina. Gradually, he felt his father hunger and became less fearful of his rage against his mother, including the ability to criticize me, push against me, as it were, without fearing that he would hurt or even destroy me. In his outside life, his premature ejaculation resolved.

An interesting scenario developed in the late part of his analysis. Since Thomas' mother was always drinking, starting early in the morning, he never knew which mood would overtake her when he arrived home from school. Sports, camp, and his cousin's home had become sites of refuge. He wanted his cousin's home to be his real home, though they were wealthier and he wasn't always comfortable there. Carl, his same-aged cousin, was a good friend but also a competitor for his aunt's attention. For his 20th high school reunion, Thomas returned to his hometown, a successful professional with a family of his own. He stayed with his cousin, since his mother had passed away. They got dressed for the occasion and then, poignantly, while straightening Thomas' tie, Carl said, "Now they'll see who you are." Thomas was touched and proud; as was I, for him.

Many months later, I referred to that moment when Carl straightened Thomas' tie; especially the way his cousin had overcome rivalrous, competitive feelings with a comment that recognized what Thomas had been through and overcome. My eyes welled with tears and my throat constricted as I repeated what his cousin had said. Thomas asked, "Are you crying?" to which I admitted I thought maybe I was. He was deeply moved and blew me a kiss when he left the office that day.

What was happening in the analytic field? Perhaps I, as a receptive organ to Thomas' ability to be erect, to be a proud, stand-up guy, was responsively moist with my tears/vaginal fluids. At the time, though, all this was not in my conscious mind; nor did my tears, or Thomas' airborne kiss, worry me. At least I thought not. I felt a special connection with Thomas and it was all good. I've written about the perils of erotic countertransference, the ways in which sexual feelings for our patients can move us to violate boundaries. Most of these cautionary tales involve defensive efforts to manage our self-neglect (Celenza, 2008; Harris, 2008; Sinsheimer, 2008) or to eroticize negative countertransference (Celenza, 2007). The so-called slippery slope is actually a dance with parts of ourselves we are unwilling to acknowledge or admit. Our patients often need to bring their sexuality into the foreground and not just dance, but tango with us; we need to be pushed and pulled, held in open embrace with a seemingly dissociated body, to be led (and sometimes to lead), to pivot, staccato-like, and then be taken on a long glide, sometimes drastically, sometimes close to the edge. The question is, Are we always up to it? What if we don't like it? What if we do?

Thomas and I continued on, meaning we proceeded with analysis in the foreground. In the background, however, there was no doubt in either of our minds that we had a 'special connection.' He felt I uniquely understood him; more—that I *felt* him. He told me how important I was to him. I was not surprised and felt the same toward him. I remember thinking, "We are sympatico. I love his sense of humor, his sensitivities." He wittily described scenes from his life; I laughed with ease and from deep inside. He said, if we were both single and had met in a different way, "I'd be all over you." I smiled and felt a mutual, resonant feeling. I also thought: It's a good thing we both have vital and satisfying marriages. I did my due diligence—I consulted with my peer group, especially in relation to the question, "Was this treatment deep enough? Was it negative enough?" All of this was in the background.

Then one day, Thomas began a session by saying, "I'm disappointed in you. I've been angry at you for a few weeks, but I haven't told you. I thought things might change, so I waited, but they haven't. I need to tell you." The only words that came to me, and I don't remember if I uttered them out loud, were, "Uh oh." He said, "You've stopped meeting me at the door when I leave. You don't get up anymore, at least not before I do, and I think you're avoiding me." I had no awareness at all that I had changed my usual habit. As with all of my patients, at the end of the hour, I would acknowledge our time was up, walk to the door and open it. There, I would say good-bye, looking each patient in the eye, as they walked toward me and out the door.

I told Thomas I was unaware of a change in me and asked him to tell me what he had noticed and how he felt. He said he felt hurt that I seemed not to trust him. He didn't want anything to change between us, but he thought I had become uncomfortable with the way we had been interacting. He did not want to be the cause of anything destructive between us, but he also wanted to feel he could speak his mind and tell me everything he felt. I promised him I would think about this more and, it will not surprise you to know that at the end of that session, I made sure I was the first one at the door.

We think we're comfortable. But what exactly was my discomfort? It wasn't the syncopation, the facile way in which we discussed his life. It wasn't even the revelation of emotion on the day I had wept, nor was it the exposure of the vulnerable little boy in me who so poignantly identified with little Thomas. We had a special way of playing—'deep play' as Jim Herzog (Herzog, 2001) would say, which had sexual overtones—but I don't think I was uncomfortable with that either. The discomfort was more in the way of a nagging guilt—Was I enjoying him too much? Did our play cross over to flirtation, in a way that seductively offered something I could not, and would not, deliver? Though he did not seem to mind, I did not know if this would always be true; more to the point, was I behaving with his best interests in mind?

Our work is sometimes a guilty pleasure, and we must always ask, Pleasure for whom? What if we enjoy it? Surely, this can be part of our work, but are we in balance, with the work of analysis in the foreground? Does each spoke contribute to the truing of the wheel?

Thomas was able to differentiate his experience of his mother with his experience of me, his wife, and other women in his life as well. In looking over this material and remembering this episode, occurring late in the analysis, I realize it may represent an unfinished remnant of the enveloping, intense, and perhaps sexualized holding I felt was my enacted counter-response to him—a receptive and safe vagina in place of the biting, castrating, and annihilating vaginas of his fantasies. But, perhaps it also represented my healthy and affectionate acceptance of him as an evolved man, grateful for the analytic work we were able to accomplish in the sense that Bolognini (1994) describes, the affectionate (erotic) transference but along with a complementary countertransference.

Discussion

What do our patients want? They say they want our love, or more pointedly, to have sex—but do they really want that? We are many things to our patients, simultaneously and equally important: analyst, woman, person, mother, father, sibling, and child—all spokes in the wheel. At any one time, a plea for love or sex is a plea from within only one of these dimensions. To respond, that is, to gratify the wish, is a gratification from within one mode of relating. The man may want a kiss, but the child does not. In the context of psychoanalysis, this multiplicity is irreducible; each spoke needs to be in balanced tension with the others.

I have come to believe that our patients do not really want us to gratify their erotic wishes, despite their vociferous protests to the contrary. But they do not want us to simply maintain our professional role either. This was the mistake of the abstinent classical analyst who refused to allow his patients to know him personally. What our patients want is not an engagement from within one single dimension (i.e., the role, the person, the professional, or the woman), but to have the multiple roles coalesce into one, as it were. Our patients will say, "I want you to touch me in a personal way, not from your professional self." But in this phrase, they are expressing a void, a problem to analyze—both a desire and dread; a need and incapacity. What they need is to expose it; what they want is for us to remain in role, but in a personal, authentic way. It is structurally like an oedipal moment, but not only that. As Davies (2003) wisely put it, in healthy families, the oedipal conflict is both won and lost. Just how is this done? I would venture to say that the parent conveys, "I would if I could."[5] Or, "In another time or place." This is what we need to convey to our patients.[6]

Our patients complain of the tease and seduction in the therapeutic context. It is tempting to think that we shouldn't go there at all. Herein lies the guilt. Are we in fact seducing and then rejecting them? But, the fact that they can be so stimulated, can feel their desires intensely and strongly, means they are expanding and deepening their experience. The effectiveness of therapeutic action is in the stirring of desire. For this, we should not apologize. The goal, to live fully and feel intensely, has always been among the many goals of psychoanalysis.

In closing, I am reminded of an interaction with my analyst that prompted a very useful exploration—it began with a flirtation. One day, I walked into his office and was about to lie down when I discovered, to my horror, a barrette on the couch. I picked it up and held it between us. I said, "You see other women?" He deftly replied, "It's a transvestite." In that one phrase, he conveyed to me his very deep understanding of my dynamics and distress. The message was, "I know you want to be my 'one and only' and I'll play along, but at the same time, I'll let you know that this is a game you need. We'll talk about it." On a personal level, I loved that he could play with me that way—funny, astute, and penetrating; sexy, professional, and deft, all in one package. Like a well-balanced bicycle wheel, he spoke to me in radial true.

Notes

1 This chapter is derived from an earlier version that won the Symonds Prize for best essay on gender and sexuality. The award is conferred by the journal *Studies in Gender and Sexuality*, and was awarded to me in 2010.
2 The question of whether the self is stable or has a core at all is a point of current controversy revolving around biological-essentialist versus postmodern, antifoundationalist epistemologies (see, for example, Mitchell, 1996, for a discussion of how these controversies relate to the construction of gender polarities).
3 In the clinical setting, it is wise to remember that a demand for love is an absence of a capacity for loving (Frayn and Silberfeld, 1986). Thus, Rachel's erotic move toward me

may represent a step in the development of her erotic life outside treatment but is not to be taken at face-value from within the treatment (Freud, 1915).
4 See Kulish (2006) for a similar idea applied to the concept of the phallic mother.
5 Compare Renn's (2013) disclosure to his adoring patient, in which he said, in effect, *I might if I weren't*. See also Chapter 5 of this volume.
6 Samuels (2000b) suggests a similar conveyance from the *good-enough erotic leader* to his citizens.

Chapter 5
Erotic countertransference revelations

> *Who plead for love, and look for recompense*
> *More than that tongue that more hath express'd.*
> *O, learn to read what silent love hath writ*
> *To hear with eyes belongs to love's fine wit.*
>
> W. Shakespeare, *Sonnet 23*, 1609

In this chapter, I wrestle with the question of the analyst's verbal disclosure of erotic countertransference.[1] Is it ever clinically indicated? How far can we allow our participation and emotional engagement with the patient to be explicitly articulated? And, most importantly, under what conditions might the disclosure of erotic countertransference be permissible and even warranted?

The need for this chapter is prompted by my work consulting on the problem of sexual boundary transgressions, but also my awareness (from supervisory settings, academic contexts, and other professional contexts) that analysts and analytically oriented therapists do communicate their loving and/or erotic feelings more than is formally reported. This clinical reality needs to be brought under the umbrella of transparent clinical discourse so that the questions and conundrums attendant to these moments can be examined and discussed.

Further, it is also prompted by the current debates, mostly within the relational literature, on the challenge of self-disclosure of such feelings. I firmly believe it is not enough to have a mandate that clinicians refrain from directly expressing all modes of feeling. Clinicians do not abide this and are not helped by such a blanket prohibition.

There are now a few (counted on one hand) examples in the clinical literature on the explicit revelation of erotic countertransference, beginning with Jody Davies' (1994) paper, "Love in the Afternoon: A Relational Reconsideration of Desire and Dread in the Countertransference," in which she revealed a courageous and controversial disclosure that she had made to her patient, where she told him that she "has had sexual fantasies about [him], many times" (p. 166).[2] In response to much of the debate that her paper generated, Davies (1998c) observed a phobic dread of erotic transference and countertransference due to the absence of theory.

To this, I add the absence of clear guidelines for technique and this chapter is an attempt to address this gap.

Almost immediately after publication, Davies' (1994) paper instigated a torrent of authors weighing in on the use, and misuse, of disclosure of erotic countertransference, with most advising against it except in unusual circumstances. Gabbard (1994) warned of unduly burdening the patient and foreclosing mourning. Benjamin (1994b) wondered about the role of power and hate in the interaction. Cooper (1998) advised "virtual disclosure," a statement that implies the analyst is willing to explore the patient's perceptions (of the analyst as a desiring other) while not definitively affirming the analyst's perspective. Both Gabbard (1994, 1996) and Benjamin (1997) emphasized the role of the analyst in protecting transitionality. Gabbard also cites Modell (1991), who writes that the asymmetry in the analytic setting is not an asymmetry of desire but an asymmetry of *the communication* of desire. Mann (1994) argues that erotic countertransference disclosure would only serve to stimulate incestuous wishes. Cornell (2009) believes direct disclosure of the analyst's personal sexual interest, or disinterest, trivializes the erotic space. Hirsch (1994) directs us to the relational-conflict model of psychoanalytic theory for guidance in making use of the analyst's private countertransference feelings.

On the other side are those analysts who argue that judicious and tactful disclosure of erotic countertransference can facilitate the treatment (see Lijtmaer, 2004, for a helpful review). Knoblauch (1995) observes other affects that often go unexplored and unarticulated due to 'something else that occurred' in the moment of erotic disclosure, such as anxiety and fear of the analyst's actions. Slavin et al. (1998) believe erotic countertransference disclosures can facilitate the demystification of infantile conflicts. Hoffman (2009) suggests that, while no single standardized mode of expression is generalizable, the "challenge for each of us is . . . to express that passionate response in a manner that is usable by each patient" (p. 635).

A more recent example is, ironically, embedded in a paper written, 20 years later, as a celebratory discussion of Davies' 1994 paper. By Jill Gentile (2013), the paper is entitled, "From *Truth or Dare* to *Show and Tell*: Reflections on Childhood Ritual, Play and the Evolution of Symbolic Life." In this discussion, Gentile describes a moment in her treatment of a patient, Mr. G, when she holds his beloved wooden baseball bat from childhood, offered to her during a session. Gentile's musings at the time included her awareness of multiple symbolic meanings for the patient, including the phallic imagery. At one point, she put the bat across her chair like a barrier and acknowledged to him that perhaps she is afraid she may get a little too excited for her comfort, if not for his, and for their work together. Despite the negation and future tense (i.e., "she may get" as opposed to "she is"), she presents Mr. G with the possibility of her embodied arousal. The use of physical objects (toys) had been frequent in the treatment with Mr. G, and Gentile has a lovely way of likening the process to play therapy, defining the various dynamics in terms of structured games, including *Hide and Seek, Truth or Dare, Show and Tell*, as well as *Lost and Found*. I have no problem with these analogies, nor with the presentation of physical objects and their use, a common enough occurrence in many treatments, usually in the form of gifts. Most importantly, Gentile keeps her eye and analytic discipline intact by exploring the meanings of the various toys at every turn, including the implied erotic messages in many.

One factor that is important to note embedded in both Davies' (1994) and Gentile's (2013) vignettes is that both authors acknowledged *a context wherein some important therapeutic work needed to be accomplished.* For Davies, it was a final moment of impasse, during the termination phase of a successful treatment that had, nevertheless, left a crucial piece of work undone. For Gentile, the moment in the treatment that led to the disclosure revolved around the patient's experience of himself as a potent man, perhaps wanting to test and claim his prowess through offering various symbolic props to his analyst. The issue I am to highlight here is that the disclosures were made with the hope and intent (at least consciously) to perform some therapeutic piece of work. We might surmise that the analyst's countertransference experience was likely to be layered, with some measure of anxiety, confusion, and/or frustration; however, these are not made explicit, and we cannot definitively know. Necessity being the mother of invention, the rationale for the disclosure followed salutary lines and, in Davies' case, included disclaimers that all other possible analytic responses had been tried and had failed. In Gentile's case, the erotic countertransference disclosure seems to occur organically, as a moment in an otherwise playful, even flirtatious, process aimed at expanding the symbolic play space. For Gentile, holding the bat created a "markedness" that served to hold the line between the concrete and the symbolic.[3] Perhaps the placement of the bat (across her lap) symbolized a similar marking, and Gentile trusted her patient to interpret these markings without confusion or overstimulation. I do not doubt the descriptions of the process in either case. In the spirit of collaboration and furthering our thinking about these crucial therapeutic choice points, I offer the following thoughts.

In contemporary theoretical discourse, including the recent colloquium conducted on the IARPP list-serve (May, 2013) on Irwin Hoffman's paper, *Therapeutic Passion in the Countertransference* (2009), there is, in my point of view, a tendency to justify analyst self-disclosure, especially when the content is positive, affectionate, loving, or even erotic, by making reference to the *mutual* dimension of the analytic relationship and adducing (I think, mistakenly) that the disclosure is encompassed entirely from within this dimension. I believe understanding disclosures in this way overemphasizes the mutuality inherent in the analytic process while minimizing, or even ignoring, the equally persistent, continual, and simultaneous dimension of asymmetry.

Clearly, we are still quaking from (and recovering from the trauma of) the classical depriving stance of abstinence, neutrality, and anonymity, whether occurring in our own personal treatments, supervisions, or other aspects of training. We can be tempted to overcorrect by emphasizing the mutual dimension of the analytic frame. It is, however, an oversimplification of the analytic process and contract. Hoffman (2009) himself asserts the complex dialectic between mutuality and asymmetry (see also Aron, 1996; Hoffer, 1996) that defines the analytic process *at all times*, whether or not we consistently adhere to this mandate. Maintaining the tension of this dialectic is our ethical responsibility and it defines a complex set of imbalances.

The undisclaimable analytic frame

In order to fully address the implications, context, and theoretical implications of analyst personal disclosure (and erotic countertransference in particular), it is important to review the intricacies and contradictions of the analytic frame. Aside from the important need to be mindful of the context in which any disclosure is made, it is imperative to keep in mind that the very dimensions that define the analytic frame (those of *mutuality and asymmetry*) also intensify the patient's experience and longing for intimate, sexual union in this context. Before entertaining the possibility of a verbal, personal disclosure by the analyst, a brief description of the complexity of the analytic frame is presented below.

First, there is the background experience of *mutual, authentic engagement*. This dimension is bi-directional in the sense that there are two persons committed to working together, engaging in a relation that will involve emotional experiences on both sides, and withstanding whatever emerges. This commitment holds out the hope for, and promise of, continued acceptance and understanding for the patient of even the most loathsome aspects of the self. Since the analysand is invited and encouraged to reveal areas of self-contempt and self-hatred, the promise of continued engagement in the face of these aspects of the self is simultaneously dangerous and highly seductive. The danger is inherent in the risk of rejection or withdrawal, despite the (sometimes overt) promise of sustained commitment. The seductive aspect coincides with the universal wish to be loved totally, without judgment or merit. Though rarely actualized, the wish to be loved totally, without having to give anything in return, remains a lifelong wish (see, for example, S. Smith's [1977] discussion of *The Golden Fantasy*). These longings are never given up but can be set aside as life fails to fulfill them. One aim of analysis is to fail the patient in tolerable ways so that the analysand may mourn these wishes and get on with her or his life.

The seductiveness of unconditional acceptance and commitment is fueled and intensified by other fundamental, universal wishes as well. These include: (a) the desire for *unity* (to be loved totally and without separateness); (b) the desire for *purity* (to be loved without hate and unreservedly); (c) the desire for *reciprocity* (to love and be loved in return), and finally; (d) the desire for *omnipotence* (to be so powerful that one is loved by everyone everywhere at all times). All of these universals figure prominently in fantasies of romantic perfection and are stimulated in the treatment setting since the treatment contract partly institutes their gratification. It can be said that the treatment frame both stimulates and frustrates these universal wishes, which will be freighted with the analysand's historical meanings and unresolved developmental trauma.

The analytic context is stimulating, seductive, and frustrating for the analyst as well. The frustration for the analyst is inherent in the second dimension of the treatment context, defined by the *asymmetric distribution of attention*. This comprises the analyst's professional and disciplined commitment to the analysand. In the psychotherapeutic and psychoanalytic setting, the treatment context is defined by the asymmetric distribution of attention paid to the patient.

We are used to thinking of the power imbalance between analyst and patient as one-way, i.e., the analyst has it and the patient does not. But this oversimplifies the structure of the analytic set-up. The axis of asymmetry is hierarchical, in that it is constituted by several power relations, yet it is not straightforward or simple. It is an asymmetry that frames several power imbalances at once, each of which is ambivalently held by both patient and analyst. On the one hand, the analysand is in a desiring or needful state (thereby vulnerable and disempowered), while the analyst, in contrast, is relatively contained in his or her need of the analysand (and is thereby empowered). This is the aspect of asymmetry that we usually refer to as the structured power imbalance in the analytic set-up. Simultaneously, however, the analysand is positioned as special (and thereby of elevated status), while the analyst is discounted in terms of the distribution of attention paid (and thereby dismissed, in terms of his or her personal needs). We know the long-term effects on the analyst of this arrangement if he or she is not mindful of self-care (Celenza, 2010b). Both types of asymmetry deepen and are concretized as the treatment progresses, in the sense that the analyst continues to learn more about the patient, but the reverse (relatively speaking) is not true. As noted previously, the asymmetry in the analytic relationship is not an asymmetry of desire, but an asymmetry of the *communication of* desire (Modell, 1991). The emotional process is mutually involving, but the content of the discourse is asymmetric. Further, the mutuality inherent in the analytic matrix is ineluctable; in contrast, the asymmetry is a matter of discipline and must be maintained continuously by the analyst.

With regard to the relationship between mutuality and asymmetry, these two axes function in dialectical relation. For example, the asymmetry deepens the analysand's need for mutual, affective engagement as a way to ameliorate the humiliating, disempowering aspects of being the continuous focus of attention. In this way, it is the facilitation and encouragement of the analysand's openness and vulnerability that makes the analyst's love and acceptance all the more important (Hoffman, 1998). Likewise, it is the extent to which the analysand reveals him or herself, especially areas of self-hatred and self-loathing, that intensifies the analyst's power in relation to the analysand. In other words, it is the analysand's self-revelations that empower the analyst and intensify the desire for a mutual, authentic engagement (deriving from the analysand's disempowerment).

In these ways, the treatment setting is a complex structure that uniquely instantiates several contradictions. Especially interesting is the way in which the treatment setting combines these two contradictory axes: the axis of equality and mutuality (a 'we're in this together' type of experience) along with the contradictory and imbalanced focus on the analysand (a 'you are in this alone' type of experience).

The treatment setting is the point at which these two axes converge, creating the paradox of a simultaneous feeling of mutuality and asymmetry, of intimacy and aloneness, and of equality and hierarchy. These are tensions that the analysand is persistently moved to resolve, to disequilibrate or level the hierarchy, so to speak, and to make contact with the authentic person behind the professional role.

Maintaining the frame in the heat of the moment

All of these structural dimensions of the analytic set-up define the boundaries of the process and cannot be disclaimed, i.e., when we accept payment for services, we symbolically accept responsibility to maintain the various power imbalances while mutually participating in the enterprise. A question I often find myself asking, when presented with clinical material that involves what I consider to be either gratuitous countertransference disclosure or a countertransference disclosure (especially erotic) borne of frustration in the context of impasse is, What happened to the focus on the patient's experience? This does not mean sidestepping the 'elephant in the room' but it does mean expressing the significance of the patient's erotic conveyance (in whatever form, e.g., a toy, a gift, a gesture, a question) *in terms of the patient's desire(s)*.

A related issue to erotic countertransference disclosure that is often raised as a rationale in favor of disclosure, especially in cases of sexual boundary transgressions, is the extent to which the patient may be viewed as a responsible adult. Additionally, there is the corollary issue of how the analyst should take responsibility for his or her participation. How one views the assumptions inferred in these questions will bear on the technical decisions and their rationales regarding erotic countertransference disclosure. Hoffman (2009) asserts that the patient is a separate person with a will, a person who is "not putty in the analyst's hands," and who has the capacity to agree, differ, and collaborate in meaningful ways (p. 619). I do not disagree with this assertion; however, I believe the quality and extent of psychological autonomy and self-control, even separateness, for all of the above-named capacities *fluctuates* during the course of treatment and, especially under the sway of an intense erotic transference, can be reduced to nil for a protracted period of time.

Further, I suggest that the development of an erotic transference and the capacity to be under its spell for a period of time is a strength, a capacity to be fully receptive to the analytic process and the intensity of affects it evokes. This capacity to surrender to the process in a more or less complete way is parallel to the classical notion of a transference neurosis, once believed to be a sine qua non of analyzability. So, I do not intend to imply that the patient is any less of an adult when under the sway of an intense erotic transference, but rather that he or she has cultivated the capacity to become fully receptive to a set of emotional reactions over which he or she may not have control for a period of time.

Because the analytic process is mutual and because we participate in it, we have varying stakes in what we want or need at any one time. This means there is the possibility of defensively disclaiming one aspect or another of this complex interchange. Our capacity for self-deception should never be underestimated, even for the highly sophisticated theoretician and experienced, seasoned analyst. For example, we can exclusively focus on our own personal meanings or intentions while denying the patients'. Often I have heard, "That phrase was not erotic, I had no intention of crossing that line," or, "I am very clear on the boundaries . . . I told her I loved her and I meant it in a Platonic way." In these statements, the analyst selectively disattends to the patient's experience or intent, including how he or she might attribute a different meaning to the very same words. It is not enough to be clear about one's own intent and there is a responsibility to refrain from engaging in actions that might be misconstrued. When we focus on the patient's experience, we engage our capacity to appreciate and monitor the asymmetry in the analytic relationship.

Further, there is frequently a minimization of the erotic potential in otherwise seemingly non-erotic language. We may desexualize, in the moment, words that at some later point may represent a highly charged conveyance. Language itself is elastic; surface and depth easily overlap manifest and latent meanings. More importantly, the treatment setting is rife with sexual metaphor—as noted in earlier chapters, the penetrating gaze and interpretative activity of the analyst can be experienced as 'coming inside.' Similarly, the background, all-enveloping support of the analyst's affirmative attitude and concrete office (including the couch itself) can engender feelings of sensual erotic longings.[4]

Comfort and clarity with erotic language

Especially for those patients whose presenting areas of distress involve sexual inhibitions, defensively eroticized activity, or compulsions, the analytic setting will provide ample opportunity to demonstrate erotic longings in metaphorized, displaced and (eventually) directly expressed modes. Conversely, sexualized material presented as pervasive or intensely preoccupying may be revealed as masking non-erotic longings. In any case, attunement to sexual metaphor and *comfort with erotic language* will be essential in aiding a patient's self-understanding and the ability to explore his or her erotic life. For many patients, the language of the treatment becomes more direct, shame-free, and thereby more intimate as the treatment progresses. This does not imply the need or therapeutic value of disclosing the analyst's erotic feelings for the patient, however, though it may be more tempting to do so with greater comfort in the discourse. I am emphasizing here a comfort with erotic language that is used to explicate and directly clarify *the patient's longings and experience*, on conscious and unconscious levels, as they arise in either disguised or direct forms. Hoffman (2009) asks, "Why, in fact, do we favor implicit over explicit forms of affirmation, indeed, implicit over explicit expressions of love?" My response is simple: We always favor explicit forms of expressions of affirmation and love, including erotic longings, *from the patient's point of view, but not from the analyst's*, because love is a four letter word.

At the same time, the appreciation of the stimulating potential of direct expressions of the analyst's erotic longing or love must always be balanced with the need to be comfortable, explicit, and non-euphemistic in expressing erotic themes. Galit Atlas (2012) recounts a moment in a treatment with a female patient when the analyst repeated, exactly in the way her patient had expressed it, an erotic phrase about a man she had been dating:

> "In the dream you give him a blowjob," [Atlas says]. Ella giggles, "Oh no, it sounds terrible coming out of your mouth." [Atlas] get[s] confused for a moment and wonder[s] whether this was not the term that she had used. "Did I phrase it differently?" [she asks]. "No, not at all," she replies, "That's exactly what I said, it's just so strange to hear it . . . it's easier to say it . . . maybe even easier to do it," she jokes . . . (p. 4)

The analyst should speak about sex in plain language, as Atlas demonstrates, especially in ways with which the patient is familiar, and the process should proceed to expand the discourse in this direction. I mention this vignette here, however, to highlight how powerful and saturated with meaning our words are to our patients. When *we* say something, it is not the same thing as when our *patient's do*.[5] It is not symmetrical nor is it predictable but, at the same time, we need to cultivate a measure of ease in speaking about sexuality and erotic life. One way to 'break the ice' in cultivating ease is to do what Atlas did, to repeat our patient's words exactly as they express their desires in order to facilitate a mutual comfort and hopefully to advance the discourse as the work proceeds. But again, this is always from the perspective of the patient's point of view.

One supervisee was uncomfortable repeating her male patient's desire to be "fucked up the ass" (his words) yet knew she had to refer to his erotic desires in some way in order to explore them. I suggested to her that she repeatedly say the phrase out loud in her car (windows closed) to acquire more comfort with his way of putting it. She did this and became more comfortable using his phrase in their work.

The delicate balance that I aim to put forth, *ease with erotic discourse while maintaining the focus on the patient's desires*, is illustrated in another clinical vignette. A patient was in the midst of an intense erotic transference for many months. He was explicitly fixated on the need to know if I was erotically attracted to him. He stated that he did not care whether I liked him or even loved him but wanted to know what my sexual feelings were for him. This quality of the transference arose in the context of his uncertainty of his desirability toward women in general and whether they wanted to have sex with him. Questions about his potency and doubts about his 'masculine' attributes were lifelong struggles and had a severely inhibiting effect on his ability to perform sexually.

At this particular time in the treatment, this patient and I were in the midst of a heated transference/countertransference dance, in which his longings and my desires were relatively in sync, and I had hoped my attraction to him would be palpably apparent to him. To be simple and direct, I was aware of being sexually attracted to him, and I hoped he could feel this, though I had not directly articulated my feelings to him, nor did I intend to do so. He consistently stated that he was unsure how I felt about him and that he needed to know; at times, he insisted he would be cured if I would only say yea or nay to this crucial question. (Believe me, it was tempting.)

One day, this patient came to our session and offered me a gift, a rectangular box covered with beautiful Asian silk. Inside were two Chinese Health Balls. (I think these used to be called *Worry Balls* and, yes, they were about the size of two testicles.) He asked me to take them out of the box and gestured how they are held "in order to release stress." I couldn't help but chuckle a bit, and I probably also blushed, but what I said was, "You want me to see and feel your potency . . . to touch your balls." Before the reader cringes with embarrassment and dismisses this interchange as one that could not possibly be uttered with either seriousness or therapeutic intent, I must add that this patient and I had cultivated a way of speaking about his sexual desires, his body, and his sexual functioning that by now was an organic part of our discourse. This was the fourth year of a moving analysis, and I knew I could speak to him using such blunt language. (This is not particularly unique to this patient and me; I try to cultivate similar plain speak with all of my patients, especially those with sexual symptoms or inhibitions. Not all patients develop an ease with such language, but I do see the development of some measure of comfort as part of the analytic work.)

At the time of this vignette, and after I had expressed the above statement, this patient seemed immediately struck, not by my language, but by how he had unconsciously displayed his desires. Because he had already directly, in words, expressed these desires to me, he was not shocked or ashamed by the unconscious meaning of his gift. He also was able to experience some pleasure in my interpretation of the possible unconscious meaning, chuckling at the stark simplicity and almost innocence of his conscious intent. It was a moment of truth (Slavin, 2013) that acknowledged in words what we each already knew he felt. Ultimately, we were both amused by his unconscious selection.

Verbal disclosure of erotic countertransference

In all of the vignettes I have read involving a disclosure of erotic countertransference, I am always left with a lingering question. Why didn't the analyst maintain her or his focus on the patient's experience rather than respond to the patient's expressed wish (at least on the surface) to be told what the analyst feels toward him or her? It is my experience that the wish to *know the analyst sexually* is invariably complicated and usually highly conflicted. And, if it is not, *it should be*, given the inherent power imbalances and (oedipal) transference structure from which the desire likely arises. Herein lies another responsibility of the analyst—to explicate the various levels of meaning in the patient's erotic desire for the analyst as someone who is virtually, or at least explicitly, unknown.

I realize all of our patients have a sense of our being, personality, and style; I do not engage, nor endorse, some impossible objectivist striving toward anonymity. But the analytic contract involves the conscious asymmetric distribution of attention and focus to remain on the patient's experience; so, why is there a push, in some extraordinary moments, to shine the spotlight on the analyst's experience? I also realize we use our awareness of our feelingful engagement at all times to receive unconscious communications and to inform our affective responses to the patient, but the responsive focus remains on the patient's experience, even if we explicitly verbalize some of the ways in which we have metabolized, processed, or experienced the patient (see Renik, 1999).

I have nothing against passion in the countertransference and in the treatment as a whole (compare, for example, Hoffman, 2009). Despite the unusual power distributions and uneven focus of attention in the analytic relationship, it is still a human interaction with ongoing mutual, bi-directional passionate engagement. In addition, our patients come to us for help with affect regulation and with desires for transformation by advancing their understanding of their emotional and erotic desires. Emotional constriction in the analyst would hardly help in this enterprise. However, too often the defensive uses of erotic feelings can mask corrupting influences in the treatment, and our capacity for self-deception must always sound a cautionary note.

Necessary conditions of erotic countertransference disclosure

I will directly address the conditions under which verbal erotic countertransference disclosure may be permissible, and perhaps even warranted, by introducing an extended vignette and then offering explicit guidelines. The context for the way in which this verbal disclosure by the analyst came about was indirect and circuitous, but it is an example of an explicit, verbal disclosure of erotic countertransference that I believe meets the conditions for which such an intervention is permissible.

A supervisee was putting together a write-up to present a case at a clinical conference, a vignette and corresponding discussion that contained a description, privately held by her, of her loving, affectionate, and erotic countertransference with her patient. In preparing for the conference, she had obtained the patient's consent to write about an interchange that had occurred during the late phase of a successful analysis and, in writing about this interchange, she described her passionate, affectionate, and erotic feelings for him in preparation for the presentation. When he gave his permission for the presentation, she invited him to read what she would be presenting with the intention that she would redact the dicey parts about her own feelings toward him. Interestingly, he refused the invitation to read her write-up, getting her off the hook for the moment. He said, "I don't want to interrupt what's going on between us right now." She prepared the write-up and presented the case at the clinical conference.

A year later, during the termination phase of the treatment, the patient asked to read what she had written. With some mixture of curiosity and trepidation, she printed out the write-up, *purposefully unredacted*, and handed it to him. He read it then and there, during the session. As I mentioned, the write-up included a description of her erotic countertransference toward him. Though it was not detailed, she explicitly said that she returned the sexual attraction that he had felt towards her. Her acknowledgments in the write-up were embedded in descriptions of love and affection for him and appreciation of his various personality attributes.

As part of the background in this case, it should be mentioned that, periodically during the treatment, this patient had expressed his longing and attraction toward his analyst. He was happily married and the treatment had solidified his bond with his wife as well. Though the analyst never explicitly told him she found him sexually attractive, she did sense that he knew how she felt, given how safe he felt he was with her and how obvious her enjoyment of him was. Several times, he stated directly that he thought he knew how she felt about him and understood she could not express her feelings directly. In short, he could *feel* their mutual attraction.[6]

After reading the write-up, which included at least two instances where she spelled out her affection for him, her enjoyment of his sense of humor, and her erotic attraction to him, he said, "I am so touched." He went on to say, "I already knew this was how you felt. In fact, I've told you how you feel about me many times! But it's nice to have it returned in an explicit way. I will keep this tucked away in my heart forever." She teared up when he said this and there was a palpable mutual appreciation for each other.

You might think this vignette and my approval of the way my supervisee handled this interchange contradicts all I have discussed thus far about verbal disclosure of erotic countertransference. To my mind, it does not, for the following reasons, all of which are interrelated. *First*, and most importantly, the patient already had surmised, sensed, thought about, and 'knew' his analyst returned his erotic feelings. How did he sense this? My supervisee is a passionate woman and does not withhold her *nonverbal responsivity* and passionate involvement in her relationships. That is different from explicitly revealing her feelings, putting them into words, and making them the focus in the session.[7] *Second*, the treatment had helped this patient hone his antennae for detecting his impact on others, in particular strengthening his ability and confidence in his capacity to erotically arouse another person. Thus, he did not need a verbal confirmation and, most importantly, the revelation of the analyst's feelings was not necessary to effect these advances in the therapeutic action. His capacity to surmise her attraction to him is a strength that partially grew out of the treatment and her disclosure was not aimed at filling a gap in his capacity to detect this. *Third*, the disclosure occurred in the termination phase of a successful analysis when the communication of the analyst's feelings was not being used to perform a therapeutic function. The revelations did not occur in the context of a treatment impasse or the analyst's frustration with unrealized gains. I believe it is acceptable to reverse the asymmetry at the end of a treatment when doing so for affectionate reasons and when the therapeutic work is largely completed. One indication that this condition is met revolves around the awareness that the disclosure is not meant to move the patient in some unfinished therapeutic direction. Nor is it meant to sidestep or circumvent important mourning. This is a difficult judgment call but one that will revolve around the analyst's awareness that the patient has demonstrated his or her acceptance of the limitations in the analytic relationship. It is crucial that this work has already been done. *Fourth*, this patient was high functioning and especially so by the end of the analysis. He was capable (in the analyst's and my judgment) of receiving this communication without confusion and without becoming overstimulated. In other words, we surmised that he would be able to retain the 'I would if I could' sentiment (see Chapter 4), the transitionality, or the 'as if' context, the persistently containing frame around her feelings for him. *Fifth*, this supervisee was aware of the performative nature of words, i.e., words *do*; they are not passive; they are actions; and the revelation of erotic feelings, especially when mutual, is a form of foreplay. This was a reason for her disciplined restraint throughout the analysis and is linked to her assessment of the patient's ability to receive this communication without becoming confused now. *Sixth*, all of these issues were being discussed in an ongoing and detailed way with a trusted supervisor, consultant, or peer group. The presence of supportive, yet potentially correcting, 'thirds' is a must, as our capacity for self-deception is an ever-present corrupting potential. *Seventh*, and finally, the analyst and supervisor(s)/consultant(s) agreed that the analyst was contained in terms of her personal needs. Monitoring our own personal needs for self-care is an ongoing responsibility, much like the need for musicians to have finely tuned instruments.

Final thoughts

I have had many patients who want to know how I feel about them. Sometimes this revolves specifically around my erotic feelings for them. They want me to 'touch' them with words as a symbol that I care for them in a personal way, beyond my professional role and beyond their being my patient. "I need something concrete to let me know you really care for me," they might say, in one way or another. The fantasy about the spoken word is that it is objectified, a *thing* that will *touch* them in a more palpable and lasting way than their silent speculations might.[8] But words have their own ambiguity and often do not last beyond the moment they are uttered.

I usually do not reciprocate a request for such signs of my caring, whether it be a loving or desiring phrase, a hug, or a meeting outside the office, but instead make it the very subject of a detailed analysis. Why do they need such an overt sign of my affection? Why is their ability to detect what I feel for them, in a personal, authentic way (not beyond my professional role but embedded within it) not speaking to them? Our focus becomes their overreliance on the concrete level of experience, overt expressions that indeed include words, in an effort to obtain an illusorily permanent reassurance that they are loved, wanted, or appreciated in a lasting way. I remind them that any concrete sign or gesture will fall flat in the absence of a resonance with what they experience within our relationship on a feeling level.

I remind my patients that words are at once ephemeral and ambiguous, that persons can lie with words in a way they cannot with feelings. I encourage my patients to explore what they know *based on what they feel* is between us so that words become unnecessary, even thin compared to the depth of attachment between us. It is as if the treatment is designed to hone their radar or antennae, directed at their own feelingful experience of the relationship, including, and especially, what they sense I feel about them.

Earlier in my career, I put how I felt about a patient into words and I regret it. This was a male patient referred to me during my internship year. He spent the first year or two letting me know directly and vociferously that he had no use for me, that I was not helping him, and that he was intellectually (and in all other ways) superior to me. I hung in there through this grueling year and did not let on that I actually (silently) agreed with him. He made me feel incompetent, unhelpful, and painfully inexperienced, as well as doubtful that I had any natural talent for this line of work. At the same time, he never missed a session. And he got better, progressing in his career, social relations, and becoming more personally appealing. He had a sharp sense of humor and endeared himself to me despite himself. He also paid me an unreasonably low fee, and I colluded with this arrangement beyond his financial need for fear of unleashing a torrent of abuse about how I did not deserve a penny higher.

After a few years, I mustered the confidence to broach the subject of raising his fee. Through a discussion with a trusted supervisor, we speculated that there was a strong, mutual attachment, despite all this angry tension on the surface, which needed to be explicitly acknowledged. I said to my patient, "Because of the love that there is there between us (or some such awkward phrasing), I've neglected to raise your fee, and I think we should talk about it." Well, the fee became a side issue very quickly, because all he heard was that four letter word. He came in the next day dressed in a suit and high with expectations that we would begin dating. It was painful for both of us to come to terms with that.

It is tempting to think that making statements, directly answering a question, will quiet inner doubts. Why not just tell the patient I like him? Or love him, especially since I do? But as one patient often put it, *"Acta non verba"*: Latin for "Action, not words" (or so he tells me). Words can have an excruciatingly short lifespan. (In effect, you just said you love me, but what about now?) The only lasting truths are the ones we feel, the ones that are informed by our guts, our ability to intuit, feel, and recognize as real what is already in the atmosphere between us. These are the skills I try to help my patients hone—to pay attention to what they know because they can *feel* it. Knowing from that level is more reliable compared to what anyone might say. After all, words hold power only as they resonate with a recognized felt inner state.

I do not mean to resurrect the prudery or wooden anonymity of the blank screen caricature, but rather to encourage a profound appreciation for the complexity of the analytic relationship, including the multitude of meanings and modes of relating emergent at any one time. While the mutuality of our participation in the analytic relationship is inescapable, unwitting, and undisclaimable, the asymmetry is our promise, our commitment to our patients and our discipline. Though it is equally rife with unconscious factors, it is more of a choice at each moment. Thereby, the promise of asymmetry is a tempting playground for self-deceptive rationalizations, deriving from our own needs, which can seduce us away from our promise of disciplined self-restraint.

Notes

1 For a selection of readings on this controversial subject, see Ehrenberg, 1992; Renik, 1993; Davies, 1994, 1998c, 2001; Gabbard, 1994, 1996, 1998; Knoblauch, 1995; Cooper, 1998; Hoffman, 1998, 2009; de Peyer, 2002; Elise, 2002a; Sherman, 2002; Barrett, 2003; Rabin, 2003; Hirsch, 2008; Kuchuck, 2012; Maroda, 2012; Atlis, 2013; Renn, 2013; Wells, 2013.
2 It is always a risk to present clinical material out of context. For the serious reader, I encourage a full acquaintance with this material and its context by reading the entire articles cited herein.
3 Personal communication, October, 2013.
4 Samuels (1985) speaks of the alchemical metaphor used by Jung in describing personality, dialogical 'fluids' and the analytical 'container.'
5 In Atlas' case, the phrase referred to a third person. How much more saturated with meaning the phrase would be if it were uttered in relation to the two of them.
6 A testament, no doubt, to mutual right-hemisphere unconscious communications accounting for their unverbalized 'knowing' of each other (Schore, 2011).
7 As Slavin (2013) has succinctly put it, "The moment of truth [is] speaking the truth, *not* disclosing it" (p. 145, italics in original). Similarly, Bollas (1983) cautions that direct expression of countertransference, "must be experienced by the patient as a legitimate and natural part of the analytic process. If it comes as a shock then the analyst has failed in his technique" (p. 12).
8 See Celenza (2011), for a related discussion on touch in the analytic setting.

Part II

Perverse scenarios revisited

Introduction to Part II

The heart is a fist wrapped in blood.

P. Marber, *Closer*, 1997

In the following chapters, I make several interconnected points of clinical relevance and theoretical interest. Chief among these is the restoration of the term *perversion* to our lexicon, given that many patients present with troubling (for them) sexualized and nonsexualized practices from which they hope to be liberated. This is not a value judgment from an outside perspective but an inescapable conclusion recognized by acknowledging the limitations placed on the individual's life and sexuality due to the adherence to perverse scenario(s). When perversion is defined and analyzed in the particular ways proposed below, the need for clinical intervention is inescapable.

In this effort, I have found the classical literature on erotic perversions to retain clinical utility, despite that there has been a persistent and deplorable history of categorizing various behaviors as perverse on their face *in a disguised effort to legislate ways of being*; a decidedly anti-psychoanalytic enterprise. Despite this profound, longstanding historical breach (ironically, a perversion in its own right[1]), the term perversion can be useful if more narrowly and relationally defined in order to describe problematic and psychically harmful or deadened modes of relating.

The following discussion is an attempt to address this problem while reformulating the term. Thus, I define perversion functionally, as a mode of relating rather than as a specific behavior or set of behaviors per se. As will be elaborated below, perversion can be characterized by the impact of its *constriction and constraint*, the hidden and unbidden (Stoller, 1986). Fundamental to the construction of perverse modes of relating is a *means/end reversal* (Stein, 2005), i.e., the use of constructive means for destructive purposes (either to the self or the other). Finally, I will discuss the clinical observation that perverse modes of relating by males are often aimed at a perceived *dangerous subjectivity of the other*, while females tend to perceive a *dangerous subjectivity within*. These dangers can be understood as organizing, delimiting, and unconsciously choreographing the dual capacities of receptivity and potency.[2] Perverse scenarios can be viewed as unconscious enactments that serve to manage and control some imbalanced reckoning with this binarial construction and the ways in which the polarities have come to define one's embodied and gendered subjectivity. Finally, I propose a schema of perverse scenarios that categorize (1) the localization of perceived dangers (within oneself or in the other); (2) the context (either dyadically or triadically conceived); and (3) degrees of severity (where a rigidly enacted perverse scenario may come to serve a transitional function as the individual's capacities for growth expand).

The reformulation of perverse scenarios

I believe some of the classical literature on erotic perversions retains clinical relevance, with the major and important exception of designating homosexuality as a pathological condition and diagnostic category. How can it be that classical literature might retain its clinical usefulness? Given that classical theorizing has arisen from within linear, mechanistic models and Enlightenment-era epistemological assumptions now rendered obsolete, how can knowledge gained from within these conceptual frameworks offer insight into contemporary conditions?

It is my claim that classical formulations of perverse scenarios still pertain to contemporary understandings because *persons engaging in perverse scenarios are essentially functioning in a one-person universe* (albeit wishful and fantastically construed). A perverse mode of relating is a fantastically construed retreat from relationality in an effort to construct a self-contained and constricted one-person universe.[3] Therefore, perverse scenarios are herein defined as an attempt to construct a one-person fantasy in order to defend against a perceived danger, experienced as either outside the self or localized within.

The construction of a one-person universe is the primary reason that I find the classical literature to retain its utility, although the reformulation carries with it the necessary recontextualization from within a two-person epistemology.[4] Perversion, therefore, is not a static entity or behavior, but an emergent process and a quality of interaction (see also Gerson, 2003; Stein, 2005; Knoblauch, 2007; Amir, 2013; and Gonzalez, 2013). Through the analyst's efforts at reparation (Hartman, 2013) or "differentiated personalization" (Khan, 1989, p. 17), the relational analyst may provide the patient with an opportunity to emerge from a one-person universe (an inert, objectified, or deadened scene) to a vitalized, differentiated, intersubjective engagement.[5]

The primary defenses of perverse scenarios involve objectification and sexualization. At the micro-level, these can be viewed as attempts to transform a threat into a manageable thing (literally, in the case of objectification, to *thing-ify*) and to transform phenomenal experience (at an affective level) into something concretely pleasurable (see Bass, 2000). However, the use of these two defenses in particular has enormous implications at the relational level. The attempt to objectify the other is an attempt to transform a two-person relational experience (along with its attendant vulnerabilities, uncertainties, and risks) into a one-person fantasy of somatic pleasure under the illusion of control and predictability.

The need for sexualization is to target and transform the affective nature of the experience from one of fear and pain to pleasure. Since affects signify object-seeking (Modell, 1975), the transformation of painful or feared affective desire (e.g., for intimacy) into a somatically oriented sexual pleasure moves a two-person scenario into a one-person, body-oriented experience, from a longing for relational engagement to a desire for (concrete, genital) pleasure.

Perceived dangers are symbolically rendered in objectified form in order to provide concrete props that then set the stage for personally meaningful scenarios unconsciously scripted to address a variety of anxieties. These scenarios, unconsciously choreographed to manage and control perceived (intersubjective) dangers (Abel-Hirsch, 2006, cited in Layton, 2013; Bonner, 2006; Purcell, 2006; Eiguer, as reported by Gonzalez, 2010) are designed to address unresolved problems of early self development, often revolving around questions of gender and the various traumas interpreted as related to one's gender identity. Though not inherently gendered, the polarization of the dual capacities of receptivity and potency can be recruited to illusorily delimit the set of challenges that otherwise would overwhelm the individual as he or she strives to organize gendered and nongendered self development. For example, Amir (2013) describes the perverse subject's language as an attempt to "penetrate that of the other only with the aim of fusing with it and paralyzing it, or in order to imprison it in a hollow, repetitious cycle" (p. 398).

Perverse scenarios are not always sexualized, but most are played out in the sexual realm because sexualization, as a defense, is an effective disguise, transformation, and distraction from unconscious anxieties. An example of a perverse scenario that is not sexualized was depicted in the film, *The Secretary*, in which the female protagonist wanted her lover to tie her to a chair and leave her for an indeterminate number of hours. This was an apparent attempt to master abandonment anxiety and little to no sexual pleasure was associated with the scenario. Along similar lines, Chassegeut-Smirgel (1984) described perversion as the destruction of the other's pleasure when the other is used coercively rather than in the service of pleasure.

The perverse quality of relating

I have always disagreed with Tolstoy's famous introduction to Anna Karenina (1954), in which he wrote, "Happy families are all alike; every unhappy family is unhappy in its own way." I believe it is just the opposite, where psychopathological systems (engendering unhappiness and originating in unhappy families) are characterized by stereotypy, repetition, sameness, and resistance to change. This is reflected in the usefulness of diagnostic manuals: inexact though they may be, it is possible to categorize and assess patterns in psychopathology. Conversely, healthy systems are growth-promoting and engender change, creativity, spontaneity, unpredictability, and novelty. Healthy systems defy categorization for these very reasons. These are qualities that engender multiple and new modes of relating; new ways of viewing the world, including fundamental paradigm shifts.

Perverse fantasies or scenarios are *the driven, unbidden.* They have a repetitive, rigidified, and ritualized nature. They are felt as compulsions (Richards, 2003), characterized by sameness and control, and are not spontaneous or creative beyond their unconscious construction. These are what McDougall (1986) referenced as addictive sexuality or neoneeds, also emphasizing the compulsive quality to these behaviors.

The sexual gratification that may accompany the perverse scenario usually becomes a conscious and self-reinforcing feedback loop; however, the fantasy itself (and the underlying anxieties it aims to manage and control) are often dystonic and restrict the individual's functioning. Persons engaging in perverse modes of relating may often be bothered by it, though sometimes this is ambivalent due to the modicum of enjoyment (usually in the form of tension release) that engaging in the scenario can provide. After a period of therapy, there begins to be an appreciation for the broader constriction in their lives, even if the perverse scenario does not become dystonic.

It is important to guard against a lapse into identifying certain behaviors as perverse rather than the qualities of relating as defined herein. Heteronormative attitudes often imply a division around sanctioned behaviors that, in this scheme, would qualify as perverse scenarios. For example, couples whose sexual play is rigidly confined to the missionary position due to anxieties associated with oral or anal desires would, in this scheme, be viewed as engaging in a perverse scenario. (See also the example of Nina in Chapter 6.)

Persons engaging in perverse modes of relating, as herein defined, feel constricted, confined, and driven. Though the drive may encompass the desire for a highly pleasurable act (i.e., sexual pleasure—and in this way, the perversion has its own impetus) it is felt as an imperative, not a choice. It may be useful to distinguish between a need and a desire in this regard; that is, persons engaging in perverse scenarios need the behavior but, if they had the choice, most would choose to be rid of it. Similarly, perverse scenarios are held close to the chest; they are often surrounded by shame. At the same time, however, the person holds onto them with a tenacious grip because the perverse scenario may be the sole channel to sexual gratification. But most importantly, they are persistently reenacted because they provide the route to address unconscious anxieties and fears.

Means/end reversal

An essential component in the use of the term perversion is the means/end reversal, *the use of constructive means or processes for destructive ends.* In this view, the perverse process is one of turning something on its head; the means-end reversal was coined by Stein (2005) as an attempt to undermine constructive ends or purposes through the misapplication of means. For example, in loving relations, there are, by definition, components of intimacy, mutuality, growth enhancement, affection, reciprocity, and nurture. A perversion of loving relations is an engagement with another person in nonreciprocal, non-intimate (objectified), harmful, and/or restrictive ways. The means through which this perverse mode of relating is often enacted is through sexual relations, a manner of relating that purportedly fosters the constructive end of healthy intimacy[6] but is used instead for destructive, non-intimate purposes (Stein, 2005; Hartman, 2013). In this sense, it is an ethical impasse as well (Benvenuto, 2003) because it transforms an inclusive process into an exclusive one. A similar notion is used by Carveth (2010) and Amir (2013); a deflection or hijacking of constructive for destructive aims.

Other writers (Stoller, 1986) refer to perversion as essentially a desire to harm within the sexual act. This is a particular application of the means/end reversal. In Stoller's coinage, perversion is 'the erotic form of hatred' in which hostility plus violence (the desire to harm) is distinguished from aggression (simple forcefulness) and is enacted in the erotic realm. Wrye and Welles (1994) see perverse object relations as those which are "anti-transformational, the opposite of health giving." They coin the phrase, 'deadlocked internal object relations' to denote the non-growth-promoting modes of relating that characterize perverse object relations. Amir (2013) describes the perverse subject's "hostile appropriation of the other's language . . . [in order to effect a] meaningless conquest" (p. 396). Hallmarks of such relations are their unchanging quality, or the absence of (i.e., constriction or destruction of) desire, the opposite of healthy intimate relating.

Motives of perverse scenarios

Usually, the perverse scenario is represented in a fantasy that is acted out (or occasionally restricted to daydreaming). If there is traumatic experience as the psychogenic referent, the fantasy may have the purpose of exacting revenge and/or correcting reality in order to turn childhood trauma into adult triumph (Stoller, 1986). This follows the same psychological principles and motivations for all traumatic experience. There is the desire to turn passive into active, to achieve mastery over the originating traumatic event, and to emerge victorious and triumphant, disavowing vulnerability or humiliation.

For Stoller (1986), the interplay of hostility and sexuality is key. His felicitous phrase, "Perversion is the erotic form of hatred" states it succinctly. He viewed perverse scenarios as a degradation of lovingness, a regression from whole object relating or a fixation on part object relating. Most importantly, Stoller (1986) recognized that perverse scenarios are ways of coping with threats to one's gender identity (the question of whether one is male or female) or gender role (confusions surrounding the sense of oneself as masculine or feminine.) As elaborated throughout this book, these confusions and restrictions can be understood as imbalanced reckonings between the dual capacities of receptivity and potency. Perverse scenarios may choreograph ways to free oneself from a constricting binarial trap in which these two capacities are polarized and split.

In a perverse fantasy or scenario, there can be elements in whole or in part that repeat the originating trauma. Historical events may be represented in the details of the perverse act and, in this way, the perverse scenario is an attempt to remember the past. According to Wrye and Welles, the perverse scenario is essentially a "normalizing narrative" (1994). The drive to remember is an effort to shore up a feeling of self-continuity, to narrate one's past and to sort out reality from fantasy. Often there is a question, "Did this happen or am I imagining it?" Sometimes there is an inchoate feeling of "I think I have done this before."

As in all traumatic repetition, there is a replay and a reworking of the dynamics in an attempt to correct the ending, address unconscious anxieties, and, in this way, reconfirm self-structure. Stoller (1986) termed this as an attempt "to fashion a better reality." There may also be an attempt to sort out ambivalence; childhood traumas engender the experience of loving what one hates or finding purpose or pleasure in pain. The attachment to destructive relationships in later life is often a reference to these early experiences where *the relation to a certain kind of (destructive) person or relationship remains more important than pleasure.*

There are many motives fueling perverse fantasies or scenarios. These are often combined; the presence of one does not exclude nor necessitate another. The motives include, but are not limited to, (1) the desire to repeat or undo trauma (in order to remember, as well as rid oneself of, intolerable affects); (2) to exact revenge through harm (as in dominate and disavow vulnerability or powerlessness); (3) to enact fantasies of omnipotence that eradicate certain feelings that threaten equilibrium (e.g., loss, goodness in oneself, desire or longing, change or uncertainty (Novick and Novick, 1991); (4) to enact the desire to deaden or deadlock object relations (Stoller, 1986; Wrye and Welles, 1994); and (5) to split and concretize the paradoxes of life (e.g., deny the difference between the sexes ... we are unisex (Bach, 1994).

Localization of perceived dangers in the self or other

In his review of the concept of perversion, Parsons (2000) notes the theoretical advance from classical drive descriptions of perversion as a defense against instinctual derivatives to a shift in seeing perversion as a defense against object-relatedness (see also Steiner, 1993; Bach, 1994; Goldberg, 1995; Coen, 1998; and Layton, 2013). Parsons' view can be taken a step further, however, where perverse modes of relating are described as a defense against a relationship to another *subject*. At a contemporary theoretical level, intersubjectivity is constituted by the relational engagement of two subjects, each with their own intrapsychic organization. Thus, historically, terms such as 'whole object relations' (in classical language) have been reformulated by placing not only objects (Parsons, 2000) but *subjects* in the foreground of an individual's psychological experience.

Parsons (2000) describes the necessary shift from "a defense against drive derivatives to a defense against object relatedness" (p. 43).[7] To this must be added that perverse scenarios represent a defense against the experience of the other *as a subject* in their own right. In this way, perverse scenarios will most fruitfully be viewed as an attempt to defend against *the subjectivity of the other* or to defend against *a dangerous subjectivity within*. From a narrower perspective, however, viewed from within the confines of the symptomatic picture and solely from the patient's point of view, it can be seen that the nature and form of the perverse scenario is an attempt to create and live in a one-person universe. In short, *the perverse scenario is an attempt to construct a one-person drama, defensively obliterating the subjectivity of the other or the subjectivity within.*

In the evolution of the concept of perversion, contemporary theorizing reformulates the term into a more elaborated understanding of what is being defended against and how the threat is localized. The two-person epistemology adds a broader framework from which to understand the construction of the perverse scenario and what constitutes a threat. For example, an unconscious threat leading to a perverse scenario may be more fully understood as the experience of difference with, and separateness from, another subject. These challenges of difference and separateness are not exactly the same, although they often constitute simultaneous and intertwined threats. Difference (otherness) is perceived as dangerous because it is unfamiliar and alien, threatening harm to the self. Beyond difference, however, is the other's intentionality, and, by extension, their subjectivity, both of which threaten harm. To reduce the subject is to reduce the threat and to deny separateness. The fantasy of merging, a common feature of perverse scenarios, is often an effort to omnipotently control these threats.

Contexts of threat

The meanings of a perverse scenario are highly individualized. When perverse scenarios are contextually examined, it is possible to discern two broad meanings or sources of threat in individuals' ways of experiencing and managing these. These sources of threat serve different functions within the interpersonal and cultural milieu. Perverse scenarios can be categorized as either *direct* or *displaced*, each of which reflects an unconscious anticipation of a source of danger. Respectively, the threat in the *direct* perverse scenario is dyadically conceived as *the dangerous subjectivity of the other or the dangerous subjectivity within.* In other words, the *direct* defense aims at obliterating the threat from within a dyadically-conceived context, either within the other or from within oneself. There is an unconscious dyad that is fantastically reduced to a one-person enactment, usually through merging with the other.

In contrast, the *displaced* defense aims to symbolically destroy some aspect of a larger culture and uses one or more objects (objectified others) to accomplish this task. The displaced defense functions in an unconsciously constructed *triadic* context. In the *displaced* perverse scenario, the threat is aimed at *the destruction of the symbolic third.*

In 2007, I applied this conceptualization to the arena of sexual boundary transgressions; I believe it can be more broadly applied to perverse scenarios as well. When making a distinction between a *direct* or *displaced* perverse scenario, the important question to ask is, "Who or what is being degraded?" The *direct perverse scenario* is an example of a classic perverse scenario in which the perverse enactment is focused directly on the threatening other or self. There is usually a felt need to degrade the self or other in an attempt to manage, control, and reduce (that is, objectify) the potentially dangerous subjectivity. This is essentially a direct (usually unconscious) dyadic scenario, in that the drama revolves around the self or other who is objectified, thereby reduced from a separate subject to an object, and is then sadomasochistically controlled. (Most sexual boundary transgressions have this structure.)

Other perverse scenarios, however, make use of a displacement object and thereby are more accurately referred to as a *displaced perverse scenario*. In these cases, the effort to degrade is not directed at the other but is unconsciously targeted toward a third person or structure (as in an organization, industry, or subculture). This third object usually has some real or fantasied authority over the individual and the perverse scenario is an attempt to act out the individual's aggression toward this object. In the case of sexual boundary transgressions, the symbol of the couch, the icon of psychoanalysis, is often used as a place to enact this perverse scenario, and the degradation is aimed at the profession. In these cases, the patient is a displacement object, a stand-in, so to speak, for an aspect of the setting or context. In this way, the perversion of the psychoanalytic process—largely aimed at corrupting the profession itself—is brought about by using the very means of healing in order to exploit and harm rather than heal, and to do so in a sometimes flagrant manner. (Note the inherent means/end reversal.)

The question of who is being degraded and whether the unconscious drama is essentially direct or displaced can be helpful in understanding the function and meaning of perverse scenarios, especially with regard to discerning the nature of the perceived danger. Consistent with this analysis is Bach's (1994) understanding of perversion as "a language of paradox refused," in which some aspect of reality is split into either/or alternatives and is then reenacted via projection. He refers to the classic example involving the shock of the anatomical difference between genders and the anxiety of losing one's penis as a result of castration. The person engaging in such a perverse scenario may adopt a fetish that serves as a concrete reminder that one has a penis and "either you see it or you don't." The analyst's role is to transform the concrete reenactment into the realm of symbolic meaning, leading to the acceptance of universal paradoxes, i.e., we are both male and female (psychologically), but only one gender (biologically). Paradox, here, can be viewed as an aspect of the symbolic third, a quality of the universe that the perverse scenario is aimed at denying.

Degrees of perverse relating

There is a distinction to make over whether a perverse mode of relating is always necessary for sexual pleasure or may be one of many channels toward sexual gratification. The latter category overlaps with contemporary views of 'perverse practices' as cultural fictions or the result of social shunning (see, for example, Dimen, 2001). *Obligatory perverse scenarios* (as in the traditional, narrow definition) classify perversions by what is required for sexual satisfaction (e.g., many fetishes fall into this category). An obligatory perversion is by definition the only route to sexual gratification and is necessary to achieve orgasm. The term *perverse enactment* represents a looser attitude. This term refers to perverse scenarios that serve important defensive functions, but are not necessary for successful performance of an erotic act. An example might include a partnered person who engages in cruising for anonymous sex in which others are experienced as external objects that are easily replaced with one another (usually an attempt to deny the importance and need of intimacy).

In my view, perverse scenarios often enough fall within current social norms or conventional sexual behavior; the sign that an individual is engaging in a perverse manner is the quality of constriction, the means/end reversal, and the element of destructiveness in the manner in which it is experienced. All of these are gleaned in the discovery of the unconscious meaning to the individual. One may ask whether a scenario is used repetitively, obligatorily, and/or ritualistically because of the psychic purpose it serves, i.e., to destroy someone or something, such as the mutuality in the sexual act.

What is *not* perversion?

In contemporary practice, it can be assertively stated that perversion is not an aberration or variant of sexual behavior relative to some cultural convention. It is not about the number of people engaging in the behavior, i.e., a deviation from a norm, as in the behavior being common or rare (Stoller, 1986). It is also not about society's moral judgments, as in a deviation from some cultural standard. These judgments shift as cultural practices change over time but, more importantly, do not fall under the purview of psychoanalytic practice. It is not for psychoanalysts to determine or legislate appropriate behavior or to define normality and thereby promote conformity. Rather, it is for psychoanalysts to promote freedom from suffering, restriction, and harm (to self or other).

Nor is perversion about homosexuality. It is true that, in perversions, one almost always finds some question of gender identity (male/female) or gender role (masculinity/femininity), but these can often be understood as deriving from a self-imposed binarial trap. The perverse scenario can often be interpreted as a way to manage from within such traps in order to address various unconscious (sometimes gendered) concerns. However, this does not point to either homosexuality or heterosexuality. Sexual orientation may or may not be conflict-laden, and in clinical practice it is my experience that there is an equal likelihood to find perverse scenarios in heterosexual as homosexual persons.

Finally, perversion does not refer to a specific behavior or concrete part of the anatomy and its usage (e.g., breast or penis). Nor does it refer to aim or object (as in homosexual or heterosexual object choice). *The only way to understand whether a person suffers with a need to engage in a perverse scenario is to understand the meaning attached to the perverse scenario,* and this will be highly individualized. Thus, a thoroughgoing, exploratory psychoanalytic psychotherapy or psychoanalysis, with a focus on unconscious processes, will be the route to constructing the meaning of the perverse scenario (see also Good, 2006, for the analysis of perverse dreams).

The issue of perversion, and the extent to which cultural convention or social construction defines and delimits its validity, has plagued analysts since the concept's early usage. Freud identified the normal infant as polymorphously perverse, and finalized his definition of perversion as the failure of repression such that infantile fantasies and behaviors are played out in adulthood (1927). Similarly, the question of perversion as deviance from a norm raises doubts about pathologization, as if the person engaging in a perverse act is a victim of societal shunning (Dimen, 2001). In my view, however, this cultural relativism misses the essential fact that persons who engage in perverse scenarios are themselves suffering with them. They tend to live constricted and repetitive sexual lives and would choose to be rid of the stereotypy if they could find another avenue for pleasure. Persons who engage in perverse scenarios are not suffering from stigma; they suffer from constriction. Stoller (1986) noted that American society (and presumably all Western societies) both stimulates and prohibits erotic expressions. He believed more repressive societies will have greater occurrence of perversions (and this is certainly borne out in clerical societies that require their priests be celibate).

Levels of perverse modes

Through his lifelong study of perverse behavior, Stoller (1986) asserted that "perverts are scapegoats who liberate the rest of us." Roudinesco (2009) similarly laments, "[perversion is] mentioned only to be condemned" (p. 1).[8] Like the moralistic judgment toward the 'bad apple' label, a common reaction to the sexual boundary transgressor (Celenza, 2007), we console ourselves that 'perversion is not us' and in this way, disavow such tendencies in ourselves (Coen, 1998; Dimen, 2001; Celenza and Gabbard, 2003). Stoller (1986) reminds us that anthropological and animal studies repeatedly show that perverse behavior is not exceptional, but is usual throughout history and across cultures.[9] Yet, the absence of discussion, paralleling the politically correct acceptance of all sexual behavior, gives the impression that there is nothing more to understand or that contemporary reworkings have made the problem disappear. Nothing could be further from the truth.

Obsolete language and knowledge tends to be expunged wholesale: if one meaning of a concept is no longer useful, it disappears along with all the other meanings associated with it. Often, the use of the term becomes taboo, while empty euphemisms prevail. While it is important to discard those conceptualizations that have proven unhelpful or false, it is just as important to retain those with merit.

Perversion has suffered such a fate, yet the concept is needed to delineate ways in which some individuals constrain and constrict themselves; it is not that perverse modes of relating have disappeared, it is that the boundaries around what is or is not perverse have shifted. If we use the criterion of constriction and constraint, some heterosexual 'vanilla' practices might be considered perverse if they are engaged in a repetitive and constrained way. It is not a particular behavior that defines perversion; it is the manner in which the behavior is engaged.

There have been recent seminal contributions to the psychoanalytic understanding of gender identity development that retain the value and foundational shaping of parent-child relations as well as "the role of fantasy as it builds the gendered child" (Corbett, 2008, p. 844). While the Oedipus myth is no longer viewed as singular in potentiating unconscious symbolism and gender identity, gender continues to be understood within the context of an array of relational matrices, including relations with parental figures, with one's body, and with important others in the social world. All of these relations exist simultaneously in real and symbolic realms and are continuously reconfigured in multiple self-systems, nonlinearly, and dynamically related (see the important contributions of several authors for a delineation of nonlinear dynamic systems theory as it relates to gender development, including Goldner, 1991; Mitchell, 1996; Dimen, 2003; Harris, 2005; Blechner, 2009; Corbett, 2009).

So, what then is pathological or perverse in relation to gender identity? Or, to put it another way, if gender development is fluid or softly assembled (as Harris, 2005a, conceives it), why are questions of gender so prominently implicated in private realms of suffering? Can we distinguish between questions of gender identity and questions of sexual orientation, opening the way for a new liberalism in terms of behaviors (Blechner, 2009) while retaining our concern for rigidity, constriction, or inhibition in sexual play? Beyond society's historical rejection of certain modes of relating, can we as psychoanalytic thinkers see through the layers of societal confusions and blunt judgmentalisms to clarify the nature of self-destructive, irrational, sadistic and/or restrictive modes of relating?

It is my view that certain relational patterns are pathological because they do destructive things to oneself and/or others. They are, by definition, anti-growth-promoting, developmentally constricting, and repetitively truncated. They cause personal suffering, and careful psychoanalytic theorizing can encompass these patterns in a way that problematizes them. This is not to ignore or minimize adaptive aspects to a particular perverse scenario or the way perverse scenarios may represent attempted solutions to pathogenic situations. It is for this reason that I conceive of *levels of perversion*, in which, at its most extreme, a perverse mode is defined by rigidity, constriction, and constraint. At some moderate level, however, perverse scenarios may serve a *transitional function*, in which an individual's enactment of a perverse fantasy is reflected upon and, in this way, opened up to more potential for play (see, for example, Bader, 1993; Corbett, 2013). (Employing the model introduced in this volume [see Conclusion: positions of subjectivity], we might say that a person transitions from engaging in a perverse mode of relating to a transitional mode when the Reflective Self is engaged.)

Notes

1. Applying perversion as defined herein, the historical designation of many behaviors as perverse is ironically constituted by a means/end reversal, employing psychoanalytic pathognomonic systems of classification for destructive, rather than diagnostically constructive purposes.
2. See McGinley and Sabbadini's (2006) essay on *Play Misty For Me* for an intriguing analysis of this film along similar lines.
3. Benjamin's (1988, 2004) concept of co-created or shared intersubjective thirdness comes to mind here, where the creation of a one-person universe represents the breakdown of this intersubjective space, especially in relation to sadomasochistic relating, doer/done-to relations, or complementarity.
4. Bach (1994) also recontextualizes perversion in many cases by noting "not only a fantasied gap in the genital area but also a gap in relatedness" (pp. 11–12). Parsons (2000), on the other hand, maintains a one-person framework by contextualizing perversion within an object-relations theoretical framework.
5. See Amir (2013) and the two incisive commentaries on her paper (Gonzalez, 2013, and Hartman, 2013) for a particularly useful presentation and discussion of perverse language games.
6. I realize this is a value judgment and not a universally accepted criterion for health, and that some may disagree (see, for example, Dimen, 2001, and Corbett, 2008).
7. Parsons explains these threats from an object relations point of view, noting that contemporary theorizing adds "an emphasis on depersonalizing the object but also merging with it . . . what is unbearable is the relationship to a *person* who has his or her own *otherness*. The *personhood* of the other is avoided by turning the person into a thing while the *otherness* of the other is avoided by the merging." (Parsons, 2000, p. 45, italics in original.) To this can be added the important conceptualization of the threatening other (personhood in Parsons' terms) as a separate and different *subject*.
8. At the same time, Roudinesco (2009) argues against the current postmodern social trend that defies "the Law" and its transgression of "the Law" or the defining of boundaries in general, such that perversion no longer has substance and "everyone is a potential pervert" (p. 135). He defines perversion as a delight in evil, wherein "access to civilization, the Law or progress is the only thing that allows us to control that part of ourselves that can never be tamed" (p. 140).
9. Indeed, Roudinesco's (2009) discussion about the differences between animals and humans helpfully focuses on the fantasy component of erotic activity, thereby deeming perversion and eroticism in the animal world an impossibility due to the absence of symbolic language and self-consciousness.

Chapter 6

Perverse female scenarios
The Objectified Self

> *She is too much, so she edits.*
> *Cuts I want, I need, I wish,*
> *Writes you desire, you require, you relish.*
> *Embellishments go next. Sassy, brash*
> *adjectives slashed for more virtuous verbs*
> *to share, to care, to give.*
> *She deletes adverbs boldly, decisively*
> *trashes showy punctuation . . .!*
> *Possessives my and mine ablated, ours pasted.*
> *She alters size, and voice, and type*
> *to fit, cuts name to mere initials with a snip.*
> *Sacrifices truth to please her readers.*
> *Now indented and neat, she adjusts*
> *her counted words to not exceed.*
> *Fits any given space.*
>
> E. Wallace, "Girl, Edited," 2004

A scene from college is indelibly etched in my memory. I was with a group of friends and, in a context I can no longer recall, I made a witty remark. Later, in retelling the story to a different group of friends, I inexplicably attributed the witty remark to my boyfriend. Luckily, he would have none of that and, though somewhat puzzled, corrected my misattribution, prompting me to wonder why in the world I had credited *him* instead of myself. (I was not at all confused about who had said what.)

Over many years, I have recalled this incident and see it as part of a familiar female malady, the tendency to disclaim power or prowess, to defer and prop up the (usually male) other, in a fantasied gesture of installing a wished-for power differential, oneself in the degraded position. Perhaps, for me, I had wanted to imbue my partner with greater gifts. More likely, I did not feel ready to embrace my own power without some guilty residue. If I am big, does that make him small? If he is small, did I do that *to him?* Will he be big enough for me? Am I too big? Presently, all of these are familiar questions with which many of my female patients wrestle. (Incidentally, I choose the metaphor of bigness and smallness precisely because it conjures bodily images and does not necessarily refer solely to genital anxieties or castration, though these may be involved for any particular individual.)

In the following, I discuss the relational function of perverse modes of relating that are often found in female[1] patients. I employ a particular definition of perversion with the hope that the word, if narrowly and clinically defined, can be recuperated and returned to our lexicon since I believe it retains useful and clinically important meanings if used in this specific way. As elaborated in the Introduction to Part II of this book, a perverse mode of relating is defined by: (1) the impact of its constriction, rigidity, repetition, and constraint (a kind of 'anti-play');[2] (2) the expression of hidden, driven, and unbidden motives (often relating to unprocessed trauma); (3) a means/end reversal (Stein, 2005), i.e., the use of constructive means for destructive purposes,[3] often involving harm (Stoller, 1986; Stein, 2005) to the other or to the self. Perverse modes of relating are subjectively experienced as noxious, depressive, unwanted, and/or constraining. Or, if pleasure is involved, there is guilt and self-punishment subsequently. In a related way, perverse modes of relating constrain and are inimical to creative play; they are characterized by monotony and ritual.

With these distinctions in mind, a perverse mode of relating is defined as *a quality of relating, not a particular behavior per se*. Perverse modes of relating are not defined by deviance from a norm, unconventionality, or atypicality, as Stoller (1986) usefully distinguished. Cultural regulations shift, yet mandate compliance, and the collusion with cultural regulations is anti-psychoanalytic.[4] To the extent that the psychoanalytic process aims to liberate and expand feelingful subjective experience, psychoanalysis subverts cultural expectations and external regulation. Similarly, to the extent that perverse modes of relating aim to constrict and/or harm, they are anti-growth promoting and are the target of psychoanalytic investigation and treatment.

Perversion may be likened to a closed feedback loop in which repetition and sameness is substituted for creativity and growth. Ghent (1990) made a distinction between surrender and submission along similar lines. Wrye and Welles (1994) use the phrase "deadlocked internal object relations" (p. 106). Kaplan (1991) puts it pithily: "Perverts do not make love, they make hate" (p. 40). Dimen (2001), in her careful navigation through cultural, moral, and political mandates, references several authors who have emphasized the absence of flexibility associated with perversion (Khan, 1979; Kaplan, 1991; McDougall, 1995). In the language employed here, perverse modes of relating can be viewed as efforts to resist the healthy striving for holistic and embodied multiplicity—a turning away from relationality in its various forms, resulting from the felt danger of enlivening or reconnecting with dissociated selves or the perceived dangers in the subjectivities of the self or other.

Embodiment

There has been much recent theorizing that aims to reconceptualize various dualities—mind/body, inside/outside, or psyche/soma (Dimen, 1998; Harris, 1998;

Kaplan, 2000). Paralleling certain transformations in contemporary philosophy, especially those writers of phenomenological hermaneutics (see, for example, Marcel, 1950; Sartre, 1956; Merleau-Ponty, 1962), the idea that we possess a body separate from a mind is already one step on the path toward reification, compartmentalization, or dissociation. Especially for Merleau-Ponty, the basic condition is holistic (see Orange, 2010, for a clear explication of Merleau-Ponty's position.)

Contemporary psychoanalytic views have incorporated these philosophical claims and hold that the body both expresses, and is the expression of, emotionally laden meaning and self-states. Affective expression viewed as an outward manifestation of the internal state, in these conceptualizations, no longer holds sway; rather, the expression *is* the state—we don't interpret joy when we observe a smile but see joy as the smile (Merleau-Ponty, 1962; Folkmarson Kall, 2009).

In a long tradition of describing the nature of being and subjectivity in terms that are immediate, experience-near, and non-reified, existential phenomenologists caution against the objectification of the body, striving instead to view the body as unified and at one with the experienced state. In Harris' (1998) words, "The body is not a thing, but a condition, a context through which I am able to have a relation to objects (and other bodies)" (p. 49). She states, "It is not, of course, that there is not a real body but that it must become sensible" (p. 43). In this way, Harris argues for an inseparability of biology and social relations, "body states and processes as inseparable from fantasy, interaction, and meaning" (p. 43).

These philosophical revelations underlie all conceptualizations of subjectivity but are particularly pertinent to the understanding of female perverse relating because of the ways in which perverse efforts seek to regulate, control, and objectify the body. Even to say I *have* a body reflects the capacity to distance from our embodiment and to objectify ourselves. When we speak of the body as separate from the mind or psyche, we are already one step along the way toward objectification, a tendency that arguably is inherent in the social fabric of Western cultures, especially in the way in which women are valued and devalued, and which paves the way for perverse usages.

From 'Embodied Subject' to 'Objectified Self'

The body as a container and expresser of psychic phenomena broadens the locus of the mind and replaces the antiquated Cartesian split between mind and body. It is not that the brain is the physiological substrate of the mind but that *the mind is embodied as a whole*. The various ways in which the body holds and expresses tension, for example, illustrate this principle.

A young female patient who had survived chronic neglect throughout childhood describes moments when she awakens "mouthing a kind of scream" without words or sound. I tell her that her body 'knows' something about her trauma that she cannot yet remember or articulate (see Pines, 1993; Lieberman, 2000; Gentile, 2006a; Orbach, 2006, for other clinical examples based on this principle).

Many individuals who make apparent efforts to enhance their physical appearance can display otherwise hidden and seemingly private preoccupations, thereby displaying unconscious wishes on the surface. In this way, private is not always hidden from view. "The fathoms of the unconscious are written on the body" as Dimen (1998, p. 66) poetically remarks. Body posture can both stimulate and reflect unconscious processes, as is sometimes evident when patients lie down on the couch or sit up in the chair in psychoanalysis (Celenza, 2005).

The body surface has also become a site of greater appreciation with reformulations of classical theorizing. Inwardness, interiority, and depth have been reified in the past as appropriate loci of the mind 'somewhere inside,' whereas past formulations have positioned the body itself as superficial, outward, and exterior. Viewed through a contemporary lens, the body expresses the mind; indeed, the body *is* the mind and psyche. Therefore, body-oriented behaviors and symptomatology acquire meaning in and of themselves—being looked at or seen (Lieberman, 2000) from the outside is legitimized. Rachel, for example, who struggles against the urge to take off her clothes during sessions, expresses her desires and fears through her use of her body. I know her by her particular use of her body as she relates to me.

A perverse mode of relating is a reversal of this mind/body unity; an attempt to disassociate oneself from some part of one's body or the experience of one's body as a whole. Concretization and objectification dehumanize or reify one's body, making it 'other' or 'not me,' i.e., 'it.' In terms of the various positions of subjectivity, and making use of the schematic offered in the conclusion of this book, there is a breakdown of the dialectical tension inherent in self-reflexive functioning (Aron, 1998), where 'I' (the position of reflecting on oneself) and 'Me' (the Subjective Object or the experience of the self as simultaneously subject and object) have become dissociated from the Embodied Subject (the experiencing self as agent or subject). 'I' reflects on 'Me' while disclaiming felt-experience, making 'Me' an 'It.' The 'Me' that is reflected upon is objectified, and the experiencing self is disavowed (in a fantasied, wishful way). More pointedly, a perverse scenario or mode of relating aims at dividing the Subjective Object (experiencing oneself as an object to others, i.e., 'Me') by constructing an Objectified Self (disavowing the experiential component of the self as object or subjective object).[5] Persons who engage in perverse modes of relating might be viewed as suffering with a *disorder of objectification.* When viewed in this manner, it is not surprising that these individuals report feeling empty, numb, or some kind of 'nothingness.' The already divided and decentered experience of the self becomes further dissociated, like an 'It' or 'Other.'[6]

When studying perverse modes of relating across genders, it is a defining characteristic that perverse scenarios involve isolation from others, an abnegation of the Embodied Subject (or an attempt to deaden feeling and turn away from whole object relations, in more classical theoretical terminology). Many perverse patterns of relating (in women as well as men) represent an attempt at a fantasied one-person experiencing; this is to be rigorously differentiated from the healthy enjoyment of solitude.[7] The withdrawal from relationality is often an attempt to disclaim or maintain dissociation from fragile self-states (earlier modes of relating, perhaps vulnerable or traumatizing patterns of experiencing) because relating to others threatens to enliven these lost or dissociated selves. (This phenomenal experience is contrasted with the Embodied Subject in relation, which is the affective and agentic experience of oneself in relation to others.)

Perverse scenarios (again, female and male alike) typically represent a withdrawal from relationality, i.e., a withdrawal from the ability to experience oneself as an Embodied Subject in relation to others. Instead, perverse scenarios are designed to obliterate the threat of the other, in particular to reduce the threat of the *dangerous subjectivity of the other* through objectification. The ways in which males tend to objectify the other, thereby obliterating their dangerous subjectivity, functions to destroy the possibility of intimacy and prevent vulnerable selves from further trauma. For females, objectification is often turned inward, localized on their own bodies, thereby substituting a dominant *Objectified Self*. As this phrase implies, the attempt is to engage the self as an object, an Objectified Self that, as experienced, is anesthetized. We could say that the Embodied Subject has been replaced by a dissociated Body Object. As Saketopoulou (2013) felicitously comments, "The body becomes bodice" (p. 2). Similarly, Ehrenberg (1992) refers to a "pattern of denying desire to the point of achieving a state of deadness and then desperately chasing aliveness in the form of unsatisfied desire" (p. 5). This conveys an experience not of solitude, but of isolation (from both others and the experiencing self).

A patient spoke of this in the following way: "It's like I'm playing a game of hide and seek with myself. I've never known the feeling part of me. It got stamped out very early, with 'I shouldn't. I have no right.' I don't know how to engage the feelings. I can feel anger, competitiveness, impatience, but I don't have nice feelings. It's hard work. When I get compliments, I dismiss it, me, them. I slap the feelings away." This patient is describing her lack of receptivity to feeling from the position of the Subjective Object, her 'self for others' as she describes these anesthetized self-states to me.

One distinction that differentiates men and women in typical perverse scenarios, then, is the tendency for men to *use others* in an attempt to objectify, whereas females *use themselves*. If perversions have been thought to be less common in females, it is only because they take a different shape and tend to be localized on, or directed against, the self, as opposed to externalized onto others. Clinically, we see a tendency for females to localize perverse scenarios on their own bodies (in contrast to males, who often use a thing outside their bodies as representative of their bodies).[8]

Thus, I am proposing a conception of the phenomenal experience of perversion for many females as centering on the creation of an *Objectified Self*. This is derived from the *Subjective Object*, the position in which one has the ability to perceive oneself as an object from an other's point of view *at the same time as inhabiting (or being) the experiencing self.* When the Subjective-Object becomes anesthetized to its own phenomenal, affective, and agentic experience, however, there can be a construction of an Objectified Self. When there is a dissociation of feeling and affective aliveness, this can be understood as relating to oneself perversely. In these instances, the creation of an Objectified Self is the outcome whereby the body, or a body part, is no longer an experiencer of affective, subjective experience, but is related to and used as a thing. The Objectified Self might be viewed as a Self-in-Itself,[9] with narcissistic or ego-centric qualities implied.

The body as fetish

Many authors currently writing about the body (Kaplan, 1991, 2006; Aron and Sommer Anderson, 1998; Dimen, 1998; Harris, 1998; Bassin, 1999; Lieberman, 2000; Orbach, 2000, 2009; Gentile, 2006a) refer to the pressures of today's narcissistic culture and the ways in which women (in particular) feel a demand to strive for an impossible ideal, especially in appearance. Within certain subcultures, thinness is at the top of the list of esteemed characteristics. When women who are obsessed with thinness enter treatment, they often attempt to have the treatment revolve around a perverse task—to subvert understanding (the process of treatment) and healthy embodied experience (the goal of treatment) toward further objectification in the pursuit of their physical ideal (see, for example, Lieberman, 2000).

The obsession of many women with their bodies (or body parts) is an obvious example of present-day culturally facilitated fetishization of the body. The meaning(s) of a particular body or body part for each individual varies, however, there are discernible trends and ways in which present-day culture accounts for these. The sanctioning of the culture, especially embedded and expressed by the fashion industry, cultivates and maintains impossible ideals for which many women strive and by which they allow themselves to be oppressed. Emphasizing the cultural and social context, Dimen (2008) has cogently described the irony inherent in the way a woman, "takes her own body as the thing that cultural representation and social relations create of it/her . . . [and thereby] participates in her own objectification, she feels uneasy if she doesn't—and uneasy if she does" (p. 3). Kaplan (1991) has made similar observations on the ways in which the fashion industry makes infantile fantasies of masculinity and femininity explicit and visually concrete, thereby enlisting the social order to preserve its own structures. But not all women fall victim to these pressures and not all women do so equally. Fragile self-esteem, dependency longings, conflicts inherent in sexual desire, and so on, comprise fertile ground for cultural mandates to take hold.

Given these conditions, it is clear that many preoccupations with one's own body can be understood as fetishized, especially to the extent that preoccupation takes the form of control over receptivity to feeling, substituting the pursuit of a culturally embedded aesthetic ideal *to the exclusion of pleasure*. The application of the definition of perversion as a means/end reversal (Stein, 2005) finds clinical utility here. The body is a sensual, aesthetic, and desire producing/giving vehicle toward intimacy. When embodied experience is geared toward enhancing the body's appeal, yet subverts the experience of intimacy and pleasure, for what purpose is this preoccupation pursued? Are the means sabotaging the ends? Is the pursuit of a beautiful body (be it thin, muscular, or voluptuous) or 'perfect' body parts (nose, lips, eyes, hair, hands, or feet) leading to greater self-confidence and an expansion of feeling or, perversely, greater self-consciousness and, as a consequence, less pleasure? Kaplan's (2006) understanding of fetishes as using erotics to "tint" (p. 8) and mask the deadening of feeling applies as well. Thus, a behavior per se is not perverse, but the quality of relating associated with it may be if it is characterized by constraint, compulsion, or deadening of affective experience. To employ the framework of the binary discussed throughout this book, receptivity and potency, we might say there is a disclaiming of receptivity (to feeling) over and against the use of the body as a (potent) object.

Consider this incident at an outdoor pool among a mix of friends and strangers. A wide range of people were lounging and swimming, with numerous different body types and in various states of undress. The sun was pleasantly shining on all when a small group of female and male body-builders (the muscle definition was truly a thing to behold) joined the party. They waited several minutes before taking outer clothing off, assuming all eyes were on them (which indeed they were). Slowly, they performed a rather awkward submersion into the tepid pool and, after several minutes, declined to join a water volleyball game that was already ongoing. They lolled about in the water for a bit and then apparently had had enough—they vacated the pool and chose conspicuously placed lounge chairs, each lying 'just so,' in poses that displayed their sculpted bodies at the most optimal angles. Not an ounce of pleasure could be gleaned on their faces; on the contrary, they seemed overwrought with self-consciousness and displayed their bodies with a studied skill. The impression was of self-objectification—in this case, by the men and women alike. My purpose is not to label body-building as perverse behavior, but to highlight the apparent lack of enjoyment in these individuals' exhibitionistic display. (Of course, I have no idea if my observation was correct. I include this anecdote to demonstrate a point—that a mode of relating to one's body can objectify the body in such a way as to eliminate pleasure. I mean to convey a mode of relating solely, not an indictment of any particular behavior per se.)

Perhaps because so many psychoanalysts are female (today), female analysts sometimes empathically resonate with their patients' preoccupations without recognizing them as perverse. We are all embedded within a culture and have blind spots relating to it, as well as our own unconscious patterns that are culturally and linguistically structured. Indeed, the preponderance of literature on male perversions, in contrast to the dearth of literature on perversion in women, may reflect a general tendency to collude with societal pressures on females to relate to their bodies perversely.

Clinical concerns

In my work with women who come to treatment with a variety of complaints centered on their body, I have found it useful to visualize a self-system that includes the construction of a self-state in which the experience of the body is objectified and the therapeutic task is to facilitate the reconnection of the women with their bodies on an affective and sensual level. I view the disavowal or dissociation of affect, i.e., the effort to divide and dissociate the Subjective Object into an Objectified Self, as the foundation of the disorder. Treatment, then, revolves around addressing this division, this wished-for divorce from the body as an experiencing and feeling agent, from the objectified body as a being for others. It is often not difficult to discern hidden fears of dependency, self-loathing, fears of sexuality, or fears of destructive envy as motives for the construction of an anesthetized Objectified Self. The creation of a concretized self dissociated from affective experience and dissociated in this particular way can also indicate a revulsion or fear of receptivity; the body, objectified thus, becomes a fantasied (perhaps conceived as phallic or 'hard') object and is fetishized.

It is possible to hear echoes here of the classical notion of penis envy and I am not averse to seeing this dynamic as relevant for some women. However, I mean to signify a broader theme. I am proposing an idea that goes beyond an unconscious struggle with a sense of inadequacy compared to men based on a concrete body part, as in genital inferiority. Nor do I presume a universal challenge for all women derived from the Oedipus Complex and the daughter's problematic identification with the maternal figure. Aspects of this classical notion of penis envy can hold some relevance for some women; however, when this is the case, the formulation must be contextualized within a two-person, relational, and social-constructivist model. Thereby, in this context, penis envy already represents a turning away from relational experience with a turn inward, refocusing on a particular body part.[10] For many women, this can represent the inhibition of feeling powerful in relation to others and the diminution of the Embodied Subject.[11] One avenue is to construct a 'Me' that is diminished because of a fear of one's power. The task, then, is to wrestle with the sense of smallness or inferiority, already a defensive transformation of the feared 'Me,' which is too big, to the more manageable 'me,' which is too small (lower case intended).

For example, I view some women with this type of constellation of symptoms and self-experience as not struggling with a (conscious or unconscious) sense of genital inferiority, but *a fear of their own (phallic)*[12] *power*. This is a fear of being too erect, a fear of assertion and thrust, a dread of either being too powerful (overshadowing and perhaps castrating the fantasied and wished-for male protector) and/or of having too powerful feelings or desires. (See Kaplan, 1991, on the myth of masculine rapaciousness and fear of phallic prowess as stolen goods; see also Harris' [2005a] explication of Riviere's [1929] thoughts on women's use of masquerade as a defense against various aggressive strivings.) In the move to concretize, and thereby manage, a symbolic body part (rather than a more cumbersome and elusive embodied relationship with others), some women can defensively and symbolically seek to replace the vagina (the too hungry, bottomless pit vagina) for a more manageable and visible, circumscribed penis.

If objectification, as a means to control the dangerous subjectivity of the other, is a hallmark of male perverse modes of relating, I suggest that a hallmark of female perversion is *self-objectification in an effort to control a dangerous subjectivity within*. A frequent danger that is often feared by women is a voracious appetite, hence the obsession with remaining thin (the expressed preoccupation in many eating disorders), which can represent a wish to control a self-image of wanting too much, desiring too much, or becoming or being too big. A woman's relation to her body often reflects these conflicts, and it is a short step to discern the link to her sexuality. (For other examples, see Evelyn's relationship to her body as a "foreign body" while appreciating her bones, hair, and hands [Pacifici, 2008, p. 117]; Olympia's use of her body as a "container-tool" requiring feminine decoration [Kaplan, 1991, p. 259]; N's conviction that her thighs are the culprit for all that ailed her [Petrucelli, 2008]; Frau L's very thin but strangely unerotic body [Springer, 1996/2006]; and *Bodies in Treatment: The Unspoken Dimension* [Sommer Anderson, 2008], for a series of creative papers on how bodies (the analyst/therapist's or the patient's) express often unspoken aspects of the treatment relationship.)

While males can struggle with their relationship to their phallic power, women can similarly fear being 'too phallic', i.e., too aggressive or forceful. (See Harris, 1997, for a related discussion of female aggression, its relationship to penis envy, ambition, and the fear of destruction; also, Kolod, 2002, in relation to the analyst's countertransference.)

The White Swan as 'Objectified Self'

Nina, from the movie *Black Swan* (Aronofsky, 2010), struggles to divide her innocent, fragile, rule-bound, and sexually repressed White Swan self from her sensual, passionate, and hedonistic Black Swan self. In the initial scenes of the movie, Nina seems to define the perfection for which she is striving as a precision-oriented, rule-following ballet technique. Thomas, her choreographer, is frustrated that she cannot lose herself in the dancing (i.e., feel into herself or be receptive to her feelingful embodiment), wanting her to allow her Black Swan to overtake her. It is as if Thomas is trying to help Nina grasp the importance of *receptivity* to sensual, embodied feeling and to find ways to *potently* express it. He tells her he sees her White Swan, a fearful and fragile embodiment who strives to perform each step with precision. He complains, however, that he cannot see her Black Swan. She cannot seem to be receptive to her sensuality, to let go of control and receive instructions from her body directly, so to speak. He wants Nina to express herself from her body, not from the self-reflective, watchful (yet disciplined) part of her embodied self. He wants her to be open to the surprises of her body and to transcend the need to be in control.

In a later scene, Thomas demands that Nina marshal her capacity to *penetrate* him and the audience with her sensuality as well. He implores her to embody her potency, in a feelingful, sensual way that is not guarded or exacting, but is strong and confident in her body's natural rhythm. He wants to be attacked and he wants Nina not only to attack the ballet steps, but to lure him and the audience into her sensuality like a spider weaving a web.

As Nina tries to perform the Black Swan (struggling to find it within herself, yet needing to squelch it when it arises), she dances with a side of herself she cannot fully tolerate or embrace. As the movie progresses, there are several scenes where she attempts to court the Black Swan, increasingly losing a grip on her more comfortable yet constrained self as her dissociated and repudiated sensual self threatens to overtake her. She must court the Black Swan and kill it at the same time. (Interestingly, none of this need be gendered or seen in a bifurcated, gendered way. The movie is about sensuality, receptivity, potency, and passion, all in Nina, as well as in another dancer, Lily, and Thomas.)

The movie begins with Nina displaying her pursuit of perfection in the White Swan. We also see symptoms that would be matters of clinical concern, including stealing (she rifles through the former prima ballerina's vanity, stealing her perfume, earrings, and lipstick), compulsive scratching of the skin on her back (metaphorically, perhaps, her swan wings), and practicing ballet until she cracks her big toe (no doubt abetted by present-day, societally sanctioned expectations of a ballerina). There are also concerning aspects of her relationship with her mother, which the movie astutely depicts, revolving around enmeshment (her mother clips Nina's nails), unconscious compliance, and guilt (her mother's own thwarted ballet ambitions are apparently being lived out through Nina), disguised maternal sadism (the presentation of a pink and white frosted cake, which she forces on Nina), and, for our purposes especially in this chapter, the overall lack of play and constriction of her sensuality.

As a pointed example beyond her dancing, Nina tries to masturbate. The intensification of her desire and pleasure is startlingly impeded by the (hallucinated or real) intrusion of her mother in her bedroom. This latter aspect of her character is emblematic of the issues I aim to highlight, i.e., the constriction and overall lack of play in her expressed area of interest and passion. Note the means/end reversal: the area of greatest personal passion lacks her embodied and affectively resonant desire. We could say that her passion lacks passion. Nina's body is objectified as it is used for others (an externally directed performance), yet lacks pleasure for herself. She substitutes perfect technique for an affectively resonant, sensually embodied, and passionate performance/play.

An interesting contrast is the ironically named Lily, another dancer in the ballet company, who seems totally at ease with herself, competes with Nina for the role, and, in some ways, helps Nina find more passion within herself. The two represent different modes of being; Nina's perverse pursuit of 'perfection' substitutes a constrained technique[13] for Lily's relaxed and exuberant play.[14]

Nina cannot get the passion of the Black Swan into her performance. What is she missing? Is it an unfettered receptivity to her feelingful desires? Is it her anxiety over being too powerful, i.e., seductive and phallic, in her own right? (Thomas' frustration includes his desire to be seduced by Nina, an 'I'm going to take you' kind of conveyance that she lacks the confidence and ease to play out.) Both poles of the dialectic (receptivity and potency) are absent in her mode of being. Thomas gives Nina a homework assignment that is not so off the mark. He tells her to touch herself and find her sexuality so that she may better inhabit the Black Swan.

In an intensely erotic scene, Nina and Lily make love while the scene depicts Nina's dissociated Black Swan (the sensuous Lily) alternately emerge through Lily and through herself. Nina sees Lily morph into herself and then back to Lily, frightening her. The two continue to have sex when Lily says, "Innocent girl," before morphing back into Nina, who raises a pillow to smother her. It is not clear if she's trying to kill Lily or this side of herself.

The movie depicts this young woman struggling with a virgin/whore dichotomy within herself analogous to the Madonna/whore perverse mode of relating often seen in men. Note as well that the virgin/whore dichotomy is played out by Nina via objectifying herself, whereas the Madonna/whore dichotomy in men is, by definition, played out via objectifying others, i.e., women. Note as well that Nina is struggling with her sensuality, an embodied experience that she seems to want to control and disavow, expunge, or kill. Were she in psychoanalysis, we might discover unconscious associations between voracity, sexuality, and desire. On an interpersonal level, this is depicted through the ways she enlists and resists Lily, her mother, and her (male) choreographer, externalizing her vitality and objectifying herself.

The fetishized self or other

Richards (2003) proposes that dehumanization of the other is the essence of perversion, a broader meaning of castration than the classical genital anxiety and, thereby, equivalent in females and males.[15] Kaplan (2006) uses the fetish as the prototype of perverse strategies and emphasizes various means to deaden aspects of affective experience, such as ambiguity, enigma, and uncertainty. Objectification is a common means to an end in perverse modes of relating. In a more broad definition of perverse scenarios, especially in the case of means/end reversal, it is possible to see examples of women engaging in the perverse use of others (as found in many male perversions). Becky, (see Introduction), illustrates the perverse use of an other, more commonly seen in males.

Why might it be that females tend to localize a dangerous subjectivity within themselves rather than in others? Here, I find it useful to consider the particular developmental challenge little girls face when grappling with the eruption of their desires within the context of the oedipal triangle. As Elise (2008) has cogently described, the little girl faces both a gender and a generational defeat in the oedipal crisis, first by registering her mother's rejection (as due to her gender), and then again, her father's—this time registered as due to her age or generation. In contrast to boys, who face only a generational defeat, girls are faced with incorporating this double rejection, ultimately internalizing a bodily based sense of shame and inadequacy.

I find this theoretical explication persuasive in explaining the greater vulnerability females seem to have and the way in which this double rejection can cause an internalizing move. Harris (1997) felicitously imagines the little boy concluding, in relation to his rival father, 'You now, me later'; in concert with this type of conception, perhaps the little girl concludes, 'Not me ever? Something's wrong with *me.*'

When female perverse relating is viewed through the broader lens of contemporary theorizing, it is possible to recognize perverse relating in women's *behaviors* that are often the focus of treatment. As noted above, however, the pathognomonic characteristic is not the behavior per se, but the quality of relating and its purpose: a means/end reversal designed to rigidify and constrict the experience of pleasure or other affective experience. (For example, compulsive shopping is deemed perverse *not because of shopping behavior* but because of its *compulsivity*. A similar distinction can be made in relation to consensual sadomasochistic relations and those characterized by fixed role assignments, see Bader, 1993; Weille, 2002.)

With this caveat in mind, common behaviors in women that are seen in present-day practice and in which the mode of relating may be viewed as perverse can include: compulsive telephone calling (Richards, 1989, 2003); compulsive shopping (Richards, 2003); anorexia nervosa (Sands, 2003; Nagliero, 2006); false wholeness or pseudo androgyny (Springer, 1996); castration fears (Grossman, 1992, 1995); fetishes (von Hug-Mellmuth, 1915; Zavitzianos, 1982; Richards, 1990; Grossman, 1995); the body as fetish (Kaplan, 1991; Becker, 2005; Eiguer, 2005); self-mutilation (Tillman, 1999); a variety of phobias (Kaplan, 1991); fear of loss of genital pleasure (Richards, 1992b); kleptomania (Kaplan, 1991; Welldon, 1995); masochism (Freud, 1924; Deutsch, 1930); vagina denial (Horney, 1933); and exhibitionism (Zavitsianos, 1971).[16]

As is also true for perversions in males, the psychoanalytic formulation of the meanings of the symptomatology reveals interweaving and multi-layered dimensions revolving around sadomasochistic desires, self-other boundary disturbances, and difficulties with affect regulation (Tillman, 1999). Further, this list is a collection of circumscribed behaviors that are remarkable for their *compulsivity* and the *driven nature of engagement*; any mode of relating might be considered perverse if it is compulsive, constricting, unbidden, and/or affectively deadening.

Notes

1 Generalizing about males and females or men and women is always fraught with inaccuracy, culture-specific stereotypes, and blunt, sweeping statements. Exceptions abound and the reality for any one individual is always more complex. Still, I propose a general mechanism that is frequently observed in clinical cases, the articulation of which can lead to fruitful exploration and elaboration in any single instance.
2 Corbett (2009) notes the frequent labeling of "resistance and play of the nonnormative" as "too easily seen as lacking in freedom" (p. 101). I aim to differentiate between behavior that is playful and creative, and behavior subjectively experienced as feeling constrained or rigidified, that subverts play and creativity. In either of these instances, however, the content of the play, especially whether it is resistive or compliant to cultural norms, is irrelevant. The distinction can be made clearer by attending to the extent to which play is engaged in an affectively enlivened way versus play in a monotonous, driven, or repetitive manner.

3 The judgment 'constructive' or 'destructive' inevitably will be imbued with cultural biases. Who is to say whether a mode of relating is either? This judgment, however, should be rigorously differentiated from any question of conventionality and deviance from a norm or moral standard. As discussed in the Introduction to Part II of this book, perversion is not an aberration or variant of sexual behavior relative to some cultural convention. It is not about the number of people engaging in the behavior, i.e., a deviation from a norm, as in the behavior being common or rare (Stoller, 1986). It is also not about society's moral judgments, as in a deviation from some cultural standard. These judgments shift as cultural practices change over time but, more importantly, they do not, in themselves, contain inherent harm or a means/end reversal for the purpose of harm or destruction.
4 I state this ironically given the extent to which psychoanalysis can be, and has been, co-opted to enforce cultural conventions. Ideally, however, it is a tool for individual emancipation.
5 Similarly, Summers (2013) refers to self-reification whereby the self is experienced as a commodity (p. 184).
6 This schematic is elaborated in the concluding chapter of this book. It is a schematic that depicts multiple ways we position ourselves in relation to others, and within our own experience, at any moment in time: *The Embodied Subject* (the pre-reflective, experiencing, or agentic self), *The Subjective Object* (the self as an object for others or 'Me'), *The Reflective Self* (the self who reflects on itself, i.e., takes itself as an object for itself or 'I') and, as discussed in this paper, the more dissociated, sometimes pathological self-structure, *The Objectified Self* or 'It.'
7 In the schematic, solitude might be conceived as the Embodied Subject-for-Itself. Though one's mind is populated with, and constituted by, identifications with others, when others are not actually present, we know we are held in mind despite material absence. Hence the experience of solitude is distinguished from isolation or aloneness in which there is the dread of emptiness or annihilation. In the latter, internalized others are not accessible in a psychologically evocative way.
8 Welldon (1996) discussed a similar idea in reference to male and female perversion, primarily as a difference in location of the object. See also Eiguer (2005) and Becker (2005).
9 See Guralnik and Simeon (2010) for a different but related conceptualization of the self-in-itself revolving around depersonalization. Also Dimen (1986) uses the term 'Subject as Object' to denote the more general experience of the self objectified by societal mandates. My emphasis in this chapter is on the ways in which the individual uses societal mandates in the service of objectification, i.e., in order to diminish affective and vital experiences.
10 Horney (1926) was the first psychoanalyst to emphasize the patriarchal underpinnings in the identification of these anxieties. She assumed a primary femininity from which many women flee in deference to a more culturally accepted yet degraded femininity. (Gediman [2005] usefully compares Horney's view to that of Riviere [1929], who viewed femininity as a masquerade designed to avoid male retribution, but within a phallocentrically structured theory.)
11 See, for example, Chassaguet-Smirgel's (1970) discussion of feminine guilt in relation to the necessary change of object in the Oedipal Complex; Butler's (1995) discussion of melancholic gender; and, in contrast, Suchet and Sand's (1999) description of performance as reflecting acceptance of disavowed gender identifications and desires in two successful female rock stars.
12 Phallic is used here in a nongendered manner, denoting a penetrating, forceful kind of power that I view as a potential in both females and males.
13 Nina's pursuit of perfection is similar to the way in which Khan (1979) describes the perversion of intimacy as a 'technique' of intimacy.

14 Another interesting contrast can be found in Balsam's 2008 paper, "Women showing off: Notes on female exhibitionism," depicting the healthy and prideful use of the body. Balsam (2003, 2008, 2012) laments the ways in which psychoanalytic theorizing has pathologized healthy female exhibitionism. See Part II for an explication of transitional perversion in this regard. This position can be contrasted with Housman's 2012 presentation, "Exhibitionism in a woman: Showing what cannot yet be told" in which Kathy dances as a substitute for intimate connection.
15 Richards (2003) maintains that the core fantasy in perversions revolves around the idea that pleasure must be wrested from a cruel adversary or a deadeningly indifferent maternal object. In another paper (1990), she supposes that the lack of discussion of female perversions is not based on a lower prevalence but on a taboo because it threatens the ideal image of maternity and maternal purity.
16 I have included many classical papers to demonstrate the point that, in my view, the classical literature on perversions remains helpful for illustrative purposes, since persons relating in a perverse manner or struggling with perverse scenarios are unconsciously creating a one-person universe (though wishful and fantastically construed). When reading the classical literature, then, it is important to remain cognizant of this formulation and not to confuse the epistemology of the classical authors with present-day understanding.

Chapter 7

Sadomasochistic relating
What's sex got to do with it?

There is a well-known aphorism about psychoanalysis, "It's all about sex. Except for sex, that's about aggression." Analogized to an archeological dig, the psychoanalytic process can sometimes miss something on the surface. A kind of 'looking behind' or 'searching beyond' has resulted in a desexualized theoretical downplay. As noted in Part I, the refocusing on object relations, interpersonal, and relational theories, along with the two-person epistemological shift in contemporary psychoanalytic theorizing, have unintentionally desexualized psychoanalysis by emphasizing object relational and especially preoedipal strains in the therapeutic setting.

Similarly, sexuality has virtually disappeared from much of the writings on sadomasochistic relating, with an emphasis instead on 'pregenital' (conceived as) non-erotic needs. In the case of sadomasochism, this theoretical downplay is even more glaring given that sadomasochistic phenomena are frequently enacted in the sexual realm. Despite the seemingly indissoluble connection between sadomasochism, aggression, and sexuality (Kernberg, 1991a, 1991b), discussions of sadomasochistic enactments even in the classical literature tend to be stripped of erotic desire, with an emphasis instead on the vicissitudes and functions of aggression. Further, the bond between sadomasochistic couples is notorious for its immutability despite intense surface conflict and manifest discontent of both members. What, if not sex, is keeping these pairs together?

On its face, sadomasochistic enactments can *seem* devoid of sexuality. Perhaps there is a sexual tie rooted so deep in the unconscious that it is difficult to discern. Perhaps such enactments aim to expunge or control sexuality so completely that it is destroyed. Much previous writing on sadomasochism discusses this dynamic and seeks to explain it. Novick and Novick (1991) assert that the attachment to a painful object relationship is a learned association. Underneath, there is the tenet that "*the need for the object overrides the need for pleasure*" (pp. 20–1); the pleasure that might have been is now destroyed.

Sadomasochistic scenarios can be conceived as attempts to omnipotently control overwhelming experience. Sexuality overwhelms by definition (see Stein, 1998, and Dimen, 2003, for observations of the 'excess' in sexual experience) requiring, as it does, tolerance of dependency, vulnerability, and self-revelation. Ultimately, orgasm requires moments of unconsciousness, a highly threatening experience for those with deep mistrust. Early experience (a lifestage of heightened dependency and vulnerability) will inevitably be evoked during sexual experience. Patients with sadomasochistic tendencies often have had overstimulating parents who did not protect them from overwhelming traumatic experiences (Novick and Novick, 1991).

Benjamin (1988) has delineated sadomasochistic dynamics as primarily revolving around the omnipotent repudiation of the need for recognition. Existential phenomenologists agree:

> We resist being determined by others and are driven to expression by the urge to explain things we have said that have not been properly understood [and] to reveal what is hidden within us.
>
> (Merleau-Ponty, 1948, p. 88)

> By taking perspective on us, others bring to light our limits and by contesting what we say about them, point to the limits of our own perspectives. I see myself limited by the other and, yet, I nevertheless need the other to give birth to me through dialogue and interaction.
>
> (Folkmarson Kall, 2009, p. 23)

Sadomasochistic relations can be viewed as a refusal of one pole in this inescapable dialectic—the denial of the ability for the other to 'give birth' and shape (as in the case of the sadist), or the refusal to acknowledge one's own shaping power of the other (in the case of masochist).[1,2] Sadomasochistic relations blur the distinction between surrender and submission (Ghent, 1990), in favor of doer-done complementarity (Benjamin, 1988).

Sadomasochism[3] is defined as a form of relating where pleasure and satisfaction are tied to suffering, either by inflicting it or receiving it. There is a manifest imbalance of power between the two members and the interactions between the members are fundamentally driven to reaffirm that imbalance. These relationships are dominated by the interplay of pain and humiliation, with overt roles usually fixed. In line with the definitions employed in this volume, it is this fixity and harm that defines such relations as perverse.

What is the glue that binds such unhappy couplings? What accounts for the solidity of this bond? As mentioned, these questions have prompted contemporary psychoanalysts to explore early, preoedipal, i.e., non-genital issues underlying sadomasochism, with the notion that primitive needs, often related to the organization and coherence of the self, explain each member's attachment to and need for the other. Although the continuous reaffirmation of the sadist's power and the masochist's disempowerment are frequently enacted in the sexual realm, the sexual dimension within these relationships is typically viewed as driven by these early, essentially non-erotic needs for recognition (Benjamin, 1988, 1994; Ghent,

1990), as a defense against loss, helplessness, or intolerable loneliness (Cooper, A., 1973; Novick and Novick, 1991), as a defense against the loss of fantasied omnipotence (Blos, 1991), denial of gender and generational difference (Chassegeut-Smirgel, 1983, 1991), or as mitigating the various dangers of autonomy, including loss, loneliness, hurt, destruction, and guilt (Renik, 1991; Coen, 1992). Stoller (1979) viewed the excitement of sadomasochism as an erotized repetition of earlier trauma, while Freud (1905), focusing on drive derivatives, viewed sadomasochism as the erotic expression of aggression. Kernberg (1991a) discusses the restriction of the range of sexual experience in perversions as the couple's attempt to elaborate and actualize aggression, specifically, "the recruitment of love in the service of aggression, the consequence of a predominance of hatred over love" (p. 46). Finally, Wrye and Welles (1994) discuss 'deadlocked internal object relations' designed to manage rage and grandiosity, deal with the fear of death, and compensate for the inability to be alone. They describe such object relational fantasies as perverse because of their intransigence and characteristic lack of vitality . . . *a place where conscious desire does not exist* (pp. 106–7, italics added).

But such preoedipal considerations need not be drained of sexuality. Benjamin (1994a) artfully observes the sexuality inherent in the (erotic) dance of healthy maternal-infant interaction (e.g., mutual gazing, gesturing, and vocalizing). She regards the desexualization of preoedipal maternal representations as consistent with the more generalized desexualization and de-eroticization of the mother in our culture (see Chapter 1 for a more elaborated discussion of these dynamics).

Further, if the language of the body, as in receptivity and potency, or openness and backbone, is applied to sadomasochistic dynamics, they can be viewed as *a polarization across the dyad* using stereotypical gender categorizations in a rigidly fixed, role-assignment (see Kaplan, 1991; Dimen, 2003; Harris, 2005b). For the sadistic/dominator, the role is *all potency* in an ongoing struggle to repudiate any trace of 'feminine' receptivity within (Kaplan, 1991). In contradistinction, the masochist is *all receptivity*, containing and receiving whatever the sadist imposes, while attempting to disavow or repudiate the stereotyped ideal of 'masculinity' within, namely, individuality, difference, potency, or agency.

Beyond discussions of sadomasochism in the context of clinical psychopathology, sadomasochistic phenomena are recognized as a ubiquitous and universal dimension of all self- and object-relations (Blum, 1991; Kaplan, 1991;[4] Dimen, 2001; Gabbard, 2012). In this broader context, the erotic dimension of sadomasochistic play tends to be regarded as a basic affect and constituent of libido inherent in the experience of erotic desire evident alongside aggressive elements. Both sexual and aggressive components comprise such sadomasochistic play and, in this context, sadomasochism is generally understood as reflecting the incorporation, recruitment, or fusion of sexuality with aggression (Blos, 1991; Kernberg, 1991a, 1991b; Bader, 1993).

The distinction between adaptive, healthy erotic play and the perverse, in my view, lies in the degree of flexibility, affective range, vitality, and freedom inherent in the overall experience, not whether sadomasochistic elements are present. The sadomasochistic scenarios typical of pathological interactions are marked by rigidity, constriction of affect, gender stereotypy, and the imposition of harm. The desexualization of sadomasochism can be understood, then, as the result of constriction, the outcome of various defensive efforts to hide, mask, or totally expunge pleasure from conscious, subjective experience. Because of its lack of salience in conscious experience, however, I believe sexuality in pathological sadomasochism has been overlooked as a basic driving force behind the destructive attachment.

With the notable exception of Bader (1993), whose work will be discussed below, most of the theoretical formulations referring to pathological sadomasochistic relating represent sexuality as a breakdown product or as a way to manage and master earlier, nonsexual needs. Without discounting the validity of such formulations, this chapter aims to put sexuality back into formulations of sadomasochistic relations by finding it in the very constraint of rigidly held gender stereotyping and fixed role assignment.

Clinical illustration

A 50-year-old professional man married his second wife in a desperate attempt to prove his devotion to her. He felt he could not win her trust any other way. They had begun their relationship with an extra-marital affair (both were married with children). He knew he was unhappily married, but was reluctant to leave his children and vacillated between the two women for several years. His current wife has never forgiven him for this and now refuses to see his children. She ultimately threatened him ("Leave your wife or I will leave you"), to which he finally responded by leaving his family and marrying her. Though this occurred more than ten years ago, she holds "the years he made her wait" over his head as proof that neither he (nor any man) can be trusted.

They live in a house with her children. He is allergic to dogs. She has a dog. He, therefore, is relegated to a study, not air-conditioned in the summer, in order to keep him away from the dog. The couple does not sleep together because the dog sleeps on the bed. He is not invited to family dinners. When he is bold enough to sit uninvited at the table, he is aware that he is not allowed to speak. The girls and their mother talk animatedly with each other; if he speaks, they stare at him coldly and do not respond. He may sit there anyway but becomes too uncomfortable to eat. If he sneezes, she will recoil in disgust; if he laughs, she will be put off by his "loudness." Like Prufrock (Eliot, 1920), he dares not eat a peach.

There is only one bathroom in the house. It has become an established rule, through various nonverbal rebuffs and territorial stakeouts, that his wife uses the bathroom first, then the girls, one of whom can preen for close to an hour. It is then his turn, and he knows he better make it quick. He also knows he is not allowed to express any desire or need for the girls to hurry, even if he is running late for work.

One morning, awaking with an urgent need to urinate and noticing that it was almost his time to use the bathroom, he gets up from his bed and waits by the bathroom door. His ever more pressing need, becoming almost intolerable, tempts him to knock and ask that his stepdaughter hurry, but he knows he will be met with a protest and possibly a spite-filled longer wait, so he does not. When his stepdaughter finally emerges, he is beside himself with urgency. She notices his discomfort and recoils in disgust, stomping off. He feels a very familiar rejection and self-loathing, looks into the bathroom, and decides he cannot now enter for fear she may return and need it. He runs out the back door of the house to urinate in the woods.

This is not sexy. These various interplays are struggles over dominance, submission, power, and control. Or, to put it another way, this couple is locked in a sadomasochistic struggle which is manifestly nonsexual. They rarely physically touch. Nor do they engage in bondage rituals. They are each essentially celibate, though hyper-attentive to each other's presence. If anything, they stalk each other, or he, at least, stalks her. She pretends to ignore him, wears a chronically disgusted or disappointed expression, and continually reminds him that she "needs her space." She is unabashedly critical of his every move. They virtually do not speak and rarely go out together. He has learned self-sufficiency, though periodically asks for a sign of affection despite her obvious communication to the contrary. Eventually he threatens to leave, which he has done on two occasions, to which she responds by becoming suicidal and begging him to return with a promise to be more affectionate. When he returns, they make passionate love once. Then the status quo returns.

* * *

At the time I originally wrote this vignette, I had been treating the husband of this couple for many years. Multiple themes had surfaced, had been extensively explored, and to a greater or lesser degree had been relived in the transference. His life had measurably improved, professionally, socially, but only in the last year had his relationship to his wife changed. Largely through the exploration of preoedipal issues, he had developed a healthy sense of autonomy and internal strength. However, it was not until the sexual dimension of his tie to his wife was explored that his feelings for her and his pathological dependency on their aggressive form of relating changed.

In the early phase of his treatment, he revealed a fear of his aggression, encapsulated in a self-representation of a life-sucking neediness that he feared would emerge with a more available or engaging woman. In effect, his wife's rebuffs held him in. This was a self-image he now reports has dissipated and I have observed his capacity to gain recognition, affection, and acceptance in other areas of his life. He is not as narcissistically fragile as when we first began.

Much of the work in his treatment has involved mourning the wished-for mother as he has realized the extent of his mother's sadistic withholding and depriving stance toward him. As an example, his mother had not spoken to him (literally) since he separated from his first wife because, as she explained it, separation and divorce are unacceptable in her moral scheme. She might visit her grandchildren and their mother (his first wife), though will leave if her son drops by. In the transference, I am experienced at times as the wished-for maternal object who responds empathically and understands his concerns. Or I am experienced as the negative, withholding maternal object who continues to deprive him of direct gratification. Alternatively, I am experienced as a negative paternal figure who frustrates and disappoints him as I silently listen but *impotently cannot* or, worse, *cruelly will not* intervene in the painful engagement with his second wife/mother.

Another focus of the treatment centered on tracking and bringing to the surface his unconscious aggression. He has realized that his wife is more outwardly aggressive than his mother was, thereby presenting a greater capacity for engagement with him. She is a new object, less incestuously tied to his mother. She has afforded him an opportunity to fight his life-long, chronically suppressed battle with his mother, all the while simultaneously actualizing his identification with her through a kind of martyrdom. It is an erotized repetition of the earlier trauma, carrying with it a hope of triumph, or at least revenge (Stoller, 1979), through identification with the aggressor.

We discussed the control he wielded through his passivity, his capacity to frustrate his wife, and engender feelings of contempt in her, which reassured him that he had an impact on her. His wife had become actively suicidal when he left her, reflecting in a dramatic way her need of him, though also making him feel trapped. He revealed a desire to see himself as a saint in comparison to her. His 'goodness,' reflected in his ability to restrain his aggression even when dramatically provoked, is a sadistic attempt to elevate himself and degrade her.

He had an idea that the more suffering he could endure, the more power he acquired to transcend the pain, and the more impotent he made his wife as he experienced her degradations. He believed he would eventually anesthetize himself against the pain, thereby becoming a stronger man. Through his engagement with her hostility and aggression, he could disavow ownership of such impulses, temporarily relieving himself of the associated guilt which otherwise dominated him, and disclaim responsibility for what is dangerous, destructive, and bad (Ghent, 1990). Further, his submission to his wife's power and fury could be seen as an attempt to feel the illusion of her protection and caring (Coen, 1992), to feel her presence, and steadfast loyalty.

The transference/countertransference matrix within which these sadomasochistic modes of relating first emerged revolved around an experience of me as sadistically withholding. For my part, I experienced him as frustrating my attempts to help him, eventually engendering an impotent rage in me. I felt hopeless, frustrated, and angry at him as he continually stopped short of asserting his needs, demanding better care from me or his wife, or becoming infuriated with the serious destructiveness in his marriage.

The sexualization of his aggression was explored, along with possible genetic roots. He recalled moments of intense longing for his mother as he, titillated by her half-clad body, watched her perform her household chores. In this way, his masochism, an identification with his mother, was discussed as a defensively sexualized repetition of his hostile aggression toward his withholding mother.

All of the above themes surfaced over time, were extensively explored and relived. Still a question persisted that I believe is worth pondering: Why doesn't he leave? What is the glue that binds them together? He said he feared he would not be as excited by another woman as he is by his wife. What is the essence of this excitement?

If this couple's interplay is viewed through a sociocultural lens, the ways in which gender roles are polarized and played out across this dyad defy the usual stereotyping. He is all receptivity; she is all potent thrust. This is their erotic interplay, associated with an unmistakable excitement. In the later phases of the treatment, I focused more directly on this dynamic.

On one occasion, I suggested that the 'tension' between him and his wife seemed intense and gripping, engaging even, despite the seeming total absence of verbal communication. He made reference to how his wife only *seems* to ignore him and how he has felt unable to ignore her. He said, "She's dangerous and I know she watches me too, though you can barely see it." I noted that danger is stimulating. He said, "She keeps me on my toes." "Or what?" I asked. There was a pause. He said, "Or I don't know. I would feel like I didn't make a difference to her, like she didn't want me. Like I wasn't exciting to her."

Parallel to this, an interesting transference-countertransference enactment occurred that demonstrated an aggressivized, but essentially erotic, interplay with me. At the start of a session, my patient entered the office and, with a shy smile, acknowledged me. I silently observed that his initial discomfort seemed to give way to sadness. I asked what was happening and he acknowledged he felt tense, but didn't know why. I asked what he noticed as he walked in the room, but he was unable to respond. He remained silent for some time. He then began to recount an exchange between him and his wife that had occurred the previous evening, characteristic of their hate-filled sadomasochistic interplay from years before. This type of interaction had diminished in recent months, so I was surprised and disappointed to hear of its return. He recounted that she had been watching T.V. with her daughters in the living room. He was being ignored and knew he was not welcome to join them. He stood at the doorway and said, "I was wondering if now would be a time you might show me some affection." She scowled and stared at the T.V. Her daughters did the same. He walked away, feeling rejected.

At this moment, I found myself unable to restrain an impatient, frustrated response whereby I said, "She doesn't *want* you to ask her! It makes her *contemptuous* when you do!" He fixed his stare now at me and looked worried. He immediately said, "You're frustrated with me too. We've talked about this a hundred times. How could I have said that to her? I wasn't going to tell you. Why did I?" We then examined what had occurred in the session, from the moment he came in up to this moment. He said, "When I saw you, you looked so inviting, so warm. You smiled when you said hello. And I felt so needy after having been rejected last night. I felt I could cry and it made me nervous. Before I knew it, I was telling you about last night." Because the interaction from the previous evening was so characteristic of the type of interaction they would have had up until about a year before this session, I wondered if he might have assumed, consciously or unconsciously, that it would irritate me, even fly in the face of our work together, and disappoint or frustrate me. I wondered *if he was moved to frustrate me* or make me angry in some way so as to defend against the longings he was feeling as we began the session. When I stated these possibilities, he agreed and added that maybe he became more sure of where he stood with me if he made me angry. He said, "It's clearer to me what to do."

These possibilities were incorporated into our understandings of his attachment to his wife. In the succeeding months, he seemed to desire her differently. For example, during one session, I interpreted his fixed stare at her after she had made an insulting remark as both hateful (which he was conscious of and readily acknowledged), functioning to monitor potential danger (he agreed and felt he had no choice since she was likely to attack him again), *and desirous*. On this last point, he wondered what I saw and meant. I elaborated, "You stare at her. A long time. Like fixed on something you *want* to look at." He responded, "I admire her meanness. For a while, it seemed the more I was repelled, the more I longed for her. Like I could control her hostility if I could get close enough, touch her body, hold her down. I wanted to. I was in awe of her ability to be so mean. Powerful, like a strength, though I know it isn't. But I feel all this less intensely now. I respect it less. I guess I don't need it as much."

In the last year of treatment, my patient's need for the aggressive overlay of their sexual interaction diminished. Unfortunately, the same could not be said for his wife, who remained untreated virtually throughout the five or six years of my treatment with her husband. He had developed a genuine autonomy and began to make overtures in a less subservient, tentative manner. Though she did not readily respond, the tension between them had become diffused. He seemed to desire her less as well; she seemed frustrated, almost a bit lost that he wasn't playing the same old game. His affective stance toward her became less dominated by a fear of her aggression against him and organized around, at least from his point of view, an appreciation of her fragility.

The eros in sadomasochism

As mentioned, the sexuality in sadomasochistic relating is most often viewed as a defensive effort to transform negatively toned experiences into positive ones, culminating in an erotized repetition of earlier trauma (Stoller, 1979; Blos, 1991; Wrye and Welles, 1994). This idea is based on an associative model, i.e., the two occurred together in childhood, and can become, or developmentally became, fused so that sex may explain the irresistible pull toward such destructive interplay. The sexuality constitutes a self-reinforcing feedback loop. This couple's interaction can be viewed as sexualized in this way, but I am suggesting that sexuality cannot be used defensively unless it is already there, unless there is something already inherently sexy in the interaction that can be selected, focused on, stoked, and enhanced. The emphasis of the non-erotic dimension of so-called sexualized experience interprets sexuality defensively and symbolically; however, this 'deliteralization of sexuality' (Samuels, 1996) requires some embodiment in the concrete and literal, or metaphor has nothing from which to derive itself.

As you can imagine, I had been forced to dig rather deep to discern the nature of their tie. The distance between them is measured and recalibrated with each step forward or back. Still I detected a subtle seduction beneath this icy dance. What follows is my construction of their possible unconscious experience, developed in the last several years of an intensive treatment with the husband of this couple.

He is relegated to the position of a disempowered, deflated subordinate who must intuit his master's desires and whims. He derives a kind of strength, however, from his constant, exquisite examination of her. He touches her with his vigilance. He is wise to her desire, knows what to verbalize and what not. Though he does not always follow her rules, he is always watching and, with his searing attention to her dynamics, he penetrates her. He knows her desire without her having to verbalize it. She receives (and requires) his vigilant looking, though at a certain distance. She exhibits herself through her ubiquitous rules so that he may know her. He feels her presence everywhere; she can feel him around her.

With his persistent requests for caring and attention, he envelops her, touches her with his awareness, surrounds her by tenaciously clinging to the rigid but clear boundaries of the relationship. She acknowledges no desire yet gets her needs met without having to verbalize what she wants. She has a telepathic lover who will answer every whim but, most importantly, who will not leave, as if every "don't" and "stop" means "don't stop."

Her rebuffs and rejections make him hard. She withholds something vital though she knows what he wants. He knows she has it to give and imagines and hopes she is teasing him. His longing intensifies as the tension between them mounts. He consciously desires to transcend the pain of this relationship and feels a strength, feels himself more erect, with each rejection. He, in turn, is in awe of her strength, her ability to aggress against him. His obsequiousness and submissive pleas makes her hard in his eyes, and he wants to control her, possess her 'phallic' power. Her ubiquitous criticism of him makes her palpable to him. She is everywhere in his consciousness. She surrounds him; he feels her. She envelops him with her persistent criticism of his every action. When she is hard, he can feel her, unlike the amorphous indifference of his mother, whom he could not psychically find or feel. He has taken her in; her rules are inside him.

The description of the sexual dimension in this couple's relating was not at the level of their conscious experience but a hidden structure concealed by their sadomasochistic interplay. I am suggesting that it is the erotic attachment that is the tie that binds and that aggression is recruited for defensive, concealing purposes, paradoxically to maintain safety under the regressive pull of sexual and preoedipal longings. Their sexuality has been aggressivized and, in this way, aggression is used to mask or defend against intolerable affects associated with sexual desire.

Such aggressivization of sexuality gives the illusion that you come from a position of strength. An aggressive gesture at once engages and holds the other at bay. It passionately invites while maintaining an unconsciously measured distance. It summons the armor surrounding and hiding one's vulnerability, making one feel protected by virtue of a self-protection, rather than relying on the other's good will. With a self-sufficient facade, this makes an otherwise highly intimate and dangerous encounter feel safe.

As in the phrase *fuck you*,[5] this erotic dance leads with aggression or, at least, it is the aggression that is most palpable. Underneath, however, is a contamination, a fusion of sexuality and aggression, even though the aggression is most salient. I believe their interaction is essentially erotic; however, it disclaims desire and need, and thereby disclaims vulnerability or sense of lack in oneself. This is the compensating organization of hate, juxtaposed on the disorganizing vulnerability of love (Bollas, 1994). To cloak an intimate engagement in hostility is to circumvent the exposure of one's vulnerability, longing, and potential defenselessness (Celenza, 1995).

Conclusion

Bader (1993) has discussed the adaptive function of sadomasochistic play aimed at the achievement of increased sexual and psychological freedom. He proposes that some forms of sadomasochistic fantasies and enactments can be liberating, as they serve to reassure the subject that the object can survive the full expression and power of his or her sexual desire. This formulation is consistent with the ideas presented here, especially in terms of levels of perverse modes of relating where certain forms of engagement may serve a transitional function. In addition, Bader's illustration aptly illustrates the erotic dimension of sadomasochism, viewed as an irreducible, driving force naturally admixed with aggression. In his words,

> The capacity to collide erotically with the object without self-consciousness or particular consciousness of the other is as important in a healthy sexual relationship as the capacity to empathize with the sexual needs and experience of the other. (p. 287)

Here, aggression is represented in collision and in the capacity to engage without consciousness of the other, i.e., the capacity to be alone, take the other for granted, destroy the other's presence as one attends to one's own self-centered, bodily pleasure. In my view, as in Bader's, this underscores the dialectical tension between the capacities for relatedness and the capacity for aloneness underlying healthy mutuality and intimacy.[6] When one pole of this tension is not tolerated, as in the couple presented here, the experience becomes imbalanced, disclaimed, and projected, as one affective dimension can defensively function to conceal the other. Bader describes an adaptive use of sadomasochistic scenarios, as they may provide a transitional play field to enact and experiment with the tension between sexual desire and aggressive power, culminating in intensifying erotic experience. However, in the pathological enactments described above, the sadomasochistic roles are prescribed in a fixed, non-playful, non-experimental fashion and function to constrict desire. The aggression is salient, and that is its function: to mask each partner's desire for the other.

Elaborating on Ghent (1990), I believe the wife in this couple cannot allow receptivity for fear of being possessed; he mistakes submission for surrender. They each substitute vigilance for caring. They desire to be overcome with feeling, to be swept away, as it were; neither can manage it without each vying to overtake and thereby control the other. Though they seek a self-affirming surrender, neither can tolerate or risk such a narcissistically challenging experience for fear of annihilation and enslavement. She mistakes his awe for adoration; he mistakes her contempt for strength.

To love ferociously,[7] with a vengeance, is to shore up the boundaries of the self and avoid feeling the full strength of one's longing to be overcome, to be possessed, or to surrender to the other. To be overtaken or to submit to the other's will allows one to disclaim ownership of the desire, need, or longing for the other. The illusion is that submission is a choice over, and against, surrender.

In Puccini's (1926) last opera, Turandot, the ice princess, the princess of death, seethes to Calaf, "No man will ever possess me; my heart burns with hatred!" Yet she invites him to solve a riddle, to exhibit his prowess, offering an opening for him to enter her. Later, after solving the riddle and demonstrating his competence to her, he penetrates her armor with the question, "Do you know my name?" He invites her to see him, dares her to look. He persists as she fearfully looks away, then finally falls under his spell. It is a seduction laced with hatred, but a seduction all the same.

Notes

1 For a series of papers on masochism as seen clinically, see Holtzman and Kulish, 2012.
2 Benjamin (1988) writes of the recognition/destruction dialectic in a similar fashion.
3 Normal or adaptive forms of sadomasochistic play are thoughtfully considered by some psychoanalytic writers (see, for example, Kernberg, 1991a, 1991b; Bader, 1993); however, for the purposes of this chapter, I will be primarily referring to maladaptive, pathological forms of sadomasochistic relating, the distinction revolving around the fixity, rigidity, and closed nature of the interacting.
4 Kaplan (1991) assertively states that masochistic fantasies accompanying sexual intercourse are so prevalent they should be considered universal. At the same time, she also states, "almost every perversion entails a variation on a masochistic script . . . [these scripts] are found in both sexes" (p. 24). However, the quality of drivenness and repetition that would qualify such behaviors as perverse is comparatively rare. She goes on to distinguish a variety of perverse scenarios that vary in prevalence, "In contrast to fetishism and transvestism, which are almost exclusively male, *sexual masochism* is much more prevalent in males in general (the ratio is about 20 males to 1 female) and especially among homosexual males (pp. 24–5).

5 In an earlier version of this chapter, the subtitle was, "Deconstructing fuck you."
6 In some ways, this tension is analogous to the dialectic between destruction and recognition (cf. Winnicott, 1969; Benjamin, 1988; Ghent, 1990).
7 These constructions are to be rigorously differentiated from Bader's (1993) notion of 'sexual ruthlessness,' which he uses to refer to the admixture of sexual excitement and aggression in mutual erotic lovemaking, where the dialectical tension is successfully contained within each member of a healthy couple. In pathological sadomasochistic interactions, this tension devolves into a polarized, rigidified scenario of dominance and submission with fixed roles for each member.

Chapter 8

Fetishes, the anal universe, and other fantasies of one-person relating

Flowers bloom and die
Wind brings butterflies or snow
A stone won't notice . . .

Watching, white moon face
The stars never feel anger
Blah, blah, blah, the end

C. Palahniuk, *Fight Club*, 2005

I begin this chapter with quotes from *Fight Club* (Palahniuk, 2005), a book arguably about male sexual perversion, or the Western male's attempt to harness, reckon, and authorize aggressive and sexual desires. In line with the themes in this book, the story is about the struggle to authorize one's needs and capacities for potency. It is a fascinating story of the various strategies the 'two' protagonists employ in order to manage, control, and experience intense desire.

Fetishes are often employed for similar purposes. In the following chapter, I define the term fetish in the strong sense,[1] i.e., as a prototype of a perverse strategy whose aim is to manage, control, and ultimately deaden vitality through the use of misleading erotic (vitalizing) imagery and symbols. An individual making use of fetishes in the strong sense will, by definition, be in need of clinical attention because of the anti-growth promoting nature of the strategy. This is in contrast to the weak sense of the term and strategy, the universal tendency to invest objects or rituals that express or exhibit desire in a non-fixed, playful, and growth-promoting manner. Fetishes in the weak sense serve growth-promoting efforts and may be viewed as transitional objects or erotically invested symbols in their own right. This chapter does *not* refer to the use of fetishistic practices or scenarios in the weak sense. The distinction I am making differentiates the use of a transitional object (fetish in the weak sense) from a devitalizing, rigid use of an object in order to expunge uncertainty and spontaneity (see Part II—Perverse scenarios revisited—for a more elaborated discussion of these distinctions).

According to Kaplan (1991, 2006), given its basic structure, the fetish is the prototype of a perverse scenario. Its use represents a psychological defense that aims to tame, subdue and, if necessary, "murder human vitalities" (Kaplan, 2006). It is almost simple in the extreme: the fetish represents the culmination of a process of externalization, objectification, and symbolization. But it is more than that, i.e., more than a transitional object. A fetish is used in a way that is repetitive and fixed. If we accept that development follows a nonlinear, circuitous path amidst multiple turns and retracings in an increasingly complex landscape, fetishes represent dead-end cul-de-sacs from which the pathway back is blocked. Further, the use of a fetish is a retreat from intersubjectivity in a fantastically construed one-person psychic world.

Fetishization is an attempt at disembodiment and objectification, the substitution of a part for the whole (Kaplan, 1991, 2006), the opposite of healthy striving for integrative, embodied relational experience. Though there is a line of thinking that cautions against pathologizing such strategies, opting instead to view all erotic activity as an attempt to address basic human anxieties, desires, and needs, I want to illuminate, and thereby place in the foreground, various perverse scenarios or fetishistic modes of relating that attempt to limit, constrain, and render inert one pole of a dialectic: the repudiated other, or the whole against the part. In the very act of repudiation, a dichotomy is instantiated whose purpose is to render dialectical interplay impossible. We could say that fetishization is a consequence, and disorder, of hierarchy, in that it rests on the repudiation of some (usually gendered) stereotype. The binary trap of receptivity/potency will often be implicated.

As noted, the construction of a one-person fantasy renders examples in the classical literature helpful in delineating (on a content level) some typical meanings of fetishistic activity. Since the classical literature is embedded in a one-person epistemology, the reported fantasies can reveal interesting unconscious meanings. Despite that many fetishes are performed alone, the accompanying masturbatory fantasies always imply the presence of others. There are usually fantasies revolving around judgments made by imagined viewers of the intactness or adequacy of the body or its parts. These are experienced either from the other's perspective or in comparison to a fantasied other, his/her body, and so on. Often, the enactment and fantasy functions to emphasize freedom from dependency on others and their associated judgments. Kaplan (1991, 2006) describes a common clinical finding in which the selected fetishes are icons that represent and revive the moment before the child recognizes the difference between the sexes, a kind of 'fem phallus,' like a piece of lace, fur, or a woman's shoe. The unconscious meaning and scenario serves to reassure that mother is not castrated; the world is as it once was, when there was no difference between the sexes, and the child was the center of the mother's universe.

A person with a fetish can seem to desexualize an erotic activity as well. Sometimes the fetishistic object does not appear (to the outside observer) as a manifestly erotic symbol. However, if there is any doubt of the sexual underpinning of a fetish, consider this example.

A married man came for an evaluation, at the insistence of his wife, for longstanding sexual inhibition. He shared with me that he was not sexually attracted to his wife and, truth be told, he had little interest in sex altogether. It took a few sessions before he revealed a foot fetish. When asked to describe his interest in (male) feet, he stated, "It's an aesthetic thing. I am enamored with their beauty. But I can control it; it's like looking at a beautiful statue." I asked if he wondered why it was feet he found so lovely. He continued, "My feet are misshapen. I have a hammer toe and I've never liked the way my feet look. I think that's the reason."

There are many aspects of aesthetic pleasure in erotic activity—beauty is a major prompt of erotic arousal. What is striking in persons who use fetishes (and what makes such use a perverse mode of relating) is the manner in which the fetish confines and constricts sexuality. The fetish is not a casual preference that brings pleasure. Rather, it is obligatory and fixed; it is necessary to the achievement of sexual arousal, and it is the only thing that makes sexual arousal possible.[2] The relationship to the fetish is repetitive and routinized; indeed, it is the opposite of play and thereby gets its designation as a perverse mode of relating.[3]

This man had an elaborate strategy to gratify his aesthetic yearning. Finding himself alone with another man (perhaps in a professional meeting), he would describe a research project he was undertaking. (This was a pretense). He would state that he was looking at the concordance between handedness and the natural direction of the foot: a right-handed person should have feet pointing in a right-ish direction, and so on. He might conjure up a few more details to embellish the project until the man was willing to take off his shoe and sock. When asked to describe the experience from then on, he would state simply, "I would gaze at his feet and enjoy it. That's it." Would he get aroused? "No." Was it in any way a sexual experience? "No," he would insist. Did he ever masturbate afterwards? Sometimes, he added, but this was only a tension release.

I would later learn that he barely felt sexual pleasure at all. Though he did masturbate to pictures of feet, his orgasms were "like little blips" and served, in his mind, only to release tension. In all, he would talk about his sexuality in a disconnected way. "I just do it. It's not arousal—It's a relief, like I say 'There, I saw it.'" (Saw what? one might ask, a question that will be discussed below.) He does not question his sexual orientation because he is responsive to women and might think about sex if he sees a picture of breasts. He has not had sexual relations with men. He mostly fantasizes about feet and adds that the fantasies are not a problem; it is simply the behavior which he struggles to control. Fantasies arise if he sees a handsome man; he will then wonder what his feet look like. If the story stopped there, it might be assumed that this man's foot fetish was not a sexual activity in some inherent or fundamental way.

Upon being given a Rorschach test, however, this man saw penises in almost every card. Deformed and misshapen, nonetheless they were penises, and he reported seeing these anatomical parts, making no connection to his foot fetish. Nor did he connect the many traumatic events and situations of his past to the development of his foot fetish. He was the second child and only boy in a family described simply as "detached." His parents never showed affection toward each other, and there was little physical contact for the children either. His mother was the disciplinarian and his father was distant. He remembers being slapped on the mouth if he misbehaved. His mother would stand before the table when dinner was ready and say, "If you want to eat, you have to come past me." In general, he said he never felt special to either parent. He interestingly commented, "I never put myself on a pedestal. I don't strive or promote myself."

These dynamics can easily be viewed as reflecting struggles and questions about castration and potency—he cannot stand tall, stand erect, or stick out. Perhaps his remembered statement, "You have to come past me" has the meaning that he cannot 'come' unless he can get beyond his mother. And most tellingly, the statement, "There I saw it" might be viewed as a reassurance that men (like him) are not castrated (viewing the foot as a displaced penis). These are the insightful speculations of classical literature reaching back to Freud (1927). There is little doubt that these play some role in this man's intrapsychic world.

Since a person who engages in fetishistic perverse scenarios, especially if the fetish is obligatory (necessary for and the sole avenue of sexual gratification), is constructing a fantasied one-person universe, the treatment situation and experience within the treatment relationship will become perverted as well. This is the application of the means/end reversal that will be evident in the analytic situation. In contemporary understanding, the analysis (a relational, growth-potentiating experience) is subverted to a one-person, rigidified, and routinized ritual. This mirrors the function of the fetish and, if the analyst does not recognize how the treatment relationship enacts the perverse scenario, the treatment process itself will likely become protracted and repetitive. A risk in treating persons trapped in a perverse scenario is that the analyst will become either a bystander or 'an uninvolved observer' (although observing is participating and, for some, the act of being seen or witnessed is a step toward relationality). Or, the analyst may imagine that he or she is not in any kind of relationship with the patient at all. In the latter instance, the analyst has become sensitized to the patient's fantasy that he or she exists in a one-person universe.

Classical formulations of perverse scenarios have adopted such a stance, hence many individuals who engage in fetishistic modes of relating that are obligatory and routinized are deemed 'unanalyzable.' Persons with fetishes are indeed difficult to treat, however, the adoption of a stance that colludes with (and thereby enacts) a fantasied one-person relatedness will only reinforce the patient's defensive construction. If the analyst takes a classical position of abstinence and anonymity, the fantasied one-person relatedness may not ever be disturbed. It may not be apparent how the act of observing and witnessing actually participates in the patient's private drama. If the analyst him or herself has schizoid tendencies, there may become a protracted 'folie á duex' of "analysis of the id by the odd" (in Blechner's [2009, p. 84] felicitous phrase).

The treatment of persons with an obligatory fetish is likely to be slow and painstaking since the ritual of fetish usage is self-reinforcing and insular. The first phase of the treatment will provide the analyst with the challenge of discerning how he or she is playing a part in the private fantasy of the patient, the so-called inner drama that the fetishist has fantastically construed. To be absent from the private world may be the first scene; however, it would be a mistake to understand this as a role that has not been cast. Usually, there is an active rejection of relating in casting the analyst into this role. Much like Searles (1961/1965) 'Out of Contact Phase' in treating psychotic patients or Slochower's (1996) phase of holding in the early part of a psychoanalysis with some particularly schizoid patients, the initial period of work in the treatment of persons who engage in fetishistic perverse scenarios is to become part of the drama, even if that means to be cast backstage for a period of time.

The man with a boot fetish

A colleague/psychoanalyst (M. Cohen, personal communication, 2011) shared the following story of a treatment he conducted over many years with John, a man who had developed an obligatory fetish with male boots. Since early adolescence, a successful but socially isolated man had collected male boots to such an extent that he eventually owned over 100 pairs. These could be boots that motorcycle riders wear but, most often, they were boots of police or military officers. He had no interest in female boots or shoes of either gender and did acknowledge that the appeal of boots was erotic. With his favored boots, he would fantasize and masturbate by stroking and rubbing the boots. He would never directly touch his penis (either while masturbating or in any other context with the exception of urination), but would rub his body against the floor to ejaculate.

Accompanying this activity with boots, were self-punitive thoughts revolving around being punished for things John did, or had done, that he imagined were 'bad.' Punishment ensued as well for what he did not do but, in his mind, should have done. Mostly, he imagined being punished for chores revolving around the boots, such as inadequately shining them. The punishments were imagined put-downs and reprimands. Though these masturbatory activities were performed alone, he fantasized being punished by various male figures, including state troopers, policemen, or his father.

When asked if he had thought about the origins of his fetish, John described having had significant problems with his feet as a child. He was required to wear special shoes due to an abnormality in the way his feet naturally pointed. His mother had prohibited him from wearing boots, but he began to collect them by stealing a pair from a store and hiding them in the woods. He would then go out in the woods, put the boots on and walk in them, discovering his great pleasure.

Further exploration of his childhood experiences revealed that John's mother was "the gatekeeper" (his word) to all others and to the outside world. He described his father as wholly absent—indeed "never available at all." His father would work all day and, once home at night, would read the paper while watching television. He communicated to his son that he did not want to be bothered. His mother was controlling and critical. At the same time, she and her son would sleep together when the father was away.

It may not surprise you to know that this man's father wore boots and this patient remembers being very attracted to them. He remembers discovering the erotic nature of boots by 7 years of age, when he would crouch under the stairway with one of his father's boots and hold them close to his chest, rubbing, and kissing them.

There are a series of pictures that this man drew as a young child. Speculation about the meaning of these became an important part of the treatment with his analyst. He insisted that they were not memories, traumatic or otherwise. To the best of his recollection, he drew them from his imagination and found them highly erotic. He began to use them to masturbate as well. They were all drawings of a father and his son, who was attempting to shine his shoes. The father was in a reprimanding, stern posture and often held a paddle or whip.

The patient described himself as depressed and anxious to the point of becoming phobic about some things. For example, he could not swim in lakes (though he was a good swimmer in pools) because he was terrified of what might be in the lake. He also seemed out of touch with his internal experience (his body-based, affective experience), given that he would often describe himself by drawing conclusions based on comparisons to others. For example, he would notice he was alone and thereby surmise that he was lonely because he would see he was the only person eating alone in a restaurant. He did not identify feeling lonely by recognizing an affective state in his body.

Murray Cohen is a classically trained psychoanalyst who has great facility in making contact with hard-to-reach patients. He is warm and engaging. He reported that the patient idealized him throughout the treatment, yet the patient also actively avoided any particularized information about him. He never commented on the various items in the office that might reflect his analyst's personality or interests. Once, Dr. Cohen greeted him on crutches, and the patient never asked about them. The analyst surmised that he was "the father that wasn't there." The analyst attempted to discuss this dynamic with John; however, the patient could not acknowledge it. In general, the patient did not think about his attachment to his analyst on a personal or emotional level. Dr. Cohen assumed that he was not in the patient's mind. He also assumed that John probably did not imagine that he, John, was in his analyst's mind either.

Yet, John got better. Through his multi-year psychoanalytic treatment, he came to understand and express the intensity of his unfulfilled longings, mostly revolving around his father. These included wishes for his father's attention, love, recognition, advice, and counsel. Though he had never had any intimate relations with either men or women in his adult life, he did establish more collegial relationships with men and women at work. His boot fetish, however, remained his only source of sexual gratification.

Consistent with the view of holistic striving and the overall assumption that 'we cannot leave anyone behind' (see Chapter 4), the treatment of this man can be viewed as reinstating the triad of mother, father, and son in an attempt to reconnect with himself as a child in relation to the wished-for father. The treatment provided the context for the cultivation of this relationship with the father, and it can be viewed that the analyst represented both the idealized father and the wished-for, accepting mother who opened the gates to the relationship with the father. Through the analyst's acceptance and acknowledgment of the patient's boot fetish, the analyst provided a context where the patient and his fantasied father could maintain their connection, symbolically through the sexualized boot. His actions with the boots might be viewed as a familiarizing and taming of the frightening father, a step toward connection.

Behind her back

Roger is a physical therapist who had several female patients submit official complaints to his licensing board that he had inappropriately rubbed his body against them during a physical examination. The women described being asked to stand up straight while he would examine their posture from behind. It was while he was supposedly touching their spine and upper shoulders during a physical examination that they could feel his erect penis rubbing against their buttocks. Roger never denied these allegations and came to treatment overwhelmed with shame and disgust with himself. He stated these were the only occurrences of such behavior and he was totally dumbfounded about why he had acted this way over a period of 5 years.

At the time of our initial meeting, Roger stated that he tried to be a good person, was religious and attended church regularly, worked hard, and loved his family. He acknowledged that he had never had extra-marital relations, though he and his wife had not engaged in sexual relations for years. He was unhappily married with several children. These complaints and the crisis that ensued led to the break-up of his marriage. He described his wife as a shopaholic, neglectful of the children, and oriented toward 'keeping up with the Joneses' in a material way. He worked full-time, did the grocery shopping, made dinner, and helped the children with their homework without realizing how exhausted he was and how imbalanced his marriage was. His wife did not work and they were severely in debt. All of this was described without resentment or bitterness. In fact, it took several months for me to realize just how oppressed and enslaved he felt—he had a 'selfless' attitude toward the way he and his wife were living. He felt it was the Christian way and he said he did not want to "run his wife down" by admitting his resentment or frustration.

We did not understand Roger's sexual behavior with his patients, however, until we delved further into his childhood history. Roger grew up in a "proper Midwestern home," in which it was considered rude or improper to be the least bit confrontational. All energies were focused on outward appearances. Neighbors and friends were not to know, for example, that his mother was chronically ill. The reality was, however, that Roger's mother was often in bed with severe migraine headaches and/or neck pain. He described the home atmosphere as a strict environment. He and his sister would have to be quiet in order to prevent waking their mother or exacerbating her headache. Child's play and, later, social contacts and parties were forbidden pleasures that would disrupt the quiet in the home. Roger's mother's symptoms were resistant to any form of treatment. On the other hand, he did note from a young age that his mother rarely followed through with any of the prescribed treatments, including taking various medications or performing relaxation exercises.

Roger believes he became a physical therapist in order to heal his mother (or women like her), despite never being able to experience his mother symptom free. During Roger's graduate training to become a physical therapist, he would often call home and instruct his mother about exercises and other treatment strategies she should adopt to control her headaches. Unsurprisingly, she would fail to follow his advice. She suffers with headaches to this day.

Pointedly, Roger's father is a guilt-ridden man who blames himself for his wife's chronic pain. Roger's father believes her symptoms were caused by an accident when he was doing some home improvement and a piece of wood fell on her. Roger believes his father has been doing penance ever since. He would sporadically work hard, sometimes two jobs at once, punctuated with long periods of unemployment, however, the cause of his periodic loss of work remained a mystery. Roger would overhear his father lament to his mother, "I couldn't get a raise," "I couldn't get ahead," and "I want to rise above."

There were interesting boundary violations that Roger endured as well, revolving around occurrences where his parents would borrow money in inappropriate ways. Roger remembers his parents obtaining a loan from the family doctor that was allegedly to help with Roger's tuition. (It was, instead, used for family expenses.) On another occasion, Roger was implored to ask his wealthy girlfriend for a loan for his family. He was deeply ashamed to do this, yet he did carry out these requests of his parents.

Roger was in his 20s when he learned that his mother had been sexually abused as a child; he wonders now what effect that had on her attitude toward him, a male. Roger recently said, "I've always had a lot of guilt. I feel like I want to confess, but I don't know for what." Roger stated that he longed more than anything to be touched and held. He has suffered with premature ejaculation for a period of time due to (he felt) his "hypersensitivity to touch." He felt he could not control his yearning yet did not masturbate because of religious prohibitions.

To say that Roger has suppressed anger toward his parents, perhaps especially his mother, would be an understatement. After a period of time in treatment, he was able to more freely express how frustrated he felt growing up and how chronically unhappy the family seemed to be. Most importantly, he talked about the way in which he felt his mother contributed to her own unhappiness, refusing to follow through with treatment regimens, seemingly cultivating her symptomatology in an effort to control the atmosphere in the home. (Whether this was actually true, or whether her headaches were treatable, is not relevant here; these are the fantasies Roger grew up believing and suppressing within himself throughout childhood and young adulthood.)

Through his treatment, Roger and I constructed the meanings of the perverse scenario he engaged with his patients. The scenario having to do with rubbing his penis against a woman (behind her back) represents a way to gratify his sexual urges without confrontation or intimacy, a way to get pleasure in the illusion that the woman does not know or cannot see him. Roger believed he was trying to gratify himself and physically contact his mother without her knowing or being aware. There is also another layer in that the fantasy of 'penetrating from behind' can be viewed as an aggressive, hostile act, given that the woman has not acceded and the act is presumably against her wishes. Finally, he also speculated that his behavior represents a muted reenactment of his mother's sexual abuse.

An anal universe

The presence of anal themes and mechanisms has long been recognized in perverse scenarios (Chasseguet-Smirgel, 1984; Stoller, 1986). This is the result of several coinciding processes: (1) on a theoretical level, the use of a hierarchical stage theory in sexual development (e.g., Freud's psychosexual stages) and the implication of regression from genital sexuality; (2) the contrast between the noxious character of anal preoccupations and the inherently pleasurable and aesthetic quality of sexuality; (3) the underlying developmental challenges of anality (power and control) and their usefulness in the defensive aspects of perverse scenarios, especially those involving conflicts with potency; (4) the psychological challenges of the anal stage, the acceptance of which ushers in the genital stage (namely, the anatomical difference between sexes and the generational difference); and finally, (5) the blatant expressions of anal concerns and rituals in patients who engage in perverse scenarios.

Chasseguet-Smirgel (1984) wrote about obliterating difference through fusion and merging, a kind of melting pot by creating an anal-sadistic universe (see Parsons [2000] for a review). Within a two-person framework, it is more easily seen how difference may be perceived as threatening, given that difference and separateness (i.e., perceiving the other as a separate subject) implies that the other has initiative; if the other is a separate center of agency, then the other is outside of one's control. Further, this implies that the other has potential aggression, conjuring up castration and other dangers.

Hugh, a 50-year-old man came to treatment because of a crisis in his marriage. His wife had just confirmed what she had long suspected, that her husband had been chronically unfaithful throughout their 25-year marriage. He acknowledged the truth in this and stated, "I have never been able to be monogamous." Hugh believed he never felt in love with his wife whom he married because their families knew each other and his mother approved of her. Though he remembered feeling sexually attracted to his wife before they married, the sexual tension between them dissipated quickly after they wed. He suffered with premature ejaculation, impotence, and a desire to "get sex over with" when making love to his wife.

Hugh is the only son of two, with an older sister two years his senior. He was very close to his mother, feeling always adored and totally accepted. She often told him he was "God's gift" and "the baby Jesus." In contrast, he had a very distant relationship with his father, who was passive, rarely expressed emotion and was uninvolved in his life. He recalled that his father was actually quite close with his sister, in striking contrast to her relationship with his mother, who was blatantly cruel to his sister. Hugh's mother was persistently verbally and physically abusive to his sister and, when Hugh recounted this to me, he insisted that witnessing her abuse had no effect on him "because I always knew I was safe with my mother. She would never turn on me." Hugh did not believe there was any fault-line in his capacity to trust women; he was the adored one, his sister was bad (perhaps deserving of abuse), and this was simply the way it was and would always be.

One way this dynamic emerged in the analysis with me related to Hugh's insistence that he felt "totally safe" with me, yet he could not lie down on the couch for over a year. He rationalized this as a casual preference to sit up, desiring to maintain eye contact; however, I had the sense that he felt the need to 'keep his eyes on me' for fear of what I might do if he turned his back. In the early part of the analysis, Hugh continued to insist that his mother's abuse of his sister had no effect on him. On one occasion, he said, "I know it's possible to have a totally safe relationship with you even if you're toxic in the rest of your life because my mother was like that." We focused on his need to separate a woman's aggression from his experience of relating with her. In the next several months of the analysis, Hugh remembered that, indeed, his mother had spanked and kicked him on several occasions. He also realized that these spankings had been incorporated into masturbatory fantasies when he was a teenager.

Over time, Hugh elaborated sadomasochistic fantasies and practices he had engaged in with previous lovers, including being whipped and given enemas by a woman whom he felt overtly controlled by, but whom he imagined he had enslaved. A reenactment of the relationship with his mother came immediately to mind (his and mine) as he recalled his mother's abuse of his sister; however, he insisted that enemas were never a part of what she did to either his sister or him. We surmised that the wish to be dominated by the woman may have been a desire to turn his mother's aggression against himself, perhaps also in response to hidden guilt he felt by witnessing his sister's abuse and being his mother's 'chosen good child.' This part of the scene might also be a way to evoke the punishing, rivalrous Oedipal father for whom he both hated and longed.

What Hugh was conscious of, however, was the method of controlling the woman in order that he might reenact the position of being out of control. It was a carefully scripted scenario including a previously agreed upon 'safe' word that, if uttered by either of them, would stop the action. Though intense sexual arousal was evoked for Hugh with this scene, he was aware that he had orchestrated the entire scene and thereby was not 'giving in' or surrendering to a set of feelings. He was not receptive to spontaneous gestures or moves initiated by his lover. He also could not penetrate a woman; he would quickly lose his erection, and the only way he could become aroused again would be through anal penetration.

Through the course of the analysis, Hugh increasingly talked about my interpretations of the meanings of his actions and fantasies as seductive penetrations. I became a figure in his fantasy life, not so much as a sexual object but as a dominatrix holding an enema bag and evincing pain by slowly adding water with pressure until his abdomen was painfully engorged. Ejaculation was not always a part of this scene. He talked about the tension release associated with the enema as a powerful attraction to the practice. We surmised that perhaps he was actualizing an identification with his mother (becoming a woman, his engorged abdomen 'pregnant' with badness, shit, aggression, or mysterious hidden desires). His desire to be anally penetrated might have represented a wish to have his father inside (more masculinity as well as closeness with him), and an overall wish to control who is penetrating whom, who is touching (spanking or beating) whom, all the while experiencing pain as some measure of punishment for his bad actions and wishes.

Conclusion

As noted, much of the content of the interpretations and meanings of the various symptomatology in this chapter can be found in the cogent and insightful writings of classical literature. Castration fears, gender concerns, and anal preoccupations are common themes in the writings of early and mid-century psychoanalysts, as well as later theoreticians of the more classical persuasion. Stoller's (1968, 1986) writings, along with the imaginative yet cogent dramas depicted in Chasseguet-Smirgel's (1984) 'anal universe,' hold important insights into the workings of a variety of perverse scenarios. I have attempted to place these important contributions into a contemporary framework and epistemology, in order to restore these ideas for clinical application. In so doing, it is possible to see how perverse scenarios render the relational world as depleted, and relegate the individual to a safer, albeit fantasied, one-person universe.

The treatment of individuals who engage in perverse scenarios is notoriously difficult. The work with Hugh had a particularly beneficial and poignant outcome. He had been a 'control case' during my psychoanalytic training[4] and participated in a lengthy analysis, more than half of which occurred after I had graduated, though he was unaware of my graduated status. One day, he began a session by discussing an employment opportunity he wanted to consider in another city. He immediately expressed concern about what would happen to me if he were to leave analysis prematurely, given that he was a training case. I told him I had already graduated, to which he immediately replied, "Mazel tov!" I was touched by his spontaneous expression of pleasure for and with me in such a genuine and immediate manner.

Many months later, Hugh began a session with a heartfelt description of lovemaking with his girlfriend in which he had finally been able to penetrate her vagina with his erect, engorged penis. His voice shook a bit as he told me he ejaculated inside a woman for the first time in his life. With heartfelt enjoyment for and with him, I was delighted to respond, "Mazel tov!" as we both teared up with joy for him.[5]

Notes

1 Distinguishing the use of fetishes in the strong or weak sense is a way to describe fetishistic practices *functionally* as opposed to identifying a particular behavior per se. I aim to emphasize here, as throughout this book, *the manner in which a practice is engaged* rather than categorizing behaviors themselves as perverse or not. For this reason, I have avoided terms such as paraphilia and neosexuality.
2 Again, I am describing fetishistic practices in the strong sense only.
3 Compare, for example, the quality of playfulness in the use of a transitional object, serving as a bridge to greater expansiveness, versus the fixity and repetitive qualities of fetishistic activity.
4 A supervised training case in partial fulfillment of the requirements of psychoanalytic training.
5 I realize this story may be read as imposing heteronormative values on a man who more naturally may have desired his own unique forms of sexual intimacies. Suffice it to say that these were Hugh's goals and values, the attainment of which coincided with a more playful and expansive quality of relating in the sexual sphere. Though he derived satisfaction from the perverse scenario he had been engaging since he was sexually active, he felt constrained by it, could not find satisfaction outside of it, and expressed the desire to be free of it since the beginning of treatment. He also did not fantasize about men and, though we explored the possibility of his having a homosexual orientation, this never resonated with him on an affective or fantasy level.

Conclusion
Positions of subjectivity—the ineluctable construction of the self

The greatest hazard of all, losing one's self,
can occur very quietly in the world,
as if it were nothing at all.
No other loss can occur so quietly;
any other loss –
an arm, a leg, five dollars, a wife, etc. –
is sure to be noticed.
S. Kierkegaard, *The Sickness Unto Death*, 1849

Throughout this book I have made reference to a useful binary, *receptivity and potency*, around which individuals may render, sift, refract, and otherwise live out their relationship to gendered and sexual being. These latter categories of being are but two of the ways in which an individual constructs meaning and interprets how, and the extent to which, they have come to terms with their personal strength and relational capacities. As discussed, this binary is not bedrock, nor is it even a polarity; it is merely one way in which an individual may display their resolution, and balanced or imbalanced reckoning, of various developmental challenges in the ongoing construction of *self*.

Similarly, contemporary theorizing has demythologized the notion of *a self* or a *core self* with the recognition of a multiplicity of selves 'standing' in some type of relation to one another. In Chapter 4, I made use of the metaphor of a bicycle wheel to depict this multiplicity, the spokes being in some balanced tension with one another connected to a moving center capable of transformation or growth. Consistent with contemporary theorizing, the idea that we have one self or a core self is now considered a convenient and wishful illusion (Butler, 1993, 2006; Mitchell, 1993, 1996; Flax, 1996; Bromberg, 1998; Davies, 1998a; Dimen, 2003; Harris, 2005a).

Yet, there is a persistent wish to reference self-experience in a continuous, holistic way[1] (Stein, 1995b). In effect, we *want* and *need* to be one person, even if it is an impossibility. There is a need to sustain the pulls of multiple states, a paradox inherent in this continual striving, in that we are simultaneously split or divided while striving for unity and wholeness. Clinically, we see patients suffer from 'fragmentation'—this psychic state should not to be confused with a multiply organized, decentered self-system. "One cannot treat an analysand as one treats the 'subject' in certain contemporary theories" (Stein, 1995b, p. 304). In the clinical setting, there is an unmistakable striving for unity, coherence, and stability, for order from chaos, even though these end-products of coherence and self-continuity might be illusory, reassuring explanatory fictions (Ghent, 1992; Elliott and Spezzano, 1996) or contradictory at a holistic level (Goldner, 1991; Benjamin, 1998; Harris, 2005a).

To speak of integration, then, refers not to a unified self so much as a *multifaceted network of self-states*, the parts of which are more or less accessible to one another. Greater access to the full variety of self-experience, including and, perhaps especially, its affective dimensions, can be conceived as a capacity to maintain a connective tension among the variety of self-states; the ability to stand in the spaces (Bromberg, 1998), achieve self-reflexivity (Aron, 1998), build bridges (Pizer, 1998), or find *radial true* (see Chapter 4) as an expressed goal of treatment.

As discussed in the introduction to this book, various self-states can be described in terms of the degree to which phenomenal experience is *receptive* (feelingful) and *potent* (agentic). A healthy state of mind is maximally both, and the embodied subject is defined by these two characteristics. *Embodiment* is sensate *receptivity* to feeling and affective aliveness. The capacity to harness one's *potency* (or authority) is what is meant by being a *subject*, i.e., the experience of articulated selfhood. Taken together in a feelingful agency is what I mean by *embodied subjectivity*.

These ideas are supported by recent developments in neuropsychological and cognitive research and are recognizable in our immediate lived experience. An overarching goal of treatment is to achieve better accessibility among complex, multiply coded, embedded systems (see, for example, Bucci's [2008] comprehensive, yet concise integration of psychoanalytic and neuropsychological/developmental findings in cognitive science).

In addition, the generation of a self-reflexive, accessible self-system is an existential need—to construct a multiply organized, relatively coherent self that is more or less continuous over time and transcendent of immediate circumstances. This striving can also be seen as a nod toward immortality, the desire to transcend the material body and attain a sense of limitless being.

A woman in her 30s tells me she has not yet begun her life—she is hiding and waiting before she chooses which path to take. She is paralyzed by several choices and frets over each possibility. She works at a job she says "does not count" because she is merely biding time until she begins her "real life." In her off hours, she lies in bed, watching videos, eats ice cream, and masturbates ... she has few social contacts because relating to others gives her a sense of becoming someone. She insists she has not yet decided when or how to begin her life. In the meantime, years have passed and she is in the same psychic place as she was in high school—not the place she describes, but in a mental state of paralysis, always about to take a step but (seemingly) never actually doing it. She has the illusion that she has not yet begun to live. I show her the irony that the reality of her life is this very façade; she lives *as she is not living*. There is no escaping the ongoing construction of selve(s) in some relation to the world. *We cannot avoid becoming someone.*[2] This *someone* derives from a continual striving for unity, coherence, and continuity, culminating in an ongoing construction of a core self feeling, the nature of 'becoming' in philosophical language, which may be illusory but is always only a work in progress.[3]

Still, there is an experiencing self that has private aspects, a potential to take a variety of perspectives (Modell, 1990), as well as unconscious motives that undergirth all of the self's positions. We strive to bring the experiencing self in some coherent relation with the more public, surface, and observable positions or perspectives. Dissociated self-states, unconscious repressed memories, and drives push for expression in varying ways, attesting to the continual need for a coherent experience of subjective embodiment.

Positions of subjectivity

The schematic offered in this concluding section (Figure 1)[4] attempts to depict states of subjectivity over which we more or less feel in some measure of conscious control and to describe the various perspectives or positions that can be distinguished. This schematic attempts to depict multiple ways we position ourselves in relation to others and within our own experience at any moment in time. The positions are conceived as potentially engaged depending on the relational interplay between oneself and others, as well as the capacity to flexibly alternate and access the various positions within one's own subjective experience: *The Embodied Subject* (the pre-reflective, experiencing, and agentic self), *The Subjective Object* (the self as an object for others or 'Me'; the public self), *The Reflective Self* (the self who reflects on itself, i.e., takes itself as an object for itself or 'I'), and the more dissociated, sometimes pathological, self-structure, *The Objectified Self* or 'It.' These positions are descriptions from the point of view of the experiencer; it is a schematic attempting to depict phenomenal subjective experience that may or may not coincide with an intrapsychic formulation constructed by an outside observer.

All of these subjective positions are rooted in and influenced by unconscious processes, defenses, and self-states categorized as *'Not Me,'* which may be comprised of dissociated unconscious images or self-states, repressed unconscious fantasies, either unencoded or encoded, the latter referring to Bollas' (1982) unthought known, and/or non-encoded, unformulated yet embodied nonconscious processes (as in Stern's [1983, 2009] unformulated experience).[5] Most of these unconscious influences are characterized by analogic/preverbal and nonverbal imagistic processing.[6]

I propose that the achievement of healthy psychological functioning is characterized by the ability to flexibly alternate among these positions as contexts

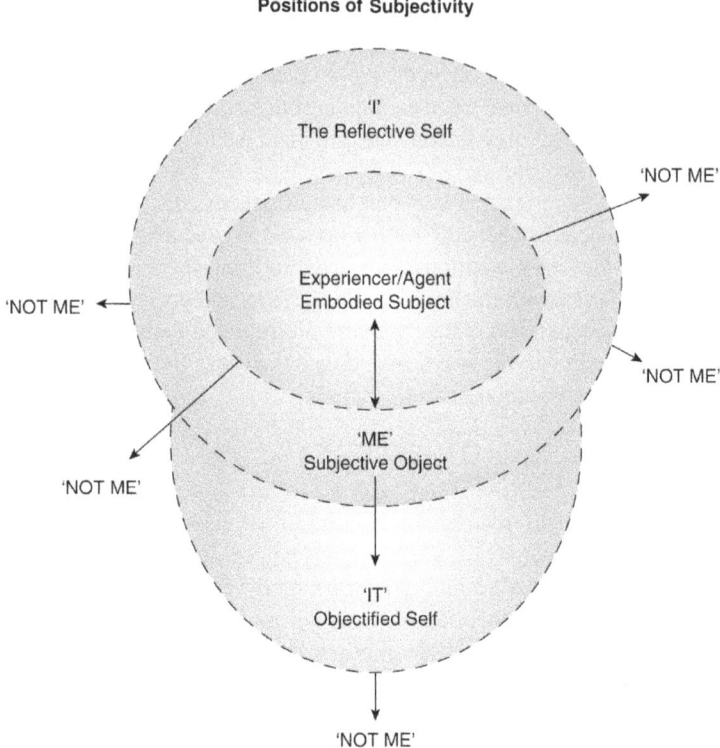

Figure 1 Positions of subjectivity

change and evoke different stances and modes of relating.[7] Such flex could be characterized by permeability or accessibility 'in the spaces between' positions[8] such that different self-states remain as potentially emergent when not engaged or actualized.[9] In a superordinate manner, this schematic multiplies; there are many Embodied Subjects as patterns evoke or engage modes of relating, cultivated through self-other identifications.

Modes of relating with another person can be characterized as primarily engaging one or another subjective position. For example, a narcissistic father (in relation to his child) might primarily engage the Subjective Object position of the child, i.e., the self as object for others. In contrast, a therapist might primarily engage the Reflective Self or the "I" position of the patient in the process of assigning meaning to experience. The capacity to flexibly alternate or engage simultaneously among multiple positions, states of being, and modes of relating is a hallmark of healthy psychological/emotional functioning and would indicate a greater potential for integration. This is captured by the striving for connectedness within and among these modes of relating with increasing affective immediacy and sense of agency, i.e., the capacity for experiencing in an embodied, self-in-relation manner.

The position of the Embodied Subject reflects the capacity for immersion in immediate experience that is, in some measure, both *affectively attuned* and *agentic*. This position can be either private (experienced in solitude) or interpersonal (experienced in relation with others.) When it is interpersonal, there is an absence of self-consciousness, as in highly familiar or intimate relationships, including the illusion of oneness with deep intimacy. (As will be elaborated below, this position is maximally *receptive* to embodied, feelingful experience; it also reflects the capacity for self-articulation or *potency*—indeed, this is what is meant by the Embodied Subject.[10]) This is the binary, receptivity and potency, that has been discussed throughout this book.

This binary emerges as an imbalanced reckoning in various positions of self-states. Thus, the schematic is not proposed as a "centered ontology of sexual difference" but refers to a decentered and multiply organized phenomenology of the psyche or self "in which subjectivity emerges through shifting multiple identifications that refer to an inconsistent though pervasive binary" (Benjamin, 1998, p. 47). In this way, I aim to account for the inclusion of various gendered experiences that transcend anatomical limits, "bigendered aspects of the self" deriving from, according to Benjamin (1998), "the postoedipal recuperation of overinclusiveness, [making] it possible to express different sexual positions in the same narrative without threat to the psyche . . . [allowing] for a kind of multiplicity regarding gender" (p. 72).

The position of the Subjective Object reflects the awareness of self-experience as an object for others that is, nevertheless, affectively attuned and agentic. This is the experience of a public self and can include the fantasy of the self from the other's point of view (a reflective function).

All of these positions can converge; that is, an individual can engage more than one at the same time, as when an individual reflects upon herself (engaging the Reflective Self) while expressing her thoughts to another (as a Subjective Object). In addition, there are certain self-states that are usually private but may become public, thereby converging with another position, as when one is immersed in an experience (from within the Embodied Subject) and then becomes aware of someone watching. This awareness moves the individual to the position of a Subjective Object, despite that he or she did not choose this. What was a private experience has now become, at least partially, public.

In the introduction to this book, the case of Becky was introduced in order to illustrate her imbalanced reckoning with her 'phallic' strivings. In the language of the proposed binary, I suggested that she can be viewed as trapped in the 'feminine' side of a traditional masculine/feminine binary, i.e., her lack of agency is a reflection of the inadequate development of her *potency* or strength. If we consider the position of the Embodied Subject as the self-state of maximal engagement, with the dual capacities of receptivity to feelingful involvement along with the potent articulation of individual selfhood, then *strengthening a person's capacity to inhabit the position of the Embodied Subject is a central clinical aim.* This can be demonstrated as Becky has moved along her trajectory during treatment.

Reprinting the case of Becky here, I have tracked the shifting and overlapping self-states as Becky moves from one position to another, all of which depict the changing perspectives she can take from within herself and the extent to which each is affectively attuned and/or agentic. I have noted the positions in italics within the vignette, with a discussion of each following. All of the positions are identified based on Becky's subjective and phenomenal experience (as opposed to my perspective in observing and experiencing her). As discussed in the Introduction, this case is an illustration of the ways in which Becky struggles with her potency—how to express herself without losing her 'femininity'—trapped as she has been in a stereotypical binarial construction of gender.

You will recall that, at the beginning of our treatment, Becky was a 53-year-old, married woman with three children. She is a highly placed executive in a Fortune 500 company. She is having an affair with a bouncer/ body-builder whom she met at a bar, and she revels in the way he "makes her feel feminine" (*Reflective Self as a Subjective Object*). From the start, Becky has struggled to break up with him, readily admitting to me, "He has no place in my life and could be dangerous to my marriage and family" (*Reflective Self as a Subjective Object*). Each session she tells me (*Reflective Self as a Subjective Object*) and herself (*Reflective Self*) that she will stop seeing him, yet ends up having sex with him (*Objectified Self*), sometimes directly after our session, despite her conviction never to see him again. He is unreliable, self-centered, and controlling; he causes her much emotional distress (*Subjective Object*) in his unavailability except when he spontaneously calls her for a quickie (*Objectified Self*).

If we examine the foregoing description, we can track the shifts in Becky's self-states, i.e., the ways in which she experiences and expresses herself from the variety of subjective positions. When she thinks about how her lover "makes her feel feminine," she is engaging her Reflective Self to observe her Embodied Subjectivity (her feelingful experience). When she states this *to me*, she is both in her reflective position and displaying her reflective capacities to me, i.e., she speaks from within her Reflective Self as a Subjective Object. Similarly, when she thinks that her lover "has no place in my life and could be dangerous to my marriage and family," she is speaking from within her Reflective Self and, when she states this to me, she is engaging her Reflective Self as a Subjective Object. Her conviction to stop seeing him is derived from her self-reflexive efforts as well, both privately and when publically stated (to me).

In contrast, when Becky "ends up having sex with him" she does so from a more objectified position—here, the question is to differentiate between herself as a Subjective Object and herself engaged as an Objectified Self. The latter position is derived from her capacity to be an object for others but disconnected from her own agentic and feelingful states. (The distinction between the Subjective Object and the Objectified Self depends on her conscious and unconscious experience of

Conclusion: positions of subjectivity

herself, i.e., the extent to which she is affectively attuned to herself in the experience and is *agentically* participating in the experience.) We know that Becky is not engaged as a Subjective Object because of her disclaimed way of describing her experience, i.e., she "ends up" having sex with him as if she did not choose to do so.

When Becky experiences and reports the emotional distress this relationship causes her, it is a feelingful state; however, it is largely derived from her experience of herself as the passive recipient of his unwanted actions. This is, for Becky, a private experience, though she can shift and reflect upon it, either with me (in her Reflective Self as a Subjective Object) or in solitude (engaging her Reflective Self). However, her passive language reveals an imbalanced reckoning within herself as a potent and receptive subject, at least in this relationship, and thereby is not reflective of an engagement with her Embodied Subjectivity.

For the purposes of the treatment, I am focused on enhancing Becky's agency and power, expanding her receptivity and affective attunement with her desires, her ability to know what she wants, as well as her capacities to reflect upon all of this. In this way, I am helping her use her Reflective Self and her experiences as a Subjective Object and Objectified Self to become more attuned to herself as an agentic or potent subject so as to gain control of her tendency to objectify herself in a non-agentic way. As her agentic capacities have developed and expanded, she has become more flexible in alternating among these positions. Her experience from within her Objectified Self (by definition non-agentic) has become more feelingful (embodied) and potent (agentic—what we usually mean by authorized or within her conscious control). It is now more accurate to describe her self-states with her lover as engaging herself as a Subjective Object or Embodied Subject as opposed to an Objectified Self.

These vignettes above can usefully be compared to a more recent interaction during our treatment. Tracking the nature of Becky's subjective positions demonstrates her transformation and, in particular, her capacity to inhabit the central position of the Embodied Subject, as she does throughout most of this vignette.

Becky was asked to give a speech extemporaneously in front of a very large audience. She described the experience to me, "It wasn't scripted and I was proud. It was spur of the moment and I felt it was really me. Like me there and me here are the same. You know that side of me; it's separate, yet connected. Afterwards, I thought of sending you a picture of Frank (her lover), then I realized I wanted you to see *me*. So you would be proud of me and for yourself too. I couldn't have done this 5 years ago, speaking my mind with such confidence. Just being myself."

In the vignette above, Becky is reflecting upon herself as she experienced her capacities to give an extemporaneous presentation. She credited herself with the ability to do so with confidence, ease, and poise. She remembered enjoying the experience, both during the presentation and, with felt-pride, afterwards. She recognized no need either to disclaim her actions or to disavow or minimize her strengths. Being a potent woman neither threatened her affectively attuned capacities nor destabilized her experience of herself as a woman. We could say that she had come to a more healthy balance of the dual capacities for *receptivity* (to affective engagement) and *potent strength* (an individuated articulation of her subjectivity). This more balanced reckoning reflects a strengthened capacity to experience herself as an Embodied Subject while flexibly alternating among other positions as well, including the capacities to reflect on herself and to engage with others without losing any sense of strength, separateness, or affective vitality.

Notes

1 I refer here to the distinction between the clinical (and developmental) need for a unified self and the constructed subject of cultural discourse, usefully clarified by Benjamin (1998) as occupying different levels of abstraction. Stein (1995b) proposes a dialectical tension between these two systems. Benjamin (1988) refers to a continually oscillating tension.
2 See Gonzalez (2013), for a discussion of the perverse attempt to "be nothing" (p. 420).
3 This core self has been referred to as decentered (Ogden, 1994), divided (Laing, 1960), continuous yet split (Benjamin, 1995; Grotstein, 2000), multiple (Mitchell, 1993, 1996; Bromberg, 1998; Davies, 1998a; Dimen, 2003; Harris, 2005a) and, only in an illusory way, 'interior' (Merleau-Ponty, 1962; Foehl, 2009; Folkmarson Kall, 2009).
4 This schematic leans heavily on the differentiations proposed by many theorists. For the interested reader, the Subjective Object includes Bollas' (1982) discussion of the relation to the self as an object, in which the individual recreates aspects of the mother's facilitation of his existence. Similarly, Dimen (2008) speaks of subject-as-object, the self as object to itself. Ogden's (1994) ideas of self and the phenomenology of subjectivity also overlap with many of these categories. Sweetnam (1996) applies the Kleinian notion of positions in a more general way in relation to gender. "The Reflective Self" denotes the position that embodies self-reflexive functioning, as Aron (1998) discusses. Grotstein (2000) denotes similar ideas in his "Phenomenal Subject and the Ineffable Subject of the Unconscious." Crastnopol (2007) discusses a spectrum of self-experience on multiple levels that include private and public domains, especially as these relate to self-esteem. Cornell (2008) also speaks of the body in relation to itself. Orange (2010) has also referred to a "body-subject." Summers' (2013) "Experiencing Subject" combines many of these positions as the essential subject of analysis. Finally, Guralnik and Simeon (2010) have investigated the processes of depersonalization and offered a model that accounts for the structuring forces of social discourse, i.e., the ways in which one's sense of personhood is recognized and interpellated (given social significance). According to them, the self-in-itself exists in a space between recognition and interpellation, where personhood either meets in synchronous relation to the social order or collides in a traumatic impasse, the latter culminating in a depersonalized experience.
5 Guralnick and Simeon (2010) make a useful distinction between repressed contents as *thing-representations* in contrast to dissociated structures that "delink states rather than things, matrixes of self-other relationships and their related affects" (p. 402).
6 See Gentile (2006a, b) for a discussion of the ways in which embodied language as primary process can be used in treatment instead of interpreting through psychoanalytic words.
7 See Howell (2005), Sands (2010) and Sweetnam (2010) for an elaborated discussion of different types of dissociation and the ability to flexibly move among a variety of conscious, nonconscious, and unconscious self-states.
8 Though this schematic is largely compatible with Bromberg's (1998) multiple self-states, I do not think it is helpful to imagine *spaces* between various positions. While

the individual is capable of positioning him/herself in such a way that can flexibly access various positions, each position too is a self-state. There is no stepping outside of a self-state, just as there is no experience that is not embodied. In effect, there are no spaces; we are always in a self-state, and we are always embodied.
9 See Hartman (2010a) for a cogent discussion of how (self) states simultaneously incorporate and resist pressures from the (social) State.
10 Benjamin (2013) comments that the term Embodied Subjectivity should be redundant; however, it is not, due to the history of mind/body duality in Western philosophical thought.

References

Abel-Hirsch, N. (2006). The perversion of pain, pleasure and thought: On the difference between "suffering" an experience and the construction of a thing to be used. In D. Nobus & L. Downing (Eds.), *Perversion: psychoanalytic perspectives. Perspectives on psychoanalysis* (pp. 99–107). London, England: Karnac.

Amir, D. (2013). The chameleon language of perversion. *Psychoanalytic Dialogues, 23,* 393–407.

Aron, L. (1995). The internalized primal scene. *Psychoanalytic Dialogues, 5,* 195–237.

Aron, L. (1996). *A meeting of minds: Mutuality in psychoanalysis.* Northvale, NJ: The Analytic Press.

Aron, L. (1998). The clinical body and the reflexive mind. In L. Aron & F. Sommer Anderson (Eds.), *Relational perspectives on the body* (pp. 3–37). Hillsdale, NJ: The Analytic Press.

Aron, L. (2006). Analytic impasse and the third: Clinical implications of intersubjectivity theory. *International Journal of Psychoanalysis, 87,* 349–368.

Aron, L. (2011). The analyst's vulnerability: How "the repudiation of femininity" remains bedrock: Ghosts, monsters, mulattoes, queers, undecidables, and other thirds. Paper presented at *The Therapeutic Action of Psychodynamic Psychotherapy Conference*, March, Boston, MA.

Aron, L. & Sommer Anderson, F. (Eds.). (1998). *Relational perspectives on the body.* Hillsdale, NJ: The Analytic Press.

Aronofsky, D. (Dir.). (2010). *Black swan.* Fox Searchlight Pictures.

Atkinson, S., & Gabbard, G. (1995). Erotic transference in the male adolescent-female analyst dyad. *Psychoanalytic Study of the Child, 50,* 171–186.

Atlas, G. (2012). Touch me know me. Erotic countertransference: From boundary violation to therapeutic action. Paper presented at APA-Division 39 Spring Meeting, Santa Fe, NM.

Atlas, G. (2013). What's love got to do with it? Sexuality, shame, and the use of the other. *Studies in Gender and Sexuality, 14,* 51–58.

Bach, S. (1994). Being heard: Attunement and the growth of psychic structure. In S. Bach, *The language of perversion and the language of love* (pp. 139–162). New York, NY: Jason Aronson.

Bader, M.J. (1993). Adaptive sadomasochism and psychological growth. *Psychoanalytic Dialogues, 3,* 279–300.

Balsam, R.M. (2001). Integrating male and female elements in a woman's gender identity. *Journal of the American Psychoanalytic Association, 49,* 1335–1360.

Balsam, R.M. (2003). The vanished pregnant body in psychoanalytic female developmental theory. *Journal of the American Psychoanalytic Association, 51*, 1153–1179.
Balsam, R.M. (2008). Women showing off: Notes on female exhibitionism. *Journal of the American Psychoanalytic Association, 56*, 99–121.
Balsam, R.M. (2012). *Women's bodies in psychoanalysis*. New York, NY: Routledge.
Barrett, M.M. (2003). Desire and the couch: Perspectives from both sides of the analytic encounter. *Psychoanalytic Psychology, 20*, 167–169.
Bass, A. (2000). *Difference and disavowal: The trauma of Eros*. Stanford, CA: Stanford University Press.
Bassin, D. (1996). Beyond the he and the she: Toward the reconciliation of masculinity and femininity in the postoedipal female mind. *Journal of the American Psychoanalytic Association, 44S*, 157–190.
Bassin, D. (Ed.). (1999). *Female sexuality: Contemporary engagements*. New York, NY: Jason Aronson.
Becker, S. (2005). Female body-self and perversion. Why women differ from men in the way they externalize their sexualized aggression. *Forum der Psychoanalyse: Zeitschrift fur klinische Theorie & Praxis, 21*(3), 242–254.
Benjamin, J. (1988). *The bonds of love: Psychoanalysis, feminism and the problem of domination*. New York, NY: Basic Books.
Benjamin, J. (1994a). What angel would hear me? The erotics of transference. *Psychoanalytic Inquiry, 14*, 535–557.
Benjamin, J. (1994b). Commentary on papers by Tansey, Davies, and Hirsch. *Psychoanalytic Dialogues, 4*, 193–201.
Benjamin, J. (1995). *Like subjects, love objects*. New Haven, Yale University Press.
Benjamin, J. (1997). Psychoanalysis as a vocation. *Psychoanalytic Dialogues, 7*, 781–802.
Benjamin, J. (1998). *Shadow of the other: Intersubjectivity and gender in psychoanalysis*. New York, NY: Routledge.
Benjamin, J. (2004). Beyond doer and done to: An intersubjective view of thirdness. *Psychoanalytic Quarterly, 73*, 5–46.
Benjamin, J. (2013). Embodiment and subjectivity: Discussion. Panel presentation at the American Psychoanalytic Association Meeting, Winter, New York.
Benvenuto, S. (2003). On perversions. *Journal Lacanian Studies, 1*, 243–260.
Birksted-Breen, D. (Ed.). (1993). *The gender conundrum: Contemporary psychoanalytic perspectives on femininity and masculinity*. London, England: Routledge.
Blechner, M.J. (2009). *Sex changes: Transformations in society and psychoanalysis*. New York, NY: Routledge.
Blos, P. (1991). Sadomasochism and the defense against recall of painful affect. *Journal of the American Psychoanalytic Association, 39*, 417–430.
Blum, H.P. (1991). Sadomasochism in the psychoanalytic process, within and beyond the pleasure principle: Discussion. *Journal of the American Psychoanalytic Association, 39*(2), 431–450.
Bollas, C. (1982). On the relation to the self as an object. *International Journal of Psychoanalysis, 63*, 347–359.
Bollas, C. (1983). Expressive uses of the countertransference: Notes to the patient from oneself. *Contemporary Psychoanalysis, 19*, 1–33.
Bollas, C. (1987). *The Shadow of the object: Psychoanalysis of the unthought known*. New York: Columbia University Press.

Bollas, C. (1994). Aspects of the erotic transference. *Psychoanalytic Inquiry*, *14*, 573–590.
Bolognini, S. (1994). Transference: Erotised, erotic, loving, affectionate. *International Journal of Psychoanalysis*, *75*, 73–86.
Bolognini, S. (2011). The analyst's awkward gift: Balancing recognition of sexuality with parental protectiveness. *Psychoanalytic Quarterly*, *LXXX*, 33–54.
Bonasia, E. (2001). The countertransference: Erotic, erotized and perverse. *International Journal of Psychoanalysis*, *82*, 249–262.
Bonner, S. (2006). A servant's bargain: Perversion as survival. *International Journal of Psychoanalysis*, *87*, 1549–1567.
Britton, R. (2004). Subjectivity, objectivity, and triangular space. *Psychoanalytic Quarterly*, *73*, 47–61.
Bromberg, P. (1998). *Standing in the spaces: Essays on clinical process, trauma and dissociation*. Hillsdale, NJ: The Analytic Press.
Bucci, W. (2008). The role of bodily experience in emotional organization: new perspectives on the multiple code theory. In F. Sommer Anderson (Ed.), *Bodies in treatment: The unspoken dimension* (pp. 51–76). New York, NY: The Analytic Press.
Butler, J. (1993). *Bodies that matter*. New York, NY: Routledge.
Butler, J. (1995). Melancholy gender – refused identification. *Psychoanalytic Dialogues*, *5*, 165–180.
Butler, J. (2006). *Gender trouble: Feminism and the subversion of identity*. New York, NY: Routledge.
Carveth, D.L. (2010). How today may we distinguish healthy sexuality from "perversion"? *Canadian Journal of Psychoanalysis*, *18*, 298–305.
Celenza, A. (1993). Toward an integration of the mind and brain. In J. Ellison, C. Weinstein & T. Hodel-Malonofsky (Eds.), *Psychotherapist's guide to neuropsychiatric patients* (pp. 617–632). Washington, DC: American Psychiatric Press.
Celenza, A. (1995). Love and hate in the countertransference. *Psychotherapy*, *32*(2), 301–307.
Celenza, A. (2000). Sadomasochistic relating: What's sex got to do with it? *Psychoanalytic Quarterly*, *69*(3), 527–543.
Celenza, A. (2005). Vis-à-vis the couch. *International Journal of Psychoanalysis*, *86*(6), 1645–1659.
Celenza, A. (2006). Hyperconfidentiality and the illusion of the dyad. Paper presented at the Philadelphia Psychoanalytic Society and Institute, Philadelphia, PA.
Celenza, A. (2007). *Sexual boundary violations: Therapeutic, supervisory and academic contexts*. New York, NY: Jason Aronson.
Celenza, A. (2010a). The analyst's needs and desires. *Psychoanalytic Dialogues*, *20*, 60–69.
Celenza, A. (2010b). The guilty pleasure of erotic countertransference: Searching for radial true. *Studies in Gender and Sexuality*, *11*(4), 175–183.
Celenza, A. (2011). Touching the patient. In S. Akhtar (Ed.), *Unusual interventions: Alternations of the frame, method, and relationship in psychotherapy and psychoanalysis* (pp. 165–176). London, England: Karnac.
Celenza, A. (2012). From binarial constraints to gender multiplicity: Steve Mitchell's contributions to gender and beyond. Paper presented at the International Association for Psychoanalysis and Psychotherapy, New York.
Celenza, A., & Gabbard, G.O. (2003). Analysts who commit sexual boundary violations: A lost cause? *Journal of the American Psychoanalytic Association*, *51*(2), 617–636.

Chasseguet-Smirgel, J. (1970). *Female sexuality: New psychoanalytic views*. London, England: Karnac.
Chasseguet-Smirgel, J. (1983). Perversion and the universal law. *International Review of Psycho-Analysis, 10*, 293–301.
Chasseguet-Smirgel, J. (1984). *Creativity and perversion*. New York, NY: Norton.
Chasseguet-Smirgel, J. (1993). Freud and female sexuality: The consideration of some blind spots in the exploration of the 'dark continent.' In D. Birksted-Breen (Ed.), *The gender conundrum: Contemporary psychoanalytic perspectives on femininity and masculinity* (pp. 105–124). London, England: Routledge.
Chodorow, N.J. (1978). *The reproduction of mothering*. Berkeley, CA: University of California Press.
Chodorow, N.J. (1995). Multiplicities and uncertainties of gender: Commentary on Ruth Stein's "Analysis of a case of transsexualism." *Psychoanalytic Dialogues, 5*, 291–299.
Chodorow, N.J. (2004). Beyond sexual difference: Clinical individuality and same-sex cross-generation relations in the creation of feminine and masculine. In I. Matthis (Ed.), *Dialogues on sexuality, gender, and psychoanalysis* (pp. 181–203). London, England: Karnac.
Chodorow, N.J. (2011). *Individualizing gender and sexuality: Theory and practice*. New York, NY: Routledge.
Civitarese, G. (in press). Between "other" and "other": Merleau–Ponty as a precursor of the analytic field. *Fort Da*.
Coen, S. (1992). *The misuse of persons: Analyzing pathological deependency* (pp. 190–208). Hillsdale, NJ: The Analytic Press.
Coen, S. (1994). Barriers to love between patient and analyst. *Journal of the American Psychoanalytic Association, 42*(4), 107–1135.
Coen, S. (1998). Perverse defenses in neurotic patients. *Journal of the American Psychoanalytic Association, 46*, 1169–1194.
Cooper, A.M. (1973). The narcissistic-masochistic character. In R.A. Glick & D. I. Meyers (Eds.) (1988) *Masochism: Current psychoanalytic perspectives* (pp. 117–138). Hillsdale, NJ: The Analytic Press.
Cooper, S.H. (1998). Flirting, post–Oedipus, and mutual protectiveness in the analytic dyad: Commentary on paper by Jody Messler Davies. *Psychoanalytic Dialogues, 8*, 767–779.
Cooper, S.H. (2000). *Objects of hope: Exploring possibility and limit in psychoanalysis*. New York, NY: Routledge.
Corbett, K. (2008). Gender now. *Psychoanalytic Dialogues, 18*, 838–856.
Corbett, K. (2009). *Boyhoods: Rethinking masculinities*. New Haven, CN: Yale University Press.
Corbett, K. (2013). Shifting sexual cultures, the potential space of online relations and the promise of psychoanalytic listening. *Journal of the American Psychoanalytic Association, 61*, 25–44.
Cornell, W.F. (2008). Self in action: The bodily basis of self–organization. In F. Sommer Anderson (Ed.), *Bodies in treatment: The unspoken dimension* (pp. 51–76). New York, NY: The Analytic Press.
Cornell, W.F. (2009). Stranger to desire: Entering the erotic field. *Studies in Gender and Sexuality, 10*, 75–92.
Crastnopol, M. (2007). The multiplicity of self–worth. *Contemporary Psychoanalysis, 43*, 1–16.

Davies, J.M. (1994). Love in the afternoon: A relational reconsideration of desire and dread in the countertransference. *Psychoanalytic Dialogues*, *4*, 153–170.

Davies, J.M. (1998a). Multiple perspectives on multiplicity. *Psychoanalytic Dialogues*, *8*(2), 195–206.

Davies, J.M. (1998b). Between the disclosure and foreclosure of erotic transference–countertransference: Can psychoanalysis find a place for adult sexuality? *Psychoanalytic Dialogues*, *8*, 747–766.

Davies, J.M. (1998c). Thoughts on the nature of desires: The ambiguous, the transitional, and the poetic. Reply to commentaries. *Psychoanalytic Dialogues*, *8*, 805–823.

Davies, J.M. (2001). Erotic overstimulation and the co–construction of sexual meanings in transference–countertransference experience. *Psychoanalytic Quarterly*, *70*, 757–788.

Davies, J.M. (2003). Falling in love with love: Oedipal and postoedipal manifestations of idealization, mourning, and erotic masochism. *Psychoanalytic Dialogues*, *13*, 1–27.

de Masi, F. (2012). The erotic transference: Dream or delusion? *Journal of the American Psychoanalytic Association*, *60*, 1199–1220.

de Peyer, J. (2002). Private terrors: Sexualized aggression and a psychoanalyst's fear of her patient. *Psychoanalytic Dialogues*, *12*, 509–530.

Deutsch, H. (1930). The significance of masochism in the mental life of women. *International Journal of Psychoanalysis*, *11*, 48–60.

Diamond, D. (1993). The paternal transference: A bridge to the erotic oedipal transference. *Psychoanalytic Inquiry*, *13*, 206–225.

Diamond, M.J. (2004). Accessing the multitude within: A psychoanalytic perspective on the transformation of masculinity at mid–life. *International Journal of Psychoanalysis*, *85*, 45–64.

Diamond, M.J. (2009). Masculinity and its discontents: Making room for the "mother" inside the male – An essential achievement for healthy male gender identity. In B. Reis & R. Grossmark (Eds.), *Heterosexual Masculinities: Contemporary Perspectives from Psychoanalytic Gender Theory* (pp. 23–53). New York, NY: Routledge.

Dimen, M. (1986). *Surviving sexual contradictions: A startling and different look at a day in the life of a contemporary professional woman*. New York, NY: Macmillan.

Dimen, M. (1991). Deconstructing difference: Gender, splitting, and transitional space. *Psychoanalytic Dialogues*, *1*, 335–352.

Dimen, M. (1998). Polyglot bodies: Thinking through the relational. In L. Aron & F. Sommer Anderson (Eds.), *Relational perspectives on the body* (pp. 64–96). Hillsdale, NJ: The Analytic Press.

Dimen, M. (1999). Between lust and libido: Sex, psychoanalysis, and the moment before. *Psychoanalytic Dialogues*, *9*, 415–440.

Dimen, M. (2001). Perversion is us? Eight notes. *Psychoanalytic Dialogues*, *11*(6), 825–860.

Dimen, M. (2003). *Sexuality, intimacy, power*. Hillsdale, NJ: The Analytic Press.

Dimen, M. (2008). Remarks on body-writing: Feminist, one-person, and two-person views. Paper presented at Division 39 Spring Meeting, New York City.

Dimen, M. & Goldner, V. (Eds.). (2002). *Gender in Psychoanalytic Space*. New York, NY: Other Press.

Donnell, M. (2013). Who's afraid of the old, gay man? *Studies in Gender and Sexuality*, *14*, 108–111.

Duvall, R. (2002). *Assassination tango*. United Artists.

Ehrenberg, D.B. (1992). *The intimate edge: Extending the reach of psychoanalytic interaction*. New York, NY: W. W. Norton.

Eiguer, A. (2005). A defiance of clinical metapsychology: Does a female perversion exist? *Intersubjectivo, 7*(1), 67–82.
Eliot, T.S. (1920). The lovesong of J. Alfred Prufrock. In *Prufrock and other observations*. New York, NY: A.A. Knopf.
Elise, D. (1998). Gender repertoire: Body, mind and bisexuality. *Psychoanalytic Dialogues, 8*, 353–372.
Elise, D. (2002a). Blocked creativity and inhibited erotic transference. *Studies in Gender and Sexuality, 3*, 161–195.
Elise, D. (2002b). The primary maternal oedipal situation and female homoerotic desire. *Psychoanalytic Inquiry, 22*, 209–228.
Elise, D. (2008). Sex and shame: The inhibition of female desires. *Journal of the American Psychoanalytic Association, 56*, 73–98.
Elliott, A. & Spezzano, C. (1996). Psychoanalysis at its limits: Navigating the postmodern turn. *Psychoanalytic Quarterly, 55*, 52–83.
Eyman, J.R. & Gabbard, G.O. (1991). Will therapist–patient sex prevent suicide? *Psychiatric Annals, 21*, 669–674.
Faulkner, W. (1951). *Requiem for a nun*. New York, NY: Random House.
Fausto-Sterling, A. (2000). *Sexing the body: Gender politics and the construction of sexuality*. New York, NY: Basic Books.
Flax, J. (1996). Taking multiplicity seriously: Some implications for psychoanalytic theorizing and practice. *Contemporary Psychoanalysis, 32*, 577–593.
Foehl, J. (2009). Discussion of "Expression between self and other by Lisa Folkmarson Folkmarson Kall." Paper presented at the Boston Psychoanalytic Society and Institute, Boston, Massachusetts.
Fogel, G. (1998). Interiority and inner genital space in men: What else can be lost in castration? *Psychoanalytic Quarterly, 67*, 662–697.
Folkmarson Kall, L.F. (2009). Expression between self and other. Paper presented at the Boston Psychoanalytic Society and Institute, Boston, Massachusetts.
Fonagy, P. (2008). A genuinely developmental theory of sexual enjoyment and its implications for psychoanalytic technique. *Journal of the American Psychoanalytic Association, 56*, 11–36.
Foucault, M. (1978). *The history of sexuality* (Vol. I). New York, NY: Vintage.
Frayn, D.H. & Silberfeld, M. (1986). Erotic transferences. *Canadian Journal Psychiatry, 31*, 323–327.
Freud, S. (1905/1961). Three essays on the theory of sexuality. *Complete psychological works of Sigmund Freud*. (Standard Edition, Vol. 7, pp. 125–243). London, England: Hogarth Press.
Freud, S. (1915/1961). Observations on transference love. *Complete psychological works of Sigmund Freud*. (Standard Edition, Vol. 12, pp. 157–171). London, England: Hogarth Press.
Freud, S. (1924/1961). The economic problem of masochism. *Complete psychological works of Sigmund Freud*. (Standard Edition, Vol. 19, pp. 157–172). London, England: Hogarth Press.
Freud, S. (1927). Fetishism. *Complete psychological works of Sigmund Freud*. (Standard Edition, Vol. 21, pp. 152–157). London, England: Hogarth Press.
Gabbard, G.O. (1994). Commentary on papers by Tansey, Hirsch, and Davies. *Psychoanalytic Dialogues, 4*, 203–213.

Gabbard, G.O. (1996). The analyst's contribution to the erotic transference. *Contemporary Psychoanalysis, 32*, 249.
Gabbard, G.O. (1998). Commentary on paper by Jody Messler Davies. *Psychoanalytic Dialogues, 8*, 781–789.
Gabbard, G.O. (2012). Masochism as a multiply-determined phenomenon. In D. Holtzman & N. Kulish (Eds.), *The clinical problem of masochism* (pp. 103–112). New York, NY: Jason Aronson.
Gabbard, G.O., & Lester, E. (1995). *Boundaries and boundary violations in psychoanalysis*. New York, NY: Basic Books.
Gediman, H.K. (2005). Premodern, modern and postmodern perspectives on sex and gender mixes. *Journal of the American Psychoanalytic Association, 53*, 1059–1078.
Gentile, J. (2013). From "truth or dare" to "show and tell": Reflections on childhood ritual, play and the evolution of symbolic life. *Psychoanalytic Dialogues, 23*, 150–169.
Gentile, K. (2006a). *Creating bodies: Eating disorders as self-destructive survival*. Hillsdale, NJ: The Analytic Press.
Gentile, K. (2006b). Words just don't cut it: Commentary on paper by Mary E. Sonntag. *Psychoanalytic Dialogues, 16*, 333–339.
Gerson, S. (2003). Response to Ruth Stein's paper, "Why Perversion." Posted for IARPP's online colloquium series, December, 2003.
Ghent, E. (1990). Masochism, submission, surrender – Masochism as a perversion of surrender. *Contemporary Psychoanalysis, 26*, 108–136.
Ghent, E. (1992). Paradox and process. *Psychoanalytic Dialogues, 2*, 135–159.
Gilligan, C. (1982). *In a different voice*. Cambridge, MA: Harvard University Press.
Goldberg, A. (1995). *The problem of perversion*. New Haven, CN: Yale University Press.
Goldberger, M. & Evans, D. (1985). On transference manifestations in male patients with female analysts. *International Journal of Psychoanalysis, 66*, 295–309.
Goldberger, M. & Holmes, D. (1993). Transferences in male patients with female analysts. An update. *Psychoanalytic Inquiry, 13*, 173–191.
Goldner, V. (1991). Toward a critical relational theory of gender. *Psychoanalytic Dialogues, 1*, 249–272.
Goldner, V. (2003). Ironic gender/authentic sex. *Studies in Gender & Sexuality, 4*, 113–139.
Goldner, V. (2011). Trans: Gender in free fall. *Psychoanalytic Dialogues, 21*, 159–171.
Gonzalez, F.J. (2010). Panel report: Perversion. *International Journal of Psychoanalysis, 91*, 380–383.
Gonzalez, F.J. (2013). Talking with chameleons: The role of language-games and setting: Commentary on paper by Dana Amir. *Psychoanalytic Dialogues, 23*, 418–422.
Good, M.I. (2006). Perverse dreams and dreams of perversion. *Psychoanalytic Quarterly, LXXV*, 1005–1044.
Gornick, L.K. (1986). Developing a new narrative: The woman therapist and the male patient. *Psychoanalytic Psychology, 3*(4), 299–325.
Gray, J. (2009). *Two Lovers*. Tempesta Films.
Green, A. (1995). Has sexuality anything to do with psychoanalysis? *International Journal of Psychoanalysis, 76*, 871–883.
Grossman, L. (1992). An example of "character perversion" in a woman. *Psychoanalytic Quarterly, 61*(4), 581–589.
Grossman, L. (1995). A woman with a nipple fetish. *Psychoanalytic Quarterly, 64*(4), 746–748.

Grotstein, J. (2000). *Who is the dreamer who dreams the dream?* Hillsdale, NJ: The Analytic Press.
Guralnik, O., & Simeon, D. (2010). Depersonalization: Standing in the spaces between recognition and interpellation. *Psychoanalytic Dialogues, 20*, 400–416.
Halberstam, J. (2005). *In a queer time and place: Transgender bodies, subcultural lives.* New York, NY: New York University Press.
Harlem, A. (2010). Exile as a dissociative state: When a self is "lost in transit". *Psychoanalytic Psychology, 27*, 460–474.
Harris, A. (1991). Gender as contradiction. *Psychoanalytic Dialogues, 1*, 197–224.
Harris, A. (1997). Aggression, envy and ambition: Circulating tensions in women's psychic life. *Gender and Psychoanalysis, 2*, 291–325.
Harris, A. (1998). Psychic envelopes and sonorous baths. In L. Aron & F. Sommer Anderson (Eds.), *Relational perspectives on the body* (pp. 39–64). Hillsdale, NJ: The Analytic Press.
Harris, A. (2005a). *Gender as soft assembly.* Hillsdale, NJ: The Analytic Press.
Harris, A. (2005b). Tomboys' stories. In A. Harris, *Gender as Soft Assembly* (pp. 131–153). Hillsdale, NJ: The Analytic Press.
Harris, A. (2008). The analyst's melancholy and the analyst's omnipotence. Paper presented at the Boston Psychoanalytic Society and Institute, Boston, MA.
Hartman, S. (2010a). L'etat c'est moi – Except when I am not: Commentary on paper by Orna Guranlik and Daphne Simeon. *Psychoanalytic Dialogues, 20*, 428–436.
Hartman, S. (2010b). Ruined by pleasure: Commentary on Steven Botticelli and Jeffrey R. Guss. *Studies in Gender and Sexuality, 11*, 141–145.
Hartman, S. (2013). On making reparation to the analyst's idolized countertransference: Commentary on paper by Dana Amir. *Psychoanalytic Dialogues, 23*, 408–417.
Herzog, J. (2001). *Father hunger.* Hillsdale, NJ: The Analytic Press.
Hilferding, M. (1911/1974). Zur Grundlage der Mutterliebe. In *Protokolle der Wiener Psychoanalytischen Vereinigung III.* (On the basis of mother–love. In (1974) *Minutes of the Vienna Psychoanalytic Society III* (pp. 112–125). New York, NY: International Universities Press.
Hirsch, I. (1994). Countertransference love and theoretical model. *Psychoanalytic Dialogues, 4*, 171–192.
Hirsch, I. (2008). *Coasting in the countertransference: Conflicts of self-interest between analyst and patient.* New York, NY: Routledge.
Hirsch, I. (2010). On some advantages of mutual sexual fantasy in the analytic situation: Commentary on paper by Christopher Bonovitz. *Psychoanalytic Dialogues, 20*, 654–662.
Hoffer, A. (1996). Asymmetry and mutuality in the analytic relationship: Contemporary lessons from the Freud–Ferenczi dialogue. In P.L. Rudnytsky, A. Bokay & P. Giampieri–Deutsch (Eds.), *Ferenczi's turn in psychoanalysis* (pp. 107–119). New York, NY: New York University Press.
Hoffman, I.Z. (1998). Poetic transformations of erotic experience: Commentary on paper by Jody Messler Davies. *Psychoanalytic Dialogues, 8*, 791–804.
Hoffman, I.Z. (2009). Therapeutic passion in the countertransference. *Psychoanalytic Dialogues, 19*, 617–637.
Hoffman, I.Z. (2013). Therapeutic passion in the countertransference. Discussion on IARPP list–serve, May.

Holtzman, D., & Kulish, N. (1997). *Nevermore: The hymen and the loss of virginity.* Northvale, NJ: Jason Aronson.
Holtzman, D. & Kulish, N. (2000). The femininization of the female oedipal complex, Part I: A reconsideration of the significance of separation issues. *Journal of the American Psychoanalytic Association, 48,* 1413–1437.
Holtzman, D., & Kulish, N. (Eds.) (2012). *The clinical problem of masochism.* New York, NY: Jason Aronson.
Horney, K. (1926). The flight from womanhood: The masculinity-complex in women as viewed by men and women. *International Journal of Psychoanalysis, 7,* 324–339.
Horney, K. (1933). The denial of the vagina – A contribution to the problem of the genital anxieties specific to women. *International Journal of Psychoanalysis, 14,* 57–70.
Housman, H.F. (2012). Exhibitionism in a woman: Showing what cannot yet be told. Paper presented at the American Psychoanalytic Association, Winter Meeting, New York, January.
Howell, E.F. (2005). *The dissociative mind.* New York: Routledge.
Jordan, J.V. (1992). The relational self: A new perspective for understanding women's development. *Contemporary Psychotherapy Review, 7,* 56–71.
Kaplan, L.J. (1991). *Female perversions: The temptations of Emma Bovary.* New York, NY: Doubleday.
Kaplan, L.J. (2000). Further thoughts on female perversions. *Studies in Gender and Sexuality, 1,* 349–370.
Kaplan, L.J. (2006). *Cultures of fetishism.* New York, NY: Palgrave/Macmillan.
Karme, L. (1979). The analysis of a male patient by a female analyst: The problem of the negative oedipal transference. *International Journal of Psychoanalysis, 60,* 253–261.
Kavaler-Adler, S. (1992). Mourning and erotic transference. *International Journal of Psychoanalysis, 73,* 527–539.
Kernberg, O.F. (1991a). Aggression and love in the relationship of the couple. *Journal of the American Psychoanalytic Association, 39,* 45–70.
Kernberg, O.F. (1991b). Sadomasochism, sexual excitement and perversion. *Journal of the American Psychoanalytic Association, 39,* 333–362.
Kernberg, O.F. (1994). Love in the analytic settting. *Journal of the American Psychoanalytic Association, 42,* 1137–1157.
Kernberg, O.F. (2011). *The inseparable nature of love and aggression: Clinical and theoretical perspectives.* New York, NY: American Psychiatric Publishing.
Kestenberg, J. (1982). The inner genital phase: Prephallic and preoedipal. In D. Mendel (Ed.), *Early female development* (pp. 81–126). New York, NY: S. P. Medical and Scientific Books.
Khan, M.M.R. (1979). Fetish as negation of the self: Clinical notes on foreskin fetishism in a male homosexual. In M.M.R. Khan, *Alienation in perversions* (pp. 139–176). New York, NY: International Universities Press.
Khan, M.M.R. (1989). *Alienation in perversions.* London, England: Karnac.
Kierkegaard, S. (1983). *The sickness unto death: The Christian psychological exposition for upbuilding and awakening (Kierkegaard's Writings, Vol. 19).* Princeton, NJ: Princeton University Press.
Knafo, D. (2008). The sexual illusionist's final trick. Paper presented at the Symposium on Erotic Transference, Center for Psychoanalytic Organizations, New York, NY.
Knoblauch, S.H. (1995). To speak or not to speak? How and when is that the question?: Commentary on Papers by Davies and Gabbard. *Psychoanalytic Dialogues, 5,* 151–155.
Knoblauch, S.H. (2007). The perversion of language in the analyst's activity: Navigating

the rhythms of embodiment and symbolization. *International Forum Psychoanalysis, 16*, 38–42.

Kohut, H. (1977). *The restoration of the self.* New York: IUP.

Kolod, S. (2002). Between women: Love and combat. *Contemporary Psychoanalysis, 38,* 315–328.

Kris, A.O. (1976). On wanting too much: The "Exceptions" revisited. *International Journal of Psychoanalysis, 57,* 85–95.

Kubie, L.S. (1974). The drive to become both sexes. *Psychoanalytic Quarterly, 43,* 349–426.

Kuchuck, S. (2012). Please (don't) want me: The therapeutic action of male sexual desire in the treatment of heterosexual men. *Contemporary Psychoanalysis, 48,* 544–562.

Kulish, N.M. (2006). Gender and transference: The screen of the phallic mother. In *Gender, countertransference and the erotic transference: Perspectives from analytical psychology and psychoanalysis* (pp. 223–239). London, England: Routledge.

Kumin, I. (1985). Erotic horror: Desire and resistance in the psychoanalytic situation. *International Journal of Psychoanalytic Psychotherapy, 11,* 3–20.

Laing, R.D. (1960). *The divided self.* London, England: Tavistock.

Laplanche, J. (1997). The theory of seduction and the problem of the other. *International Journal of Psychoanalysis, 78,* 653–666.

Layton, L. (2004). *Who's that girl? Who's that boy? Clinical practice meets postmodern gender theory.* New York, NY: Routledge.

Layton, L. (2013). "A bend towards truth": A relational rethinking of perversion. Paper presented at Massachusetts Association for Psychoanalytic Psychotherapy, March.

Lerner, H. (1976). Parental mislabeling of female genitals as a determinant of penis envy and learning inhibitions in women. *Journal of the American Psychoanalytic Association, 24S,* 269–283.

Lester, E. (1985). The female analyst and the erotized transference. *International Journal of Psychoanalysis, 66,* 283–293.

Levine, S.S. (2009). *Loving psychoanalysis: Technique and theory in the therapeutic relationship.* New York: Jason Aronson.

Lichtenberg, J.D. (2008). *Sensuality and sexuality across the divide of shame.* New York, NY: The Analytic Press.

Lieberman, J.S. (2000). *Body talk: Looking and being looked at in psychotherapy.* Northvale, NJ: Jason Aronson.

Lijtmaer, R.M. (2004). The place of erotic transference and countertransference in clinical practice. *Journal of the American Academy of Psychoanalysis, 32,* 483–498.

Lingiardi, V. (2007). Dreaming gender: Restoration and transformation. *Studies in Gender and Sexuality, 8,* 313–331.

Long, K.M. (2005). Panel report: The changing language of female development. *Journal of the American Psychoanalytic Association, 53*(4), 1161–1174.

Mann, D. (1994). The psychotherapist's erotic subjectivity. *British Journal of Psychotherapy, 10*(3), 344–354.

Mann, D. (1997). *Psychotherapy: An erotic relationship.* New York, NY: Routledge.

Marber, P. (1997). *Closer.* New York, NY: Grove Press.

Maroda, K.J. (2002). *Seduction, surrender and transformation: Emotional engagement in the analytic process.* New York, NY: Routledge.

Maroda, K.J. (2012). *Psychodynamic techniques: Working with emotion in the therapeutic relationship.* New York, NY: Guilford.

McDougall, J. (1986). Identifications, neoneeds and neosexualities. *International Journal of Psychoanalysis, 67*, 19–31.
McDougall, J. (1992). *Plea for a measure of abnormality.* New York, NY: Brunner/Mazel.
McDougall, J. (1995). *The many faces of Eros.* New York, NY: Norton.
McGinley, E. & Sabbadini, A. (2006). "Play Misty for me" (1971): The perversion of love. *International Journal of Psychoanalysis, 87*, 589–597.
Merleau-Ponty, M. (1948). *The world of perception.* (O. Davis, trans.). London and New York, NY: Routledge, 2004.
Merleau-Ponty, M. (1962). *Phenomenology of perception.* New York, NY: Routledge.
Miller, J.B. (1976). *Towards a new psychology of women.* Boston, MA: Beacon Press.
Mitchell, S. (1993). *Hope and dread in psychoanalysis.* New York, NY: Basic Books.
Mitchell, S. (1996). Gender and sexual orientation in the age of postmodernism: The plight of the perplexed clinician. *Gender and Psychoanalysis, 1*, 45–73.
Modell, A. (1975). A narcissistic defence against affects and the illusion of self-sufficiency. *International Journal of Psychoanalysis, 56*, 275–282.
Modell, A. (1990). Transference and levels of reality. In A. Modell, *Other times, other realities* (pp. 44–59). Cambridge, MA: Harvard University Press.
Modell, A. (1991). Resistance to the exposure of the private self. *Contemporary Psychoanalysis, 27*, 731–736.
Munoz, J.E. (1999). *Disidentifications: Queers of color and the performance of politics.* Minneapolis, MN: University of Minnesota Press.
Myers, H. (1987). How do women treat men? In G. Fogel (Ed.), *The psychology of men* (pp. 262–275). New York: Basic Books.
Nagliero, G. (2006). Anorexia and perversion: Some reflections about the psychopathogenesis of anorexia nervosa in adolescents. *Analytische Psychologie, 37*(143), 58–78.
Novick, J. & Novick, K. K. (1991). *Fearful symmetry: The development and treatment of sadomasochism.* New York, NY: Jason Aronson.
Ogden, T. (1994). *Subjects of analysis.* Northvale, NJ: Jason Aronson.
Orange, D. (2010). *Thinking for clinicians: Philosophical resources for contemporary psychoanalysis and the humanistic psychotherapies.* New York, NY: Routledge.
Orbach, S. (2000). *The impossibility of sex: Stories of the intimate relationship between therapist and patient.* New York, NY: Simon and Schuster.
Orbach, S. (2006). What can we learn from the therapist's body? In J. Schaverien (Ed.), *Gender, countertransference and the erotic transference: Perspectives from analytical psychology and psychoanalysis* (pp. 198–209). London, England: Routledge.
Orbach, S. (2009). *Bodies.* New York, NY: Picador.
Pacifici, M.P. (2008). The coconstruction of 'psychoanalytic choreography' and the dancing self: Working with an anorectic patient. In F. Sommer Anderson (Ed.), *Bodies in treatment: The unspoken dimension* (pp. 103–125). New York, NY: The Analytic Press.
Pajaczkowska, C., & Ward, I. (2008). *Shame and sexuality: Psychoanalysis and visual culture.* London, England: Routledge.
Palahniuk, C. (1996). *Fight Club.* New York, NY: W.W. Norton.
Parsons, M. (2000). Sexuality and perversion a hundred years on: Discovering what Freud discovered. *International Journal of Psychoanalysis, 81*, 37–49.
Perel, E. (2007). *Mating in captivity: Unlocking erotic intelligence.* New York, NY: Harper Perennial.

Person, E. S. (1985). The erotic transference in women and men: Differences and consequences. *Journal of the American Psychoanalytic Association, 13*, 159–180.

Petrucelli, J. (2008). When a body meets a body: The impact of the therapist's body on eating–disordered patients. In F. Sommer Anderson (Ed.), *Bodies in treatment: The unspoken dimension* (pp. 237–253). New York, NY: The Analytic Press.

Phillips, S. H. (2002). The overstimulation of everyday life: II. Male homosexuality, countertransference, and psychoanalytic treatment. *Annual of Psychoanalysis, 30*, 131–145.

Phillips, S. H. (2003). Homosexuality: Coming out of the confusion. *International Journal of Psychoanalysis, 84*, 1431–1450.

Pines, D. (1993). *A woman's unconscious use of her body: A psychoanalytic perspective*. London, England: Virago Press.

Pizer, S. (1998). *Building bridges: The negotiation of paradox in psychoanalysis*. New York, NY: Routledge.

Puccini, G. (1926). *Turandot*. Milan, Italy: Ricordi & Co.

Purcell, S.D. (2006). The analyst's excitement in the analysis of perversion. *International Journal of Psychoanalysis, 87*, 105–123.

Pynchon, T. (1973). *Gravity's rainbow*. New York, NY: Penguin.

Rabin, H.M. (2003). Love in the countertransference: Controversies and questions. *Psychoanalytic Psychology, 20*, 677–690.

Reis, B. (2009). Names of the father. In B. Reis & R. Grossmark (Eds.), *Heterosexual masculinities: Contemporary perspectives from psychoanalytic gender theory* (pp. 55–72). New York, NY: Routledge.

Reis, B., & Grossmark, R. (2009). *Heterosexual masculinities: Contemporary perspectives from psychoanalytic gender theory*. New York, NY: Routledge.

Renik, O. (1991). The Biblical book of Job: Advice to clinicians. *Psychoanalytic Quarterly, 60*, 596–606.

Renik, O. (1993). Analytic interaction: Conceptualizing technique in the light of the analyst's irreducible subjectivity. *Psychoanalytic Quarterly, 62*, 553–571.

Renik, O. (1999). Playing one's cards face up analysis: An approach to the problem of self-disclosure. *Psychoanalytic Quarterly, 68*, 521–539.

Renn, P. (2013). Moments of meeting: The relational challenges of sexuality in the consulting room. *British Journal of Psychotherapy, 29*, 135–153.

Richards, A.K. (1989). A romance with pain: A telephone perversion in a woman? *International Journal of Psychoanalysis, 70*(1), 153–164.

Richards, A.K. (1990). Female fetishes and female perversions: Hermine Hug-Mellmuth's "A case of female foot or more properly boot fetishism" reconsidered. *Psychoanalytic Review, 77*(1), 11–23.

Richards, A.K. (1992). The influence of sphincter control and genital sensation on body image and gender identity in women. *Psychoanalytic Quarterly, 61*(3), 331–351.

Richards, A.K. (2003). A fresh look at perversion. *Journal of the American Psychoanalytic Association, 51*(4), 1199–1218.

Riviere, J. (1929). Womanliness as a masquerade. *International Journal of Psychoanalysis, 10*, 303–313.

Roudinesco, E. (2009). *Our Dark Side: A History of Perversion*. (D. Macey, trans.). Cambridge, England: Polity Press.

Roughton, R.E. (2002). Rethinking homosexuality. *Journal of the American Psychoanalytic Association, 50*, 733–763.

Saketopoulou, A. (2011). Minding the gap: Intersections between gender, race and class in work with gender variant children. *Psychoanalytic Dialogues, 21*, 192–209.
Saketopoulou, A. (2013). Discussion of Celenza's "Perverse female relating and the creation of an objectified self." Paper presented at the winter meeting of the American Psychoanalytic Association, New York, January.
Samuels, A. (1985). Symbolic dimensions of Eros in transference-countertransference: Some clinical uses of Jung's alchemical metaphor. *International Review of Psychoanalysis, 12*, 199–214.
Samuels, A. (1996). From sexual misconduct to social justice. *Psychoanalytic Dialogues, 6*(3), 295–321.
Samuels, A. (2000a). *Politics on the couch*. London: Profile Books.
Samuels, A. (2000b). The erotic leader. *Psychoanalytic Dialogues, 10*, 277–280.
Sands, S.H. (2003). The subjugation of the body in eating disorders: A particularly female solution. *Psychoanalytic Psychology, 20*(1), 103–116.
Sands, S.H. (2010). On the royal road together: the analytic function of dreams in activating dissociative unconscious communication. *Psychoanalytic Dialogues, 20*, 357–373.
Sartre, J.P. (1956). Existential psychoanalysis. In J. P. Sartre, *Being and nothingness* (pp. 557–575) (H.E. Barnes, trans.). New York, NY: Philosophical Library.
Schaverien, J. (1995). *Desire and the female therapist: Engendered gazes in psychotherapy and art therapy*. London and New York: Routledge.
Schaverien, J. (2002). *The dying patient in psychotherapy: Desire, dreams and individuation*. New York, NY: Palgrave/Macmillan.
Schaverien, J. (2006a). Men who leave too soon. In J. Schaverien, *Gender, countertransference and the erotic transference: Perspectives from analytical psychology and psychoanalysis* (pp. 15–31). London, England: Routledge.
Schaverien, J. (Ed.) (2006b). *Gender, countertransference and the erotic transference: Perspectives from analytical psychology and psychoanalysis*. London, England: Routledge.
Schiller, B.M. (2012). Representing female desire within a labial framework of sexuality. *Journal of the American Psychoanalytic Association, 60*, 1161–1197.
Schore, A.N. (2011). The right brain implicit self lies at the core of psychoanalysis. *Psychoanalytic Dialogues, 21*, 75–100.
Searles, H.F. (1959) Oedipal love in the countertransference. *International Journal of Psychoanalysis, 40*, 180–190.
Searles, H.F. (1961/1965). Phases of patient-therapist interaction in the psychotherapy of chronic schizophrenia. In H.F. Searles (1965), *Collected Papers on Schizophrenia and Related Subjects* (pp. 521–559). NY: International University Press.
Sedgewick, E. (1990). *Epistemologies of the closet*. Berkeley, CA: University of California Press.
Shakespeare, W. (2000). Sonnet 23. In S. Booth (Ed.), *Sheakespeare's sonnets*. New Haven, CN: Yale Nota Bene, Yale University Press.
Sherby, L.B. (2013). *Love and loss in life and treatment*. New York, NY: Routledge.
Sherfey, M.J. (1966). The evolution and nature of female sexuality in relation to psychoanalytic theory. *Journal of the American Psychoanalytic Association, 14*, 28–125.
Sherman, E. (2002). Homoerotic countertransference: The love that dare not speak its name? *Psychoanalytic Dialogues, 12*, 649–666.
Simon, B. (2013). Is there a psychoanalytic contribution to the ethics of sexual relationships? Paper presented to the Association for Psychoanalytic Medicine, April, New York.

Sinsheimer, K. (2008). Having a heat wave: The analyst's vulnerability to boundary violations. Paper presented at Division 39, Spring Meeting, San Francisco, CA.

Sinsheimer, K. (2010). Calling on the hotline for your love: Further elements in erotic countertransference in the consulting room. Paper presented at Division 39, Spring Meeting, Chicago, IL.

Slavin, J.H., Rahmani, M., & Pollock, L. (1998). Reality and danger in psychoanalytic treatment. *Psychoanalytic Quarterly, 67,* 191–217.

Slavin, J.H. (2013). Moments of truth and perverse scenarios in psychoanalysis: Revisiting Davies' "Love in the afternoon." *Psychoanalytic Dialogues, 23,* 139–149.

Slochower, J. (1996). Holding and the fate of the analyst's subjectivity. *Psychoanalytic Dialogues, 6,* 323–353.

Smith, S. (1977). The golden fantasy: A regressive reaction to separation anxiety. *International Journal of Psychoanalysis, 58,* 311–324.

Sommer Anderson, F. (2008). *Bodies in treatment: The unspoken dimension.* New York, NY: The Analytic Press.

Spezzano, C. (1998). The triangle of clinical judgment. *Journal of the American Psychoanalytic Association, 46,* 365–388.

Springer, A. (1996). Female perversion: Scenes and strategies. *Journal of Analytical Psychology, 41,* 325–338. Also in J. Schaverien (Ed.) (2006) *Gender, countertransference and the erotic transference* (pp. 184–197). New York, NY: Routledge.

Stein, R. (1995a). Analysis of a case of transsexualism. *Psychoanalytic Dialogues, 5,* 257–289.

Stein, R. (1995b). Reply to Chodorow. *Psychoanalytic Dialogues, 5,* 301–310.

Stein, R. (1998). The poignant, the excessive and the enigmatic in sexuality. *International Journal of Psychoanalysis, 79,* 253–268.

Stein, R. (2000). 'False love' – 'Why not?' Fragments of an analysis. *Studies in Gender and Sexuality, 1,* 167–190.

Stein, R. (2005). Why perversion? 'False love' and the perverse pact. *International Journal of Psychoanalysis, 86,* 775–799.

Steiner, J. (1993). *Psychic retreats.* London, England: Routledge.

Stern, D.B. (1983). *Unformulated experience: From dissociation to imagination in psychoanalysis.* Hillsdale, NJ: The Analytic Press.

Stern, D.B. (2010). *Partners in Thought: Working with Unformulated Experience, Dissociation and Enactment.* New York, NY: Routledge.

Stoller, R. (1968). *Sex and gender.* New York, NY: Science House.

Stoller, R. (1979). *Sexual excitement.* NY: Pantheon.

Stoller, R. (1986). *Perversion: The erotic form of hatred.* London, England: Karnac.

Stolorow, R. (1975). The narcissistic function of masochism (and sadism). *International Journal of Psychoanalysis, 56,* 441–448.

Suchet, M. (2011). Crossing over. *Psychoanalytic Dialogues, 21,* 172–191.

Suchet, M., & Sand, S. (1999). Performing desire: Musical expressions of female sexuality. *Psychoanalysis and Contemporary Thought, 22,* 365–382.

Summers, F. (2013). *The psychoanalytic vision: The experiencing subject, transcendence, and the therapeutic process.* New York, NY: Routledge.

Sweetnam, A. (1996). The changing contexts of gender: Between fixed and fluid experience. *Psychoanalytic Dialogues, 6,* 437–459.

Sweetnam, A. (2010). Activating and enlivening ourselves and our patients: commentary on paper by Susan H. Sands. *Psychoanalytic Dialogues, 20,* 393–399.

Szmarag, R. (Reporter.) (1982). Special panel A: Erotic transference and countertransference between the female therapist and the male patient. *Academy Forum*, *26*, 11–13.

Taniguchi, K. (2012). The eroticism of the maternal: So what if everything is about the mother? *Studies in Gender and Sexuality*, *13*, 123–138.

Tansey, M.J. (1994). Sexual attraction and phobic dread in the countertransference. *Psychoanalytic Dialogues*, *4*, 139–152.

Thurer, S.L. (2005). *The end of gender: A psychological autopsy*. New York, NY: Routledge.

Tillman, J.G. (1999). Erotized transference and self–mutilation. *Psychoanalytic Review*, *86*(5), 709–719.

Tolstoy, L. (1954). *Anna Karenina*. (R. Edmons, trans.). New York, NY: Penguin.

Tyson, P. (1986). The female analyst and the male analysand. Presentation to the San Francisco Psychoanalytic Institute, 1986.

von Hug-Mellmuth, H. (2013). Un caso di feticismo del piede, o meglio degli stivali. *Rivista di Psicoanalisi*, *59*, 179–183. (orig. 1915. A case of female foot, or more properly boot fetishism.)

Wallace, E. (2004). Girl, Edited. *The American Psychoanalyst*, *38*(1), 14.

Watt, D.F. (1990). Higher cortical functions and the ego: Explorations of the boundary between behavioral neurology, neuropsychology and psychoanalysis. *Psychoanalytic Psychology*, *7*, 487–527.

Weille, K.-L.H. (2002). The psychodynamics of consensual sadomasochistic and dominant–submissive sexual games. *Studies in Gender and Sexuality*, *3*, 131–160.

Welldon, E.V. (1995). Female perversion and hysteria. *British Journal of Psychotherapy*. *11*(3), 406–414.

Welldon, E.V. (1996). Two perversions in men and women. *British Journal of Psychotherapy*. *12*(4), 480–486.

Wells, H. (2013). Client's perspectives on therapist's self–disclosure. Unpublished doctoral dissertation, Massachusetts School for Professional Psychology (MSPP), Newton, MA.

Winnicott, D.W. (1969). The use of an object and relating through identification. In D.W. Winnicott (1971) *Playing and Reality* (pp. 86–94). NY: Basic Books.

Wolfe, M. (2010). Hello 911? I'm on fire! Paper presented at Division 39, Spring Meeting, Chicago, IL.

Wrye, H.K., & Welles, J.K. (1994). *The narration of desire: Erotic transferences and countertransferences*. Hillsdale, NJ: The Analytic Press.

Yanof, J.A. (2000). Barbie and the tree of life: The multiple functions of gender in development. *Journal of the American Psychoanalytic Association*, *48*, 1439–1465.

Yeats, W.B. (1928). Among school children. In R.J. Finneran (Ed.) (1996), *The collected poems of W.B. Yeats: The tower* (p. 194). New York, NY: Scribner.

Young-bruehl, E. (1996). Gender and psychoanalysis: An introductory essay. *Gender and Psychoanalysis*, *1*, 7–18.

Zavitzianos, G. (1971). Fetishism and exhibitionism in the female and their relationship to psychopathy and kleptomania. *International Journal of Psychoanalysis*, *52*, 297–305.

Zavitzianos, G. (1982). The perversion of fetishism in women. *Psychoanalytic Quarterly*, *51*(3), 405–425.

Index

abuse 132, 133, 134
adolescents 39
affairs 7–9
aggression 16, 18, 24n4, 40; anal themes 133; displaced perverse scenarios 94; erotic transference 38, 44, 47–58; fear of patient's 39, 55; murderous feelings 50–52, 63–64; perversion 91; sadomasochism 113, 115, 117, 119, 121–122, 123; sexual ruthlessness 124n7; sexualization of 48–49, 118–119; unconscious 118
ambivalence 92
Amir, D. 89, 91, 98n5
anal themes 133–135
analysts: asymmetric relationship with patient 21, 40–41, 73–74, 75–76, 77, 80, 84; erotic transference 19–20, 21, 38, 58n9, 62; fetishes 128–129; mutuality 73–74, 75–76; patient's desire for sexual relationship with 41, 42–43, 47, 53, 57n2, 63, 81; sexual boundary transgressions 24n5, 47, 54, 56–57, 60, 62–63, 76, 94; threatened by patients 56–57, 58n9; *see also* countertransference; transference
analytic frame 73, 74–76
anger 50, 56
anorexia nervosa 110
anxiety 40, 47, 73, 90
Aron, L. 144n4
arousal 127, 134
assertion 7, 8, 10
asymmetry 21, 40–41, 72, 73–74, 75–76, 77, 80, 84
Atkinson, S. 39
Atlas, G. 78
attunement 31, 42, 141, 143

authenticity 23
autonomy 3, 4, 23

Bach, S. 94, 98n4
backbone 3, 4, 7
Bader, M.J. 116, 122–123, 124n7
Balsam, R.M. 35n5, 35n7, 112n14
Benjamin, J. 25, 72, 98n3, 114, 115, 123n2, 141, 144n1, 145n10
bicycle wheel metaphor 60–61, 64, 68, 69, 137
binaries 3, 6, 10, 27
bisexuality 7, 10, 64
Black Swan 107–109
Blechner, M.J. 62, 128
body 2, 7, 21, 100–101; as fetish 104–105, 110; maternal erotic transference 26, 27; perverse scenarios 102, 103, 105–107; *see also* embodiment
'body loveprinting' 26
body therapy 29
Bollas, C. 27, 84n7, 139, 144n4
Bolognini, S. 16, 68
Bonasia, E. 24n2, 45n2
boot fetish 129–131
boundary transgressions 24n5, 47, 54, 56–57, 60, 62–63, 76, 94
breast 25, 30
Bromberg, P. 144n8
Bucci, W. 138
Butler, J. 111n11

Carveth, D.L. 91
castration 44, 128, 133
castration anxiety 35n5, 94, 110, 135
Chasseguet-Smirgel, J. 48, 89, 111n11, 133, 135

Chodorow, N.J. 2
classical literature 41, 88, 112n16, 113, 126
Coen, S. 20, 38
Cohen, M. 129, 130
compulsivity 90, 110
constriction 95, 96, 97, 100, 116
consultation 54–55
containment 26
Cooper, S.H. 72
Corbett, K. 7, 97, 110n2
Cornell, W.F. 72, 144n4
countertransference 19, 39, 41, 43, 71–84; changes in 49, 63–64; disclosure of erotic countertransference 18, 71–73, 76, 79–82, 83; empowerment 40; erotic transference inhibited by 42, 55; guilty pleasure of 59–70; love and hate 56; sadomasochism 118, 119; sexualization 20
Crastnopol, M. 144n4
cultural expectations 2
culture 2, 3, 95, 96; body fetishism 104; Western 11n2, 11n5, 11n7, 25, 101

Davies, J.M. 69, 71–72, 73
'deep play' 68
defenses 19, 21, 88, 92, 139
degradation 49–50
dehumanization of the other 109
dependency 21, 42, 47–48, 49–50, 106, 114
depression 30, 33, 50, 53
desexualization 34, 77; fetishes 126; of the mother 25, 115; of psychoanalysis 15–16, 17–18, 113; sadomasochism 116
desire 9, 16, 18, 21, 40, 125; asymmetry of the communication of 72, 75; erotic countertransference 63, 72; erotic transference 19–20; inhibited 37; preoedipal 25; sadomasochism 122, 123; therapeutic action 69
destructiveness 50, 95, 97, 118
development 3
dialectics 3, 4, 22, 23
Diamond, M.J. 6, 12n15
difference 27, 31, 42, 93
Dimen, M. 11n6, 16, 100, 102, 104, 111n9, 144n4
direct perverse scenarios 93–94
displaced perverse scenarios 93, 94
dissociation 4, 20, 102–103, 106
dreams 18, 59

drug use 28
Duvall, R. 47

Ehrenberg, D.B. 103
Eliot, T.S. 116
Elise, D. 109
Embodied Subject 102, 103, 106, 111n6, 139–144
embodiment 1, 4, 9, 16–17, 100–101, 138, 139; *see also* body
enactments 87–88, 95, 122, 123
enemas 134, 135
envy 50, 51, 53, 106
erectile dysfunction 6–7, 23–24; *see also* impotence
the erotic 15, 16, 27
erotic transference 16, 17–18, 19–21, 24n3, 68, 78–79; aggression 47–58; capacity to be receptive 76; gender of analyst 38, 39, 47–48, 58n9, 62; maternal 25–35, 37–39, 42–45
erotic urges 34–35
ethnicity 31
Evans, D. 38
exhibitionism 23–24, 110, 112n14
experience of the other 1
Eyman, J.R. 57

false wholeness 110
fantasies: analyst's own 71; 'body lovepriting' 26; erotic transference 19, 33, 34; feminine guilt 48; fetishes 126; gender and sexuality 3; infantile 96, 104; male 48; masochistic 123n4; maternal 44; merger 40, 43, 63, 93; murderous 50–52, 63–64; one-person 88; perverse 88, 90, 91–92, 97, 115; sadomasochistic 122, 134; unconscious 139; universal wishes 74
fashion industry 104
fathers: case illustrations 8, 40, 129–131, 132, 134, 135; gender roles 21; oedipal crisis 109
Faulkner, W. 6
fear: analyst's fear of patient 39, 50, 51, 55; Objectified Self 106
femininity 3, 4, 5, 7, 104, 111n10; culturally defined 2; experience of both maleness and femaleness 32; maternal fantasies 44; passive feminine ideal 8; sadomasochism 115; stereotypical gender binary 6, 24, 48, 57n4, 141, 142; *see also* women

feminism 2, 3, 7, 42
fetishes 109, 125–136, 136n1; anal themes 133–135; body as fetish 104–105, 110; boot fetish 129–131; foot fetish 127–128; male 123n4
Fight Club 125
Flawless 4–5
flirtation 68, 69
Fogel, G. 6
Folkmarson Kall, L.F. 22, 114
Fonagy, P. 15
foot fetish 127–128
fortitude 4
Freud, S. 17, 96, 115, 128, 133

Gabbard, G.O. 39, 57, 72
Gediman, H.K. 111n10
gender 1–2, 3; embodied 21–23; gender blend 6, 9, 10; gender of analyst/analysand and erotic transference 38, 39, 47–48, 58n9, 62; gender role confusions 91, 95; identity 27, 44, 89, 91, 95, 97; as marker of difference 4, 6, 62; multiplicity 5–6, 141; opposite-gendered selves 62, 65–68; power relations 40–41; stereotyping 5, 37, 48, 55, 57n4, 115, 116; Western culture 11n2, 11n7; *see also* femininity; masculinity
genitals 10; *see also* penis; vagina
Gentile, J. 72–73
Gentile, K. 144n6
Ghent, E. 100, 123
Goldberger, M. 38–39
Goldner, V. 4
Gonzalez, F.J. 144n2
Green, A. 16
Grotstein, J. 144n4
guilt 118, 132; analyst's 41, 42, 68, 69; *Black Swan* 108; feminine 48, 111n11; perverse modes of relating 100; sadomasochism 115
Guralnik, O. 111n9, 144n4, 144n5
gynocentrism 3

Harris, A. 1–2, 101, 106, 110
Hartman, S. 145n9
hate 56, 91, 100
Herzog, J. 68
heteronormativity 90, 136n5
heterosexuality 95, 97
Hilferding, M. 25, 35n2
Hirsch, I. 72

Hoffman, I.Z. 72, 73–74, 76, 77
holding 4, 18, 23, 26, 68
Holmes, D. 39
homoeroticism 30–31, 63
homophobia 62–63, 65
homosexuality 30, 62–63, 65, 88, 95, 123n4
hopelessness 50, 51, 53
Horney, K. 111n10
hostility 48–49, 63–64, 91, 118–119, 120, 122; *see also* aggression
Housman, H.F. 112n14
Howell, E.F. 144n7
humiliation 39, 42, 44, 49–50, 51, 56, 114
hysteria 30

idealization 21, 40, 53, 56
identifications 61–62; *see also* self-other identifications
identity: construction of 11n4; gender 27, 44, 89, 91, 95, 97; *see also* self
impotence 37, 39, 133; *see also* erectile dysfunction
incest 21
integration 10, 21, 138, 140
intersexed persons 11n9
intersubjectivity 2, 92, 98n3
intimacy 3, 4, 10, 23, 47; analytic relationship 76; difficulties with 28; embodied 16–17; erotic urges 34–35; healthy 122; loving relations 90; perverse mode of relating 91; perversion of 111n13

Jordan, J.V. 27

Kaplan, L.J. 9–10, 12n14, 100, 104–105, 106, 109, 123n4, 125–126
Kavaler-Adler, S. 35n1
Kernberg, O.F. 24n4, 47–48, 115
Khan, M.M.R. 111n13
Kierkegaard, S. 137
kleptomania 110
Knoblauch, S.H. 72
knowing, modes of 27
Kohut, H. 20
Kulish, N. 70n4

language 77–79, 83, 96
Laplanche, J. 26
Lester, E. 39
libidinization 20
libido 16, 115

Lichtenberg, J.D. 24n1
licking 27
Lingiardi, V. 12n12
loneliness 30, 115, 130
love 19, 34, 49, 50; countertransference 56, 83; expressions of 77–78; lost selves 66; transference 47; wish for 74

Mad Men 4
'manliness' 37
Mann, D. 15, 72
Marber, P. 87
masculinity 3, 4, 5, 7; culturally defined 2; experience of both maleness and femaleness 32; infantile fantasies 104; sadomasochism 115; stereotypical gender binary 6, 24, 48, 57n4; *see also* men
masochism 48–49, 110, 114, 119, 123n4
masturbation 61, 108, 127, 129, 130
maternal transference 25–35, 37–39, 42–45
McDougall, J. 26, 90
McGinley, E. 98n2
means/end reversal 87, 90–91, 95, 98n1, 100, 104–105, 108, 109, 128
men: erotic transference 38, 39, 47–48, 58n9; forbidden feminine wishes 10; masochism 123n4; objectification 103; perverse ways of relating 87; sexual boundary transgressions 57; *see also* fathers; masculinity
mental masturbation 20
merger 27, 29, 31, 32, 40, 43, 45, 63, 93
Merleau-Ponty, M. 1, 15, 22, 25, 101, 114
Mitchell, S. 69n2
Modell, A. 72
mothers 9, 25–27, 44; *Black Swan* 108; case illustrations 33, 39–40, 43, 51, 66, 117–119, 127–128, 129, 131–135; desexualization of 115; gender roles 21; mother-infant relationship 1, 25, 26; oedipal crisis 109
multiplicity 5–6, 22–23, 61–62, 65, 68, 100, 137–138, 141
murderous feelings 50–52, 63–64
mutuality 73–74, 75–76, 90, 95, 122

narcissism 47, 104
'negative oedipal position' 39
neglect 26, 101
nonverbal communication 81
normality 95

Novick, J. 113
Novick, K.K. 113

object relations 15, 17, 25, 91, 92, 98n7, 115
objectification 88–89, 101, 102, 109; *Black Swan* 108, 109; experience of the body 105–106; fetishes 126; male/female differences 103; self-objectification 104, 105, 106–107
Objectified Self 102, 103–104, 106, 111n6, 139–143
obligatory perverse scenarios 94–95
oedipal conflict 21, 38, 69, 109
Ogden, T. 144n4
omnipotence 74, 92, 115
one-person universe 88, 93, 98n3, 102, 112n16, 126, 128
openness 3, 4, 7, 75
orality 30
Orange, D. 144n4

pain 89, 114, 135
Pajaczkowska, C. 24n1
Palahniuk, C. 125
paradoxes 92, 94
parents: good enough 10n1; polarization of parental relations 27; power differential with child 40; *see also* fathers; mothers
Parsons, M. 92–93, 98n4, 98n7
patriarchy 5
peer supervision 52–53, 54, 82
penetration 4, 7, 18, 23, 31, 43; aggressive 52; analysts 21; *Black Swan* 107; masculinity 24
penis 7, 23, 94, 127, 128; *see also* phallus
penis envy 106
Perel, E. 6–7
Person, E.S. 38
perverse enactments 95
perversion 21–22, 87–88, 125, 135; anal themes 133; dangerous subjectivity 87, 92–93, 94, 103, 106–107, 109; degrees of perverse relating 94–95; direct and displaced 93–94; female 99–112; levels of perverse modes 96–97; means/end reversal 87, 90–91, 95, 98n1, 100, 104–105, 108, 109, 128; motives of perverse scenarios 91–92, 100; perverse quality of relating 89–90; reformulation of perverse scenarios 88–89; what it isn't 95–96; *see also* fetishes

phallic power 8–9, 106, 107
phallic striving 5, 6, 21–22, 141
phallocentrism 3, 5
phallophobia 7
phallus 7, 12n13, 23, 64; *see also* penis
phenomenology 22, 101, 114
phobias 110
physical objects 72–73
play 68, 97, 110n2, 115
pleasure 16, 89; degrees of perverse relating 94, 100; fear or loss of 110; sadomasochism 113, 114, 116
postmodernism 2, 3, 22–23
post-structuralism 2
potency 3–4, 6, 8, 9–10, 137, 138; anal themes 133; *Black Swan* 107, 108; body fetishism 105; conversational dialectics 22; cultivation of capacity for 48; dangerous subjectivity 87; difficulties with 37, 49; Embodied Subject 141–142, 143–144; fetishes 126, 128; gender role confusions 91; phallus 7; sadomasochism 115; *see also* impotence
power 2, 40, 53; imbalance in analytic relationship 40–41, 54, 57, 75; phallic 8–9, 106, 107; sadomasochism 114; sexual boundary transgressions 57; women's fear of their own 106
powerlessness 49–50
premature ejaculation 66, 132, 133
preoedipal issues 21, 117; desexualization of psychoanalysis 15, 16, 113; erotic maternal transference 25, 27, 29, 35n1, 38, 42; sadomasochism 114, 115, 121–122; sexualization 20
prostitutes 49
pseudo androgyny 110
psychoanalysis 16–17, 60, 69; desexualization of 15–16, 17–18, 113; embodiment 101; erotic transference 38; gender identity development 97; multiplicity 68; perverse modes of relating 100; perverse scenarios 94, 96; sadomasochism 114; *see also* analysts
Puccini, G. 123
purity, desire for 74
Pynchon, T. 59

'radial true' concept 61, 64, 69, 138
rape 48

receptivity 3–4, 6, 9–10, 23, 31, 137, 138; analysts 21; *Black Swan* 107, 108; body fetishism 105; conversational dialectics 22; cultivation of capacity for 48; dangerous subjectivity 87; difficulties with 37; Embodied Subject 141–142, 143–144; fetishes 126; gender role confusions 91; sadomasochism 115
reciprocity 74, 90
re-embodiment 23
re-eroticization 23
Reflective Self 97, 111n6, 139–143
regression 133
rejection 50, 51, 119, 121
relationality 2, 3, 4, 11n6, 16, 100, 102–103
Renn, P. 70n5
repression 96
revenge 50, 91, 92, 118
Richards, A.K. 109, 112n15
Riviere, J. 12n14, 106, 111n10
romance 33–34; *see also* love
romantic idealization 21
Roudinesco, E. 96, 98n8, 98n9
ruthlessness 124n7

Sabbadini, A. 98n2
sadism 108, 114
sadomasochism 40, 110, 113–124, 134; desexualization of psychoanalysis 16; direct perverse scenarios 94; merger fantasy 43, 63; sexual boundary transgressions 56; sexualization 21
Saketopoulou, A. 103
sameness 27, 29, 31, 42, 65
Samuels, A. 10n1, 70n6, 84n4, 121
Sand, S. 111n11
Sands, S.H. 144n7
Schaverien, J. 12n13, 38
Schiller, B.M. 11n8, 11n11
Searles, H.F. 24n7, 57, 129
The Secretary 89
Sedgewick, E. 11n3
seduction 26, 47, 56, 57, 69, 74, 123
self 4, 22; aggression 50; core feeling of 10, 60, 64–65, 137, 139, 144n3; lost selves 64–65, 66; maternal erotic transference 26–27; multiplicity 22–23, 61–62, 97, 137–138; Objectified Self 102, 103–104, 106, 111n6, 139–143; opposite-gendered selves 62, 65–68; Reflective Self 97, 111n6, 139–143; *see also* identity; subjectivity

168 Index

self-deception 77, 80, 82, 84
self-disclosure 18, 71–73, 76, 79–82, 83
self-hatred 50, 74, 75
self-mutilation 110
self-objectification 104, 105, 106–107
self-other identifications 4, 7, 48, 60, 64, 65
self-psychology 20
separation 21, 30
sexual boundary transgressions 24n5, 47, 54, 56–57, 60, 62–63, 76, 94
sexual orientation 95, 97; *see also* bisexuality; heterosexuality; homosexuality
sexual ruthlessness 124n7
sexual transference 19, 57n2
sexuality 1, 3, 17, 28; desexualization of psychoanalysis 15–16, 17–18; expression of 2; fear of the power of 37; fetishes 127; healthy 16; preoedipal 16, 25; sadomasochism 113–114, 115, 116, 120–122
sexualization 19, 20–21, 24n8, 30, 44–45; of aggression 48–49, 118–119; perverse scenarios 88–89
Shakespeare, W. 71
shame 44, 90, 131
Simeon, D. 111n9, 144n4, 144n5
Simon, B. 16
Sinsheimer, K. 62–63
skin contact 27
Slavin, J.H. 72, 84n7
Slochower, J. 129
social order 2
solitude 3, 4, 111n7
splitting 56
Stein, R. 6, 90, 138, 144n1
stereotyping 5, 6, 10, 37, 57n4; analytic relationship 21; erotic transference 48; femininity 55, 142; sadomasochism 115, 116
Stern, D.B. 139
Stoller, R. 91, 92, 96, 100, 115, 135
Stolorow, R. 20
strength 49
Subjective Object 102, 103, 106, 111n6, 139–143
subjectivity 2, 5, 8, 101, 102; 'borrowed' 43; dangerous 87, 92–93, 94, 103, 106–107, 109; embodied 4, 9, 138; positions of 139–144; *see also* self
submission 123, 124n7
Suchet, M. 111n11
sucking 27

suicidality 48–49, 52, 57, 117
Summers, F. 111n5, 144n4
supervision 52–53, 54, 82
Sweetnam, A. 144n4, 144n7
symbolic third 93, 94

Taniguchi, K. 25
termination of therapy 54, 81–82
thinness 104, 107
the third 54, 55, 64, 82, 93, 94
thrust 7, 23, 43
Tolstoy, L. 89
tomboys 1–2
touching 27, 29–30, 34
trans persons 1, 5
transference 16, 17–18, 19–21, 24n3, 68, 78–79; aggression 47–58; capacity to be receptive 76; empowerment 40; gender of analyst 38, 39, 47–48, 58n9, 62; maternal 9, 16, 25–35, 37–39, 42–45; sadomasochism 118, 119; *see also* countertransference
transference neurosis 76
transvestism 123n4
trauma 91, 92, 115
Two Lovers 66

the unconscious 17, 61
unity, desire for 74

vagina 66, 68, 106, 110
violence 91; *see also* aggression

Wallace, E. 99
Ward, I. 24n1
Welldon, E.V. 111n8
Welles, J.K. 25–26, 27, 44, 91, 92, 100, 115
Western culture 11n2, 11n5, 11n7, 25, 101
women 5–6; bodies 104, 105–107; erotic transference 38, 39, 48, 55, 58n9; feminization of the profession 55; forbidden masculine wishes 10; objectification 103; perverse scenarios 87, 99–112; *see also* femininity; mothers
words 77–79, 82, 83
Wrye, H.K. 25–26, 27, 44, 91, 92, 100, 115

Yeats, W.B. 37
Young-Bruehl, E. 11n2

Lightning Source UK Ltd.
Milton Keynes UK
UKHW020015240919
350327UK00006B/39/P